Understanding
Linux®
Web Hosting

Understanding Linux® Web Hosting

Don Denoncourt and Barry Kline

Understanding Linux® Web Hosting

Don Denoncourt and Barry Kline

First Edition
First Printing—July 2002

Corporate Offices:
125 N. Woodland Trail
Double Oak, TX 75077 USA

Sales and Customer Service:
P.O. Box 4300
Big Sandy, TX 75755-4300 USA
877-226-5394

www.MCPressOnline.com

For information on translations or book distribution outside the USA or to arrange bulk-purchase discounts for sales promotions, premiums, or fund-raisers, please contact MC Press Corporate Office at the above address.

Acknowledgements

I'd like to thank Luanne H. Eckenrode, friend, editor, and goddess of the written word, who cheerfully waded through my chapters and now knows more than she ever wanted to about Linux. You're the greatest!

—Barry Kline

I'd like to thank and dedicate this book to Jim Stanicki. Jim got me interested in this field, gave my my first job, and trained me on how to be a coder. Jim taught me how to attack technology with intelligence, enthusiasm, and humor.

—Don Denoncourt

Contents

Preface

As the Internet continues to grow, more and more people find the notion of publishing their thoughts to the World Wide Web quite intriguing. Some people want to share their hobbies with the world and make new friends with similar interests. Others like to post information and pictures where their families can find them. Still others are just plain exhibitionists. Whatever the reasons, the web holds a fascination that few can ignore.

Most Web publishers are content with posting static web pages, and, for them, the Web space provided by their Internet Service Providers (ISPs) is sufficient. But for businesses and technically advanced individuals, static pages simply are not adequate. Both need something more.

Today, the hot Web technologies involve server-side programming. There are many server-side technologies from which to choose, but one of the leading is based on Sun System's Java language. Any time you visit a Web site and find in your browser a URL that references a file with the extension ".jsp", you are experiencing server-side Java in action. Java programs run unchanged on any platform for which a Java Virtual Machine is available, including personal computers from Apple or Intel-based PCs running Linux or Windows. And Java scales right up through the bigger iron, such as the eSeries machines from IBM. Thus, the knowledge that you gain programming on your personal computer scales automatically!

This book is a guide to setting up a complete environment for yourself on which to learn about this wonderful technology. When you're done, you'll have a system replete with a database management system, a Web server as well as server-side Java. And you'll know how it all works. Because the whole shebang is based on Linux, that wonder of the open-source era, everything you learn herein is applicable to any platform on which Linux will run. This includes Apple hardware, Intel and Intel-compatible hardware, and, of course, the eSeries by IBM.

We hope that you enjoy your exploration of these exciting technologies. We certainly enjoyed mapping your journey.

1

Why Linux

The Linux operating system was initially available merely as a UNIX clone for Intel-based workstations. Linux has grown, however, from Linus Torvalds' 1991 school project for Finland's University of Helsinki to be the only operating system that runs on all major computing platforms, including IBM's eServers, Sun's platforms, and Intel's complete line of processors, from the 386 to the 64-bit Itanium. Linux gained worldwide attention in the mid-1990s when it became one of the dominant operating systems used for Web hosting.

Early adopters of the Web used Linux for two main reasons:

1. It's free.

2. As a UNIX platform, it can run a variety of excellent Internet server applications, most notably the Apache Web server and sendmail.

Linux is also a full multitasking operating system, which means it can run many processes concurrently. Internet server machines need to be able to multitask so that they can run concurrent processes such as email, Web servers, and relational databases, thus being able to respond to numerous simultaneous requests from remote users. Personal workstations need to be able to multitask so the user can view the screens of multiple applications—such as a spreadsheet, a text editor, and a personal organizer—at the same time.

As a UNIX platform, Linux runs a wide variety of powerful Internet server applications. Besides Apache and sendmail, Linux can run software such as Network File System (NFS), a file server for Linux and UNIX file systems; SAMBA, a file server for Windows NT file systems; and Domain Name Service (DNS), a facility that converts human-readable domain names like "www.ibm.com" to the cryptic Internet Protocol (IP) addresses required by the Internet.

Today, Linux is used heavily in businesses because it proved its reliability as a server platform during the dawn of the Internet revolution. Initially, however, IT (Information Technology) directors scoffed at the idea of using "free" software such as Linux for mission-critical applications. Nevertheless, Linux sneaked in the back door of corporate America. The networking experts who were given the task of setting up and maintaining Internet applications were comfortable with the stability and reliability of Linux. These networking personnel, without asking management, began to use Linux to host their Internet applications.

The product-approval process at most companies revolves around the signing of purchase orders. Since Linux is free, however, networking personnel didn't have to cut purchase orders. As a result, management often had no idea Linux had been deployed at their companies. When Linux began to receive positive trade press, and the stocks of companies like Red Hat started to explode, many IT directors asked their networking experts to try Linux, only to find out it was already being used.

Who Needs Linux

Linux is a great operating system for colleges and universities, not only because it's free and runs on old computers that other operating systems can't handle, but because all the code for Linux comes with it. Students can research the code, make modifications, reconfigure, and recompile the entire operating system. In fact, Linux enhancements and bug fixes quite often come from the computer-science departments of universities.

Linux is a good host for a desktop graphical user interface (GUI). The desktop metaphor of a GUI allows users to organize application windows on their monitors in the same way that they organize papers and books on their desks. A desktop GUI also enables the point-and-click capabilities of a mouse, where a picture represents an action that will occur when the user clicks on it. GUIs have improved the usability of computer applications, and today's users expect a GUI environment for their PCs.

GUI Choices

Unlike Microsoft Windows, Linux does not have an integrated GUI. Linux is a part of the *open source* movement that frees you from proprietary solutions. If Linux had an integrated GUI, it would be picking the desktop GUI for you. When you install Linux, you pick from a variety of choices available for system software, including your choice of a GUI environment. The two most predominate Linux GUIs are KDE (*www.kde.com*) and Gnome (*www.gnome.org*). KDE is more Windows-like, while Gnome is more sophisticated with greater potential for application integration through object-oriented interfaces. (For this book, one of the authors used KDE as his desktop GUI, while the other used Gnome.)

Desktop GUIs like KDE, Gnome, and Microsoft Windows do not, by themselves, provide a complete set of application software. They just come with basic facilities such as file browsers, email clients, and configuration software that allows you to add application software. When you purchase a PC with Microsoft Windows preinstalled, a suite of office products is often included in the price (*bundled*). These office suites typically include, at the very least, a word processor and a spreadsheet.

With proprietary software solutions such as Microsoft Office, you pay a premium for the office software. With Linux, you have freedom of choice for office software. You can pick from a variety of options, from free open-source solutions like Sun's StarOffice (which was used to write this book), to pay-for-view solutions like Applixware/Anyware (*www.vistasource.com/products/*) and WordPerfect Office (*www.corel.com/products/linux.htm*).

Linux Origins

Linux is considered a new operating system. Because it is UNIX-based, however, much of the technology behind it is over 30 years old. In 1969, Ken Thompson and Dennis Ritchie, two software engineers at AT&T Bell Labs who had previously worked on the Multics (Multiplexed Information and Computing Service) operating system, began developing a portable operating system. They called this operating system "Unics" as a pun on Multics. (The *c* later mutated to an *x*.)

To make their operating system portable, Thompson and Ritchie had to develop a language that was not bound to a specific platform, and so the C language was born. The C source for their entire UNIX operating system could be copied and then recompiled on various platforms. Because AT&T Bell Labs made the C source code for UNIX freely available, several UNIX variants emerged: BSD (Berkley Systems Division) UNIX, Sun Microsystems's SunOS, and AT&T's System V. After the federal breakup of AT&T, however, Bell Labs' UNIX was legally considered to be a commercial asset of AT&T. As a result, companies that wanted to use UNIX had to formally license it.

The various vendors who began to license UNIX rights from AT&T ended up tweaking their own flavors of UNIX so that they could lock their customers into their particular variant. Despite these "UNIX wars," as they were called, UNIX was still very successful, and most technical colleges had UNIX in their curriculum.

To circumvent UNIX licensing, Andrew Tannenbaum, the author of several highly successful books on operating systems and compilers, created his own flavor of UNIX, called MINIX, for the sole purpose of teaching UNIX to college students. Much later, the University of California at Berkley also created a UNIX derivation called FreeBSD that, like MINIX, was intended to be freely modifiable and distributable. Today, however, the most well-known and successful free version of UNIX is Linux, created by Linus Torvalds.

In the early 1990s, Torvalds, then a graduate student at the University of Helsinki, became tired of the limitations of MINIX. He began to develop Linux as his own version of UNIX for the Intel platform. Through Internet newsgroups and forums, Torvalds invited other computer scientists to assist with his pet project. On October 5, 1991, the initial version of Linux, 0.02, was released. Version 1.0, the first business-quality version, was made available in March 1994.

Linux has received so much positive press that its adoption rate has exceeded that of any other UNIX variation, including IBM's, AT&T's, and Sun Microsystems'. Interestingly, FreeBSD (*www.freebsd.org*), which is comparable to Linux in features and quality, has nowhere near the acceptance rate, mostly because of bad timing. While Linux was the darling of the press, BSD was in litigation with AT&T to determine whether BSD UNIX contained propriety Bell Labs material. By the time BSD was free from the litigation, Linux had gained the industry momentum.

The History of Microsoft Windows

Linux is often compared to Microsoft's operating systems. Because of the "Linux or Windows?" question, it is worthwhile to briefly review the history of Microsoft Windows. Microsoft got its start in 1983 because IBM wanted an operating system for its new IBM PC. IBM could have developed its own operating system for the PC. In fact, an excellent operating system was already available at one of their research divisions. However, because IBM was under investigation by the federal government for having a monopoly, it began to search for an outside software firm to develop the PC's operating system.

Bill Gates' mother happened to find out about IBM's search and suggested that an IBM executive acquaintance of hers give her son a call. At that time, Gates' expertise was in the development of BASIC compilers, but when IBM asked if his company (which only amounted to a couple of people at the time) could create an operating system for the PC, he said yes. Gates bought the rights to an existing operating system for $40,000, tweaked it to IBM's specifications, and called it Disk Operating System (DOS). Shrewdly, Gates asked IBM for royalties on DOS rather than a lump-sum payment. Millions of PCs were sold with DOS bundled, and Microsoft started its rise to dominance.

IBM soon realized that PCs required a more powerful operating system than DOS, so it asked Microsoft to partner with it in the development of a multitasking operating system. Microsoft agreed, and the two companies began the collaborative development on what would become OS/2. While Microsoft was developing OS/2 with IBM, however, it was also developing its own new multitasking operating system. Thus, soon after OS/2 was introduced, Microsoft came out with Microsoft Windows.

OS/2 was superior to Windows because OS/2 was a full multitasking operating system, while Windows sat on top of DOS and faked multitasking capabilities. Nevertheless, partly because Windows was backward-compatible with DOS applications, and partly because of Bill Gates' marketing genius, Windows became the dominant PC operating system, while IBM's technically superior OS/2 product floundered.

Later, Windows 95 and Windows 98 provided improved GUI capabilities, but the operating system still crashed regularly, and users began to accept rebooting their machines daily as an acceptable part of owning a PC. Even in the 1980s, operating system crashes, whether on personal workstations or corporate servers, should not have been acceptable because sophisticated multitasking operating systems had been available since the 1970s.

It wasn't until the introduction of Windows NT that Microsoft provided a full multitasking operating system. (Meanwhile, OS/2 floundered to the point of being discontinued.) With Windows NT, Microsoft finally produced an operating system that could be compared to Linux. Still, NT was known to crash regularly, and many system administrators found that for true reliability, they needed to have one NT server per application: one for Web serving, one for file serving, and one as a Domain Name Service. In 2000, Microsoft came out with Windows 2000, and the reliability of Windows 2000 as a server has been far superior to its Microsoft predecessors.

Linux Growth

When Linux version 1.0 was introduced in 1994, the first people to use it were UNIX programmers who wanted UNIX-based systems at home. They found that not only was Linux a solid operating system for their Intel-based PCs, but it also had many of the same capabilities as the UNIX operating systems running on the costly mid-to-large systems at their workplaces.

As mentioned earlier, when the Internet explosion hit, network administrators were given the task of getting their companies on the Web. That task required additional hardware and software. Rather than going through the laborious procurement process, these networking administrators pulled 386 and 486 PCs that could no longer run the latest versions of Windows, loaded Linux, and configured those boxes as Web servers. Networking administrators also found that they could recompile the Linux operating system with only those features required for a specific server, thus enhancing performance.

Many of the early adopters of Linux used their home-based Linux systems and their knowledge of UNIX to deploy personal Web sites. A significant number of these personal Web sites evolved into commercial sites. What better operating system for an Internet startup than one that runs all the required TCP/IP software, is solid, robust, and stable, yet free?

Corporate American began to take notice of Linux, and the rate of Linux-hosted Web sites skyrocketed to 17 percent of the server market (source: International Data Corporation, *www.idc.com*). By 1998, that number was 25 percent and, in 2000, Linux gained the number-two spot behind Windows 2000 in the server operating-system market, with 27 percent of the market. IDC predicts that the Linux operating environment worldwide will achieve a 25 percent compound annual growth rate through to 2003.

Cost Effectiveness

Virtually all businesses require cost justifications for new directions. Although the Linux operating system is free, there are other costs to consider. First, there is the question of technical support, both internally and externally. Then, there is the question of whether or not Linux is a verifiably reliable, stable, and secure platform. If a company dedicates a thousand work-hours to the deployment of a Linux-based Web site, and it fails, that's a loss of perhaps $100,000. Even if the project were a success, would an NT or Solaris server solution have been less costly? To answer the question of server costs, companies need to look at three factors: hardware, software, and support.

Hardware Costs

Linux can run on any existing hardware. In fact, it is known as the "universal OS" because it runs on all kinds of devices, from wristwatches like the one in Figure 1.1 to high-end platforms such as those provided by Hewlett Packard, IBM, and Sun.

Figure 1.1: To demonstrate the portability of Linux, IBM installed it on a wristwatch.

Of course, a company won't be running its Web server off a wristwatch, but many small companies are running Linux-based Web servers off old Intel 486s and low-end Pentiums. At the other end of the scale, larger companies can opt to install Linux on existing IBM, Sun, or Hewlett-Packard hardware. IBM's iSeries even allows companies to run Linux on the same machines as legacy OS/400 systems, using a facility know as *logical partitioning*, or *LPAR*. In fact, using LPAR technology, the iSeries can run up to 32 virtual Linux operating systems on one iSeries platform. IBM's gargantuan zSeries platform, shown in Figure 1.2, takes the capabilities of LPAR even further: a single zSeries machine can host literally thousands of virtual Linux operating systems.

Figure 1.2: The IBM zSeries platform is able to concurrently run thousands of virtual Linux operating systems.

If a company has existing hardware, however, why wouldn't it simply use that platform's native operating system instead of Linux to host the Web server? The answer is two-fold:

1. Linux has some of the best Internet software.

2. There are far more Internet professionals with Linux experience than those with, say, IBM OS/400 or OS/390 Internet experience.

Furthermore, the Linux professional base is growing exponentially, while the professional base for all other operating systems (except Windows) has leveled off.

Even if a company opts to purchase new hardware for Web serving, the required hardware for Linux will be equal to or less than that required for other platforms. The hardware requirements will be equal if you run the Linux operating system using the default product installation, but it can be less if you factor in the reduced size of the Linux operating system recompiled to contain only the required software components.

Software Costs

You have already learned what Linux costs—it's free. Costs for other operating systems can range anywhere from $800 to as much as $100,000, depending on multiuser licensing fees. But what about all the other software required to host a Web server? You'll need several products that support TCP/IP, the low-level protocol of the Internet. Obviously, you'll need a Web server, and you'll probably also need an email server. Linux, unlike other operating systems, has its TCP/IP modules fully integrated. For Web serving and email, the various Linux distributions bundle the world-class open-source products Apache HTTP server (*www.apache.org*) and sendmail (*www.sendmail.org*), along with many other Web-hosting products.

An important piece of software vital to the hosting of a robust Web site is a *Web application server*. While Web servers (also known as *HTTP servers*) basically serve only static, unchanging Web pages, Web application servers work in association with HTTP servers to serve dynamically constructed, interactive pages. When a user's request for dynamic information comes into the HTTP server, it forwards the request to the Web application server. The Web application server, in turn, uses Java application code to dynamically construct a Web page that responds to the user's request. The Web application server then forwards this page to the HTTP server, which sends it to the user's Web browser.

The cost of Web application servers is not a consideration for whether or not to use Linux because all Web application servers (except Microsoft's Internet Information Server) run on almost all operating systems. IBM's WebSphere, for example, runs well not only on all of IBM's operating systems (OS/400, OS/390, and AIX), but also on Solaris, HPUNIX, and Linux. WebSphere's closest competitor, BEA's WebLogic, also runs on a wide variety of operating systems, including Linux. In addition, the open-source Web application servers available, most notably Apache's Tomcat, run on many operating systems, including Linux.

Support Costs

Having discounted hardware and software costs, the only real concern is support costs. The big question that companies have about "free" software is who's going to support it? For Linux, the answer is multifaceted. One source of support is the Linux user community, which, in 1997, was awarded "Best Technical Support" from *InfoWorld*. The Linux user community is made up of technical experts who are ready to freely assist new Linux users. The community is accessible through a wide variety of newsgroups available from such sources as Usenet (*www.usenet.com*) and Internet Relay Chat (*www.irc.org*).

Many corporate executives, however, want to put a "suit and tie" on technical support. They want to pay to ensure the quality and availability of these services. Formal support for Linux is available from a variety of sources, the first and most obvious being the Linux distributors. These distributors, some of whom are shown in Table 1.1, sell installation CDs for Linux that come with bundled open source software, an installation program, and a limited amount of phone and Web support. Most of these distributors also offer extended support programs. In fact, much of their revenue streams comes from technical support for Linux.

Table 1.1: Major Distributors of Linux	
Distributor	**Home Page**
Caldera OpenLinux	www.caldera.com
Debian Linux	www.debian.com
Slackware Linux	www.cdrom.com/titles/os/slackwar.htm
Red Hat Linux	www.redhat.com
SuSE Linux	www.suse.com

Many other third-party firms, such as LinuxCare (*www.linuxcare.com*) offer distribution-neutral support for enterprise Linux environments. If you want the best "suit and tie" possible for Linux, however, go to

IBM (*www.ibm.com/linux*), which spent $1 billion on Linux development in 2001 alone. IBM can work with any size company and provides Internet and voice technical support 24 hours a day, seven days a week.

Stability

Two other questions need to be answered before IT directors agree to deploy a Web site on a new platform:

1. Is the platform stable?

2. Is the platform secure?

A company that expects to derive revenues from a Web site can't have that revenue stream disrupted. Even if the Web server goes down for a short time, the Web site loses credibility, and customers might opt to click over to a competitive site to purchase the product.

UNIX systems in general are highly stable, and Linux platforms have been known to run for years without crashing. One of the authors of this book, as the systems manager for a large OS/400 shop, installed Linux on an outdated Intel 486 machine to provide a Domain Name Service for his OS/400-managed network (before OS/400 provided a DNS product). The system ran uninterrupted for over a year before its disk drive crashed. Linux was simply moved to another outdated machine, and the DNS server is still running today.

Windows NT administrators will tell you that the most stable way to run an NT network is to use one machine per server application to avoid crashes. In contrast, one Linux server can host all the TCP/IP services required for a network and a Web site without conflicts. More recent versions of Windows are much more stable than NT, but it seems a little late for Microsoft to come out with stable operating systems. This is especially true when you consider that in 1994, when Windows 3.1 was the best system offered by Microsoft, Linux users were exploiting the full multitasking, 32-bit, protected virtual memory capabilities of Intel processors.

There is no need to compare Linux's stability with other UNIX operating systems because they all benefit from similar UNIX technologies, so they all have comparable stability ratings. However, Linux is not as stable as IBM's iSeries OS/400 or zSeries OS/390 operating systems. The question of whether to use OS/400 or OS/390 to host your Web site, though, is not a question of stability, but of technical support. There are far more networking experts available for Linux than for OS/400 and S/390 combined, and the number of Linux experts is growing every day.

Security

Many layers of security need to be in place for a Web site. Internet users must go through these layers to get to the application software and data files. One of the first layers of security, known as a *firewall*, is software designed to block destructive attempts to enter an area. Firewall software does such things as exclude users who attempt to access a machine using well-known entry points like File Transfer Protocol (FTP) and terminal emulation (telnet). On most operating systems, firewall software must be separately procured, installed, and configured. Linux, however, has an integrated firewall.

Most operating systems have user profiles set up, so that a person cannot access a platform without entering a user name and password. Linux has a robust security strategy, where users are added to the system by a network administrator. The administrator assigns an initial password for the user (which can be changed later by the user). Even after the user is logged into the system, Linux has another level of security: *file-level security*.

Each file on the Linux machine is qualified to be accessed by three types of users: *owner*, *group*, and *user*. The owner profile associated with a file is typically that of the user who created the file (although this can be changed). The group profile associated with a file is that of a *namelist* of profiles set up to simplify application security into groups of users. The user profile, which is not special like owner or group, basically means everybody other than the file owner and the namelist associated with the group profile.

Permissions to read, write, and execute a file are assigned for each of these three user types. For instance, a Web page stored as a text-based HTML file on disk might have the owner name *Denoncourt* and the group name *webpgmr* assigned to it. The owner and the group have read and write privileges assigned, while the user has only read privileges. That way, if a user not in the group of Web programmers attempts to modify or delete that HTML file (maliciously or otherwise), the attempt will fail.

There is one other special security level known as the *root user*. Only the system administrator (and his or her backup) should know and use the root password because someone logged in with that profile can do absolutely anything with the system.

Many other operating systems have similar file- or object-level security, but Linux has something that no other operating system can boast: daily kernel updates available with security bug fixes. Because the complete source for Linux is available to all Linux users, when a security breach is found, anybody with the appropriate technical skill can fix that breach and make that fix available to the Linux community.

To the Internet crackers of the world, there's a big philosophical difference between cracking open-source Linux code and cracking closed-source code like Windows. The crackers tend to fix the breaches discovered in Linux and publish those fixes, while with Windows, they simply publish how they cracked the system. After all, they can't fix Windows—they don't have the code. Plus, some crackers resent Microsoft's dominant position in the market, preferring the freedom associated with Linux. There truly are, then, far more developers working on improving Linux security than Microsoft has working on its security. As a result, Linux security fixes are published daily.

Linux Software

The wide variety of software for Linux can be divided into two groups: open-source and commercial. The various Linux distributions bundle many of the open-source products on their installation CDs. They even have options during the installation process to load the various products. We've already introduced sendmail, the Apache Web server, and Apache's Tomcat Web application server, but there are a number of other open-source products for developing and hosting Web applications.

Commercial applications will require a *relational database* (*RDB*). Various open-source RDB products are available, such as MySQL (*www.mysql.com*) and PostgreSQL (*www.postgresql.org*). Java is the predominant (non-Microsoft) application programming language for the Web, so you'll also need a *Java Development Kit* (*JDK*). Your Linux distribution CD probably already has a Linux JDK, but if not, they are available as free downloads from a number of sources. The most obvious source is Sun (*http://java.sun.com/products*), since it created the Java programming language, but Linux JDKs can also be had from sources such as BlackDown (*www.blackdown.com*) and IBM's AlphaWorks (*www.ibm.com/java/jdk/*). Many corporate Web sites have found IBM's JDKs to be faster and more stable than Sun's.

You'll need more than Java and an RDB to develop a Web site, however. You'll need a graphical desktop environment (like Windows), a Java integrated development environment, and editors for developing Web pages. Microsoft, of course, bundles the Windows desktop environment with its operating system. Since Linux, on the other hand, is about choice, there are numerous desktop environments available. As mentioned earlier, the two best-known are Gnome (*www.gnome.org*) and KDE (*www.kde.com*). Both are on all the major Linux distribution CDs.

With a graphical desktop installed, you'll next want an *integrated development environment* (*IDE*) for Java. A Java IDE allows you to type source code, compile it, and then debug it before deploying it to your production Web site. Once again, several products are available as free downloads, such as Sun's Forte for Java (*http://java.sun.com/forte/jjf*); IBM's VisualAge for Java (VAJ), Entry Edition (*www.ibm.com/software/ad/vajava/download.htm*); and Borland's JBuilder (*www.borland.com/jbuilder/ foundation/*). Note, however, that each of these free Java IDEs lacks some of the sophisticated features found in various commercial versions.

Up to this point, we've concentrated on open-source or free software for developing and deploying a commercial Web site. To host a really sophisticated Web site, however, you might want to look at commercial software. The open-source relational databases, for example, don't contain all of the features available in the commercial products of Sybase, Oracle, or IBM's DB2 UDB. Similarly, open-source Web application servers do not scale as well as IBM's WebSphere, BEA's WebLogic, and Sun's iPlanet. The three open-source Java IDEs just mentioned (VAJ, JBuilder, and Forte) have commercial versions that provide integration tools and wizards to simplify development and deployment of Web applications. For more about Linux software, and many other Linux issues, see the sources listed in Table 1.2.

Table 1.2: Hot Linux Web Sites	
Site Name	Home Page
Slashdot	www.slashdot.org
Linux Today	www.linuxtoday.com
LWN.net	www.lwn.net
Linux.com	www.linux.com
Linux	www.linux.org
Just Linux	www.justlinux.com
Linuxnewbie.org	www.linuxnewbie.org
Linux Programming	www.linuxprogramming.com
Linux Central	www.linuxcentral.com
Linux Planet	www.linuxplanet.com

Open Source Is Not Free

With the wide availability of open-source products, it's important to understand the open-source movement. Richard Stallman, an MIT scientist, missed the spirit of sharing source code that prevailed in the early days of UNIX. So, in 1984, Stallman began the GNU project (*www.gnu.org*), which had the mission statement of creating a free UNIX-like operating system. (The name is a recursive acronym that stands for "GNU's not UNIX.") To organize work on the GNU project, Stallman created the non-profit Free Software Foundation (FSF). The FSF seeks to promote free software and eliminate restrictions on its copying, redistribution, understanding, and modification.

When open-source developers speak of "free" software, they are referring to the users' freedom to run, copy, distribute, study, change, and improve the software. To ensure these rights, the FSF created the GNU General Public License (*GNU GPL*). The GNU GPL is essentially a copyright, but its proponents prefer to call it a "copyleft" because it does the opposite of copyrighted software—it increase the rights of users. There are several other open-source software licenses, such as the Open Source Initiative (OSI) and the Apache Software License.

Regardless of the organization, the licenses at the top of every open-source file are relatively similar. As an example, the following is a summary, in everyday language, of the Apache Software License, Version 1.1:

1. Don't rip the tag off—Like those warnings against ripping labels off of sofas, you're not supposed to delete the copyright off the top of a source file. While you probably won't be selling your sofa any time soon, you very well might be selling your code. And sooner or later, someone, perhaps a competitor, will recognize that code as open-source.

2. If you create new code, it gets the label—New code that enhances open-source code gets the same copyright. This prevents a vendor from making mild enhancements to an open-source OS or server and calling the whole thing its product.

3. Tell the users where the code came from—All documentation must credit the organization that controls the open-source code.

4. Don't use the organization's name—You can't go around saying your application is endorsed by the open-source organization unless you've gotten permission to use the name of that organization.

5. If it breaks, it's not their fault—So don't expect to sue the Apache Software Foundation.

The first two items are the big ones because they effectively say that any software with open-source copyrights will always be open source. The organization that originated the code might die, but the code lives on forever.

The last thing to keep in mind about open-source licenses is that they contain no verbiage that prohibits anyone from making money off distributing or supporting open-source products. That's how Red Hat, Caldera, Debian, and SuSE make their money. One well-known Web site, CheapBytes (*www.cheapbytes.com*), legally resells a copy of the Red Hat distribution CD, among other open-source software, for just a couple of dollars (plus shipping), rather than the $100 or so that CD would cost from Red Hat itself. Of course, you don't get the Internet and phone support you would if you purchased directly from Red Hat.

Linux Today

In late October 1998, two highly confidential Microsoft emails concerning its strategy against Linux leaked to the open-source community. The Open Source Initiative, a nonprofit organization, called them the "Halloween documents" because of the curious date on which they were received. Those documents are accessible today at *www.opensource.org/halloween*. They clearly show that Microsoft was highly concerned about the threat of Linux specifically, and open source in general, to its market dominance. Microsoft noted that IBM was taking a lead role in optimizing the open-source Apache HTTP server for NT. The document further stated that the "worst-case scenario" would be if IBM adopted Linux.

Microsoft's worst-case scenario came true. In late 2000, Lou Gerstner, IBM's chief executive officer, stated that IBM would spend $1 billion on Linux in 2001. Gerstner is quoted as saying, "Linux can do for business applications what the Internet did for networking and communications: make computing easier and free from proprietary operating systems."

IBM's billion dollars went a long way to changing the perceptions of many corporations that Linux was not adequate for commercial applications. There were two major problems with Linux as a business OS: the lack of quality *symmetric multiprocessing* (*SMP*) to improve speed and scalability, and the lack of a *journaled file system* (*JFS*) support to improve recoverability. (For more about JFS, see *www.ibm.com/developerworks/library/jfs.html*.) Among many other Linux projects, IBM has been developing Linux solutions for both SMP and JFS. Both of these projects require a huge base of code, and IBM contributed most of the code base required for JFS. Remember, because of the open-source licenses, any enhancements that IBM makes to existing open-source products are also open-source.

Besides contributing to open-source Linux, IBM was one of the first major software vendors to create Linux versions of its products. Today, you can run DB2 UDB, WebSphere, Domino, MQSeries, VisualAge for Java, and Tivoli on Linux.

IBM intends to make a return on its billion-dollar investment by selling its world-class eServers hardware and DB2 UDB, Domino, Tivoli, and WebSphere software. As an example of how IBM has already cashed in on Linux, in late 2000, Telia, the largest ISP and telecommunications company in Scandinavia, replaced 70 Sun servers with one IBM zSeries. The zSeries machine today hosts more than 1,500 virtual Linux servers. With that one zSeries machine, Telia is able to easily start a new server in less than five minutes whenever it gains a new client. The IBM-Telia deal is worth about $3 million. As another example, IBM signed a deal to sell 15,000 Linux computers, software, and support to Lawson, a Japanese convenience-store chain.

Although Linux might lack business application software for such things as payroll, manufacturing, or sales, the best use of Linux is not for business applications. Instead, it is for server applications like these:

1. Domain Name System (DNS)

2. FTP, mail, news, proxy, and search servers

3. File servers

4. The Apache HTTP server

Universal OS

Linux is quickly becoming known as the "universal OS" because, regardless of the operating system a company uses for its legacy applications, it uses Linux for its Web server. That Linux-based Web server then communicates with legacy applications and databases to retrieve the information required for Internet applications.

Large IT shops are beginning to host their Internet applications with Linux running in one or more logical partitions on their iSeries or zSeries machines, while continuing to run their legacy applications in an LPAR running that platform's native operating system. Smaller IT shops are beginning to run their Linux-based Web sites on low-cost Intel-based machines, with their legacy applications running an Internet connection away. Regardless of which platform Linux is deployed on, these companies are able to take advantage of Linux's integrated security features, the industry-standard Apache Web server, sendmail, and either IBM's WebSphere bundle or Apache's open-source Tomcat product for the Web application server. These companies' bread-and-butter business applications still run as they have for the last twenty or thirty years. Because they are hosting their Web sites with Linux, however, they are able to take advantage of high-quality, low-cost Internet hosting software. And, because there is an ever-increasing number of Linux Internet professionals available, they are able to find the talent required to develop, deploy, and maintain their Web sites.

End of Chapter Review

Key Terms

C language	Graphical user interface (GUI)	TCP/IP
Desktop	Linux user community	UNIX
Disk Operating System (DOS)	Multitasking	User profile
File-level security	Open source	Web application server
Firewall	Operating system	Web hosting
Free Software Foundation	Personal computer (PC)	Web server
GNU	Root user	

Review Questions

1. What are the costs to be aware of when considering Linux?

2. What are the two most popular Linux GUIs?

3. List three server applications that Linux can run.

4. What is the dominant programming language for the Web?

5. How do Linux distributors drive revenue, in light of open source?

Programming Assignment

Exercise 1: Visit Some Linux Web Sites

1. Report on a recent topic.

2. Find a major implementer of Linux.

Exercise 2: Review Various Open-Source Licenses

1. Find out about the GNU GPL at *www.gnu.org*.

2. Find out about Apache's license at *www.apache.org*.

Exercise 3: Find Open-Source Products

1. List six open-source products, other than those mentioned in this chapter.

2

Distributions

In the previous chapter, Linux is referred to as an operating system because that's what most people call it. Actually, however, Linux is not an operating system. It is, instead, the *system kernel* of an operating system. This distinction is important, so we'll explain it first, before discussing Linux distributions.

What's in a Name

Most casual computer users have little idea of what's going on "under the covers." Most believe that, when the word processor is active, it is the only program running. Actually, a running computer that appears to be sitting idle is, in fact, quite busy. Many processes and threads are running all of the time. To satisfy yourself that this is true, go to a Windows computer (other than Windows 95 or 98), press Ctrl-Alt-Delete (the famed "three finger salute"), and then click on Task Manager. When it starts, click the Processes tab, and you'll see a list of some of the processes currently executing. These tasks will appear even if you have no user applications active.

It is the job of an operating system to schedule the resources required to run each of these processes, plus whatever you add with your applications. At the very least, each process requires some memory and CPU time to run, and most processes require some kind of disk access to retrieve data. The operating system must perform a juggling act to keep all of this running, ensuring that no process gets starved for resources too long. This problem manifests itself in slow response times. An in-depth discussion of operating systems is beyond the scope of this book, but this basic understanding will be helpful when setting up your Web server.

To fully appreciate what an operating system kernel is, think of your computer as an integrated combination of software and hardware. Figure 2.1 shows this combination drawn as a layered rectangle. Communication between layers can be accomplished only by going through all intervening layers.

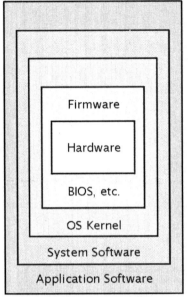

Figure 2.1: The hardware-software hierarchy.

The hardware components of the computer are at the core of the integrated mass in Figure 2.1. This core includes the memory, CPU, video system, I/O system (keyboard, communications, USB ports, etc.), and storage (hard drive, CD, floppy). Enveloping the core is a layer of software called *firmware*. This layer is supplied by the hardware's manufacturer to provide a means for communicating with other software. Firmware is also called *embedded software* because it's typically burned into read-only memory (ROM) or in some kind of electrically erasable programmable read-only memory (EEPROM), which can be updated using manufacturer-supplied programs.

The next layer out is the operating system kernel. Through software modules known as *device drivers*, which can be provided by the manufacturer or written by enterprising open-source programmers, the kernel can communicate with the hardware. The kernel "owns" all of the hardware resources. Any program that requires a resource, such as a chunk of memory, must request it from the kernel. In fact, the kernel is responsible for the allocation of all of the computer's resources, including CPU time. It provides the scheduling so that all processes get a chance to run, arbitrating between conflicting requests for resources. Most importantly, it provides protection between processes, so that some errant program instructions in one process can't cause damage to another.

The next software layer out is the system software. This layer is an adjunct to the kernel and extends the services that the kernel provides. An operating system is the combination of the kernel and the system software.

The kernel could function without this software, but the computer would be, in effect, spinning its wheels and accomplishing nothing. The system software adds whatever functionality is required to make the computer operate in the role to which it is assigned. For example, a workstation computer has significantly different functionality than, say, a network server, and thus will have different pieces of system software loaded. A network server has little need for a sophisticated video system, since it is probably text-based and has no GUI capability. Therefore, it will not have the system software dealing with graphics loaded onto its hard drive.

The outer layer of software is the application software. This might include the Apache Web server, the DB2 Universal Database (although on the AS/400, DB2 is tied into the system software), and the Gimp graphics editor.

It's easy for the distinction between system software and user application software to become blurred, particularly because system software such as Windows and Linux typically includes so much application software. Most people tend to classify any software that's available for multiple operating systems or for end users (such as a word processor) as an application. If the software modifies the behavior of the operating system in some way, or operates directly on objects within the operating system, then it is considered system software. After all, if it walks like a duck and quacks like a duck...

GNU/Linux

Arguably the biggest reason UNIX doesn't have a bigger share of the market is because, early on, every company that wrote some UNIX-like operating system did so from the kernel layer up. Layers of software above the kernel were written to that specific kernel specification. This snowballed all the way up through to the application software layer. As a result, it became very difficult to port an application written on one variation of UNIX to another. Software companies had to have different versions of their applications for each version of UNIX to which they marketed their products. This became an incredibly expensive proposition and a very unattractive business model. To combat this, what became the IEEE Portable Applications Standards Committee was formed, and the POSIX (pronounced "pahz-icks") standard developed. This standard was developed by extracting the best points of all the existing variants and then codifying the result. Application software written on one POSIX-compliant variation of UNIX can be ported to another with relative ease.

The software that has brought Linus Torvalds fame and fortune (well, fame anyway) is a kernel. It's the layer of software right above the firmware layer. Torvalds designed Linux to be POSIX compliant. The system software that becomes an operating system when combined with the kernel was provided by the GNU project. The resulting operating system is properly called GNU/Linux. This is a major point of contention among purists, as referring to GNU/Linux as simply Linux minimizes the contribution of GNU and the Free Software Foundation to the Linux phenomenon. So, keep in mind, whenever you see or hear anything about Linux, that GNU had a great deal to do with it. Even though we use the simpler term "Linux" in this book, we do so while recognizing the contribution of GNU and the Free Software Foundation.

Definition of Distributions

Now that you know about kernels, you need to know what a distribution is. To give a complete explanation, we must first look at how "techies" had to historically obtain copies of Linux.

You might not have ever installed an operating system on you computer before because most big-name computer manufacturers provide one (typically, Windows) pre-loaded. If you *have* done a Windows installation, the process has probably been to insert a CD into a CD-ROM drive, power on the computer, and then follow the on-screen instructions. Modern Linux distributions have made the installation process equivalent to that of Windows. This has not always been the case.

When the Linux kernel was initially made available (long before it became version 1.0), the only option you had was to download its source code from an FTP site (the Web as we know it was in its infancy), and then compile it on another system, copying the resulting binaries onto diskettes. Once you had the kernel successfully running, you had to go back to the Internet, and then download and compile the various source files for each of the required system programs and utilities, being ever mindful of the dependencies between programs (i.e., one program requires another). The resulting binaries would then be copied to diskette for installation on the target system. In short, you had to completely handcraft your Linux system. Given the complexity of this task, it's no wonder that the only users of the early system were hackers (in the positive sense of the word) with UNIX backgrounds. Their interest was primarily the potential to bring their beloved UNIX environment home to their personal computers without having to pay for the privilege.

It is unlikely that Linux would have achieved the status it currently enjoys had this situation remained unchanged. Fortunately, the need to simplify the Linux installation process became apparent, and some enterprising individuals decided to bundle together all of the tools, compiled and ready-to-run, into a package that could be installed by "mere mortals." Included in this package was a set of installation scripts that would modify the installation, based on the answers the user supplied to the script's questions. Thus, the concept of a distribution was born. The short definition of a distribution, then, is this:

> A distribution is a GNU/Linux system and associated utilities, bundled together into a package along with installation and/or configuration scripts (programs), which tends to be the center of many religious wars in the Linux community.

We'll expand this definition later.

One of the first popular Linux distributions was Slackware, developed and maintained by Patrick Volkerding. Slackware started as a floppy-based distribution, with the various parts of the OS divided into several lettered series of diskettes. There was a diskette set for the kernel, one for networking, one for compilers, and so on. It also had an installation script that seemed to ask a never-ending series of questions. Worse, the script wasn't very forgiving: you could not change the answer to any question without restarting the installation. This could be a major irritation if it happened toward the end of the process.

For all its warts, however, Slackware was a major step forward. It still wasn't ready for the average user, since it required quite a bit of knowledge to use. However, it did allow people who wanted to use Linux to do so without having to jump through hoops, particularly those who didn't have an additional computer on which to compile the source files needed to get Linux running. Slackware is still a viable distribution that has been updated with each new Linux kernel. The distribution is now available on a bootable CD-ROM, and the installation script is much more user-friendly. For all its improvements, though, Slackware is not for the beginner. It still requires some knowledge to install effectively.

Anyone Can Do It

Now that you know the basics of distributions (also called *distros*), you might wonder who creates them. The answer is simple: anyone can create a distribution because, as mentioned in chapter 1, both the kernel and GNU software have been GPLed. That means there is no legal encumbrance preventing someone from creating a distro, other than that of releasing any software based upon other GPL software with the same copyright. The result can be distributed as the author wishes, complete with the code that came from other sources. That's the beauty of open-source software.

Contrast that with the commercial model practiced by companies such as Microsoft. Suppose a company called Slick Software sold a compelling package to manage widgets. How long do you think Microsoft would permit Slick to bundle a copy of Windows with its own widget software? The answer is obvious. On the other hand, Slick could bundle a Linux distribution with its software without any problem at all. Again, that's the beauty of open-source software.

Since anyone can create a distribution, the question becomes not, "Who creates the distributions?" but rather, "Why do they create them?" The list of reasons is probably as long as the number of distributions, but certainly would include the following:

- *Because they can.* The early adopters of Linux came from the hacker community. This group is notorious for reinventing the wheel, if for no other reason than the sheer joy of the learning experience. We fully understand and endorse this "roll-your-own" philosophy, if that's what gives you pleasure.

- *For a specific purpose.* Although there are the do-it-yourselfers who create distributions for their own sake, a more likely reason to build one is to meet a specific need. Perhaps you need an extremely compact Linux system to act as a firewall. Or maybe you need a small one to turn those old 486s you have lying around into capable X terminals. Assuming that you can't find a current distribution that fits the bill (which for the two reasons just mentioned is unlikely), you can always custom-build one that is not too big, not too small, but just right for your purposes.

- *To build a better mousetrap.* Sometimes you find a distribution (call it *A*) that would be just perfect for your needs if only it had *x* (a list of essential features, by their omission of which the authors of *A* have proven themselves to be imbeciles). One classic example of this is the Mandrake distribution. Early distributions of Red Hat would install a kernel compiled for the Intel 80386 processor and its clones. It was simple to do this, as the 386 kernel would run on any Intel processor that was a 386 or better, since Intel designed its processors to be backward-compatible. The problem with this approach is that the kernel doesn't take advantage of any of the performance enhancements designed into later processors. To avail yourself of these speed enhancements, you'd have to compile your own kernel. This isn't a major undertaking, but it does seem somewhat inelegant.

  This is where the Mandrake distribution comes in. The original Mandrake distribution was based on Red Hat, but with everything compiled to be optimized for the Pentium-class CPUs. Installing Mandrake on a CPU lower than a Pentium virtually guaranteed that you'd be plagued with kernel-panics and mysterious system lock-ups, since there were machine instructions embedded in its executables that a 486 or lower couldn't understand. (For the record, Mandrake has evolved way beyond its original *raison d'être* and can no longer be called an optimized Red Hat clone. However, it is an excellent example of the open-source philosophy in action.)

- *As a value-added commercial product.* The term *value-added* means that the product is in some way enhanced (has additional value) over a standard version of the same product. If Slick Software had a distribution that included their famous widget management application, you would call it a value-added commercial product. Typically, the price for this distribution would be the cost of the widget application and perhaps a small amount to cover the cost of the distribution media. There wouldn't be any licensing fee for the operating system because Slick wouldn't have to pay anything for it.

  Although Slick probably wouldn't create a distribution for its software, since there are already so many available, it could modify an existing one and add its own software to it. This would make Slick's application very attractive to a business that wanted to use it on computers dedicated to the widget application. All that an IT manager of one of these businesses would need would be a computer with an empty hard drive and Slick's distribution CD. (Slick Software is, of course, a hypothetical example. The next section discusses some real-world commercial distributions.)

Choosing a Distribution

Choosing a Linux distribution is a lot like any software project. You must first determine your requirements. Typically (but not always), you'd choose the application software prior to picking the operating system. Since you are reading this book, we can assume that the application software you want includes a Web server, a database, and various other sundries to make the project go. Linux is a good fit, so you've settled on using it for your project.

So what differentiates one distribution from another? To answer that question, check out any of the Linux newsgroups. Or get on an Internet Relay Chat, like *#linux*, and see what "everyone" has to say. Observe what questions are being asked and what, if any, distribution is mentioned in either a positive or negative light. Keep in mind that, for some reason, the choice of distribution seems to become a personal thing with many people. Derogatory comments about a given distro are likely to get you into a flame war, so tread lightly, and choose your words carefully if you want to ask anything. Judge like you're grading a test on a curve, discounting the high and low comments about a distribution, and you should come away with a reasonable view of its highlights and flaws.

For the less adventurous, another way to compare and contrast the various distributions is to go to *www.linuxlinks.com* and check out the "Distributions" link. The number in parentheses is the number of distributions in this site's database. At the time this book was written, there were 219. Click on the link, and you'll see short descriptions of each distribution, as well as links to a number of special-purpose ones, including those that are floppy-based, built for security, or built for international use (with appropriate language fonts for double-byte character sets, such as those used in Asian and Middle Eastern countries).

The short descriptions given on the "Distributions" page hardly do the distributions justice. To compare them all, you'd have to follow the link to each one's home page, where you could read about its design goals, features, and included application software. This would be a really time-consuming chore. To narrow down your selections, ask yourself what you need or want to do with your Linux machine.

If you have specific application software in mind, the choice might be fairly straightforward. For instance, if your company has a requirement to use Corel's WordPerfect Office 2000 suite or its CorelDRAW program, use Corel's distribution. This is particularly true if you're going to buy hardware that's approved for use on Corel's distro, since you can ensure that the hardware will be supported.

But what if you have hardware already sitting in your office onto which you'll load Linux? In this case, pick a distribution that has a Linux kernel new enough to support your hardware, assuming that one exists. In most cases, bleeding-edge hardware gets support for Windows long before Linux because manufacturers will write drivers for Windows before delivering hardware to market. After all, they want to sell hardware, and since Windows has the lion's share of the desktop market, the drivers must be ready. With a few exceptions, Linux support for a piece of hardware comes after it is available to the general public.

While some manufacturers write Linux drivers, most of the time, the best the Linux community gets from the manufacturer is the hardware specifications. The actual software engineering has to be done in the open-source community. And they can't do that until the hardware can be purchased. The moral is to pick a distribution for which there is active development. If you do, you won't have to wait too long until new hardware gets supported.

Speaking of support, remember to consider long-term support for your system when picking a distribution. The cost of an operating system is just a small part of the total cost of ownership (*TCO*) for any computer system. You still have to keep the system running. Even though Linux is miles ahead in the purchase-cost race, and is arguably ahead in the stability (and, therefore, TCO) race, you're going to need to maintain your system, since your software and hardware requirements will change over time. You'll need someone to do that. The current reality is that the number of qualified Linux gurus available to do maintenance is eclipsed by the number of qualified Windows gurus available, but that will change over time.

The myth that "everyone" is a Windows guru (after all, they use the OS on their home PC, so that makes them experts) gives the perception that obtaining support for a Windows box is trivial. It is this perception that gives "the suits" a warm, fuzzy feeling when adopting Windows as the server operating system over Linux. Since Windows is a tangible product, with a tangible cost, produced by a not-insignificant company, it is an easier choice for the corporate world. After all, you know where to obtain support, should the need arise.

The corporate argument against Linux stems from the necessity of support. The clients who use our services can always call on us to support their systems—at least until we hit the lottery, retire, or meet an untimely demise. We're not being trite when making that statement. Those thoughts have crossed the minds of more than one of our clients. An exit from their world could prove problematic. Fortunately, it's a problem that can be solved by selecting a distribution for which support is available.

Although not the only one, Red Hat is one such company. Red Hat derives some revenue through the retail sale of its distributions, but its business model is predicated on selling support services. After all, you wouldn't want to bank on a company selling software that legally can be downloaded from the Internet, or purchased once and then loaded on hundreds of systems. It doesn't matter where your copy of the Red Hat distribution comes from; Red Hat's retail package doesn't have a fancy holographic seal or product ID you need to key in. Regardless of your software's pedigree, you can purchase a support agreement from Red Hat that suits your needs. That availability of support, along with the warm embrace of companies like IBM, has legitimized Linux in corporate circles.

So, how do you choose a distribution? Simple:

- Pick one that supports the hardware on which you're going to load it.
- Pick one that includes applications you'll want or need to use.
- If you're going to use it in a corporate environment, pick one that is mainstream, with ongoing development. Obscure or special-purpose distributions are inappropriate for the business world.

For the purposes of this book, we chose Red Hat Linux.

Chapter Summary

The entity known as the "Linux operating system" is, in fact, comprised of the Linux kernel and system software from the Free Software Foundation. So, the proper name for Linux is GNU/Linux.

A distribution is made up of the kernel, system software, application software, and installation/configuration tools, bundled together in a particular way to satisfy specific requirements defined by the distribution's author. A distribution should be selected according to how closely it supports the hardware and software requirements of the application for which the Linux machine is to be used. The selection should always be made with an eye toward the availability of support from outside sources.

And most importantly: never post a message to a Linux newsgroup stating that a given distribution is unequivocally the best one. Them's fightin' words.

End of Chapter Review

Key Terms

Application software	GPL software	Red Hat
Distribution	Hardware	Slackware
Firmware	Mandrake	System software
FTP site	Operating system kernel	Total cost of ownership
GNU/Linux	POSIX standard	Value-added

Review Questions

1. Besides Linus Torvalds, which other entities must be credited with making Linux what it is today?

2. Explain what is meant by "total cost of ownership" with regard to obtaining a Linux system.

3. Describe the importance of the kernel to an operating system.

4. What standard enabled Linux to become a player in the computer industry?

5. How does Red Hat, a popular Linux distribution, appeal to corporations?

Programming Assignment

Exercise: Investigate Linux Distributions

1. List the current retail prices of four Linux distributions.

2. Describe the different features of the distributions.

3

Installation

Since the title of this chapter is "Installation," you could reasonably assume that it contains a step-by-step set of instructions on how to accomplish this task. Well, forget that idea. Such a document is already available for Red Hat Linux, titled (non-coincidentally) "The Official Red Hat Linux x86 Installation Guide." This document is available in printed form with the Red Hat boxed set, and in both HTML and Adobe PDF format on the distribution CDs and the Red Hat Web site (*www.redhat.com/support/manuals*). There is no need to reinterpret that document's information here. Besides, any well-crafted instructions added here would be obsolete by the time you read them. Instead, this chapter focuses on installation issues that would otherwise typically be learned through trial-and-error.

Preparation Is the Key

Preparation is the key to successfully installing an operating system. This is particularly true when you are dealing with a computer that will be used as a server. A server, unlike a desktop workstation, is expected to be available to multiple users, typically on a 24-hour basis. Once a server is placed online, its maintenance, upgrade, or reconfiguration typically involves some serious planning so that the system downtime can be minimized.

It is bad enough to have to make changes to a server due to increasing capacity requirements (although this can be a good problem, if it means that server use is on the increase). It is even worse if you need to go through the exercise due to some short-sightedness or lack of planning on the part of the original system architect. System downtime will, at the very least, erode your users' confidence in the server and, perhaps, in your abilities. At the very worst, the downtime will cost your company money in lost sales or productivity, especially if the server happens to be hosting an e-business application. And that just might cost you your job.

In the context of a Linux server, preparation includes the following steps:

1. Ensure that the hardware is supported by the operating system.

2. Ensure that the hardware has sufficient capacity for the tasks that you plan for it.

3. Determine what software you need for the server. (Most server software is bundled with the operating system, but you might need to gather some from additional sources. Ensure that you retrieve the documentation and software updates during your quest.)

4. Decide how to carve up the disk real estate.

5. Plan your backup and recovery strategy.

6. Install, configure, and test.

Each of these steps is discussed in detail in the following sections.

Is Your Distribution Compatible with Your Hardware?

As discussed in the previous chapter, hardware compatibility can be a major issue when selecting Linux as your operating system of choice, since it does not always support the latest gizmos and gadgets. Fortunately, the manufacturers of those products target the home user, where the "sizzle" factor sells more product than does actual need or utility. Since you are building a server, you are dealing with an area where Linux excels and where unsupported gizmos are unlikely to be a factor. You still need to do your homework, however, to ensure that you don't have any nasty surprises during installation.

Highest on the compatibility checklist is the platform's architecture, on which you plan to install Linux. Unlike Windows, which runs only on Intel or compatible hardware (Windows NT does run on the DEC/Compaq Alpha chip, but is no longer supported), Linux is available on a number of different platforms. So, it is imperative that you get the distribution for your architecture. Because the focus in this book is Linux on Intel-compatible platforms, we need the Red Hat distribution for the "x86" platform. Be sure you get the distribution for your target platform.

Next in priority is compatibility with disk interfaces. Currently, two different interfaces are commonly in use. The first, *SCSI* (Small Computer System Interface), is typically used in server and workstation machines. SCSI has been around for a long time, and the equipment that uses it is usually of high quality and reliability. SCSI has two main benefits: performance and compatibility. Except for the very low-end controllers included with page scanners, SCSI controllers include their own processors. These processors handle the communications between the peripherals and the main system, which increases the performance of the system as a whole. At the time of this writing, the maximum transfer rate available for a SCSI-based system is 160 Mb/second. Since SCSI has been around for such a long time, it's almost a foregone conclusion that the SCSI controller you want to use will work just fine with Linux, particularly if it's from a mainstream manufacturer.

If SCSI has any downside, it would have to be cost. Along with the higher performance and reliability comes a higher price. SCSI devices are manufactured with higher-quality parts and within finer tolerances than other device types, which increases their production costs. Since they are sold in fewer numbers than their consumer-grade equivalents, there aren't as many items over which the costs can be distributed, resulting in a higher per-unit cost.

The topic of unit cost leads to the second common disk interface: *IDE* (Integrated Drive Electronics). In addition to SCSI, early interfaces included MFM and RLL, both of which were limited in their performance capabilities. A cheaper, yet better-performing, alternative was created that moved the "smarts" from the controller card onto the hard drive itself—hence the term *integrated*. IDE was a major improvement over its MFM/RLL predecessors, offering better performance at a lower cost. Although it wasn't a contender in performance compared to SCSI, it was a step up for the burgeoning PC industry. A later version, *EIDE* (Enhanced Integrated Drive Electronics) added both speed and the ability of the drive to report its geometry (how many heads/sectors/cylinders it has) to the computer's BIOS, making hardware installation much easier for the average user to tackle.

Why should this be of any interest to you? Because EIDE is one of those gizmos we alluded to earlier. The high CPU/bus speeds available in today's modern PCs have highlighted the relatively dismal performance exhibited by the disk subsystems. A CPU running at 1GHz has exactly the same performance as one running at 33MHz if both are awaiting the arrival of some data from the disk subsystem. To combat this phenomenon, and to give you another way to compare the performance of your system with that of a neighbor's (thus spawning a hardware upgrade), manufacturers have come up with some more enhancements, with specifications known as UDMA-33, UDMA-66, and UDMA-100. These drives can transfer data at 33 Mb/second, 66 Mb/second, and 100 Mb/second, respectively, so the I/O bottleneck isn't as much of a problem as it once was. Unfortunately, these are new kids on the block, and controllers for them aren't supported by many out-of-the-box Linux distributions. Fortunately, however, Red Hat is fairly up-to-date and can handle many of the commonly available controllers. To be safe, though, you'll need to check.

Although we have discussed only the CPU and drive interface hardware so far, you should take the time to make a checklist of all your computer's hardware, and then check the hardware compatibility list to see if all of it is supported. Red Hat users can check *http://hardware.redhat.com* to find a good list of compatible products. Two other resources are the "Linux Hardware Compatibility HOWTO" (*www.linuxdoc.org/ HOWTO/Hardware-HOWTO/*) and the "Linux Hardware Database" (*http://lhd.datapower.com*).

No matter which Linux distribution you choose, make sure that the hardware you choose is supported. Although many of the major PC vendors now offer computers with Linux preloaded, thus guaranteeing hardware compatibility, you will probably be loading Linux onto hardware you've decided to recycle. Ensuring that your distribution either directly supports or can be made to support your hardware will make the installation process much less irritating. It is time well spent.

How Big Is Big Enough?

One confusing aspect of building a server is determining the minimum hardware requirements. Although Linux has become famous for its ability to make older and less powerful equipment sing, you must have sufficient hardware resources to handle requests in a timely manner. If you don't, your users will look elsewhere. Other than advice like "just purchase a server-class machine to start off with," there are few hard and fast rules to the alchemy of server-building. Nevertheless, keep in mind the following tips.

- Buy the fastest disk hardware you can afford. As mentioned earlier, a CPU that's waiting for the arrival of data from the disk subsystem is an idle CPU, regardless of its speed. For applications that include a lot of disk I/O, such as a database server, faster disk hardware will keep the CPU supplied with data to work with, thus minimizing idle time. The newest Ultra-160 SCSI system is always a good bet, but the EIDE UDMA-100 hardware is no slouch either.

You can improve your disk subsystem performance by spreading the disk requests over multiple units. With this setup, multiple disk arms can be working simultaneously. If you can afford to do so, install more than one disk drive and partition them so that the workload is distributed evenly across them. (You'll see how to do this shortly.) If you do install multiple drives, particularly if they are EIDE drives, be sure to install them on separate I/O channels. Most motherboards support at least two IDE channels; by using both, you'll increase your available I/O bandwidth, further enhancing performance.

- Stuff as much RAM into the box as you can. Linux has a real talent for managing memory. If the physical RAM exceeds the total required for the current processes, it will use the excess as a cache for data that would normally be sent straight to disk. It will also store recently accessed data in memory. If a request is made for data that is still in cache, it will be retrieved from there instead of involving another request to the disk subsystem.

  In short, more RAM can make up for slower disk performance. You can, conversely, try to compensate for less RAM by increasing the swap partition on the disk drive, but this will decrease the system's performance because of the relative performance differences between real memory and virtual (disk-space) memory.

- Consider your CPU performance. This is where the numbers become more difficult to pin down. As you know, Linux is a multitasking operating system, meaning it can do many things at the same time. Well, not really. Actually, the CPU works on one task, then switches to the next. It does the switching quickly enough to give the illusion that everything is running at the same time.

  Although a complete discussion of how it selects which task to execute next and how much time it spends on a given task is beyond the scope of this book, you need to consider which tasks you plan to run on the same server. If you run your Web server on one machine and have a separate computer for your database, even a 233 MHz Pentium might be fast enough for your Web server. On the other hand, if you plan on running the database on the same machine as your Web server (which might not be a great idea if you expect many intense queries to the database), you might need a CPU that has cycles to burn. A long-running query can easily soak up enough CPU time to make additional connections to the Web server appear sluggish and to make the server seem unresponsive. Naturally, you want to avoid this situation.

  You might also want to consider purchasing a motherboard that can handle multiple CPUs, which enables symmetric multiprocessing (SMP). Older versions of these motherboards can be bought quite inexpensively. Linux will balance requests across the various CPUs, helping to keep a heavy-duty database query from hogging all available CPU cycles.

As you can see, it is somewhat difficult to give explicit hardware recommendations because of the variation in job mixes encountered in different installations. We know that you still would like some kind of recommendation, though, so here goes:

A low-volume Web server, or one that would be a great development machine, would consist of a Pentium Pro/Pentium II or faster processor, at least 128 Mb of RAM, and a relatively fast disk-drive system. This assumes that the server will be dedicated to this task and not used simultaneously as a workstation. A workstation implies the use of the X Window system (the Linux GUI) and its inherent memory requirements, which would necessitate a corresponding increase in memory and CPU capacity.

Acquiring the Pieces and Updates

After you have picked up the Red Hat Linux distribution, one of the first things you'll want to do—either before the installation if you have another Internet-connected computer, or immediately after the installation—is go to Red Hat's errata page (*www.redhat.com/errata*) and retrieve all of the updates for your distro. The Linux community is very quick to produce patches for errant software, particularly if those patches fix a recently discovered security hole.

Furthermore, the distribution will undoubtedly be missing some of the software you will require for your Web server. Almost all distros include the Apache Web server (which is the one we recommend), so that base is covered. However, if you intend to use Java to provide dynamic content to your site (which we also recommend), you'll need a Java virtual machine (JVM) for Linux. There are number to choose from. You can obtain a Linux JVM from the original suppliers, BlackDown, at *www.blackdown.org*; from IBM at *www.ibm.com;* or from Sun Systems at *http://java.sun.com.*

Once you have acquired the JVM, you'll need some kind of servlet container in which to run the server-side Java programs you'll be running. A good choice, if you have the hardware to run it, is IBM's own WebSphere. The open-source alternative, Tomcat, is great for lightweight systems. It is available at *http://jakarta.apache.org.*

It is the rare site indeed that doesn't use some kind of database management system. Included with your Red Hat package are two open-source favorites: MySQL and PostgreSQL. You'll need to check out the Web sites for each of these to find out which one best suits your needs. MySQL can be found at *www.mysql.com* and PostgreSQL can be found at *www.postgresql.com.* If you need a commercial database, you can hardly go wrong with IBM's own DB2 Universal Database for Linux, which is the same database available on IBM's S/390 (zSeries) and AS/400 (iSeries) platforms. DB2 does, of course, cost money, while the open-source alternatives are free. The alternative you choose depends on your needs.

This list of software requirements is not meant to be all-inclusive; instead, it is designed to get you thinking about your needs. You will be much more likely to have a successful installation if you select your software and read the associated installation documentation prior to the actual installation.

Carving Up the Disk Real Estate

On a clear disk you can seek forever. (Ancient Computing Proverb)

One of your tasks during the installation of Red Hat Linux (or any operating system, other than DOS/Windows) is to carve your disk into at least two, but probably more, logical chunks of varying sizes. When created under DOS/Windows using the **fdisk** program, these chunks, called *partitions*, make a single drive appear to the operating system to be multiple drives. Thus, a physical drive, divided into two parts, would appear to Windows as drives C: and D:. (Actually, if you had more than one drive, you could dedicate the entire drive to a single partition.)

Information about each partition, such as its size and partition ID (the type of file system written on the partition), is stored on the drive in a data structure known as the *partition table*. This table is capable of storing information for up to four partitions, referred to as *primary partitions*. One of these partitions can be created as a special type, known as an *extended partition*, which permits the drive to be divided even further.

Figure 3.1 shows a disk drive partitioned with **fdisk** into a primary partition (which would appear to Windows as C:) and an extended partition. A logical partition (which would appear as D:) has been created within the extended partition. This extended logical partition allocates only one-third of the space available in the extended partition. The remainder is left unallocated. Once the disk has been partitioned, each of the partitions needs to have a file system written to it before Windows can use it. The program to accomplish this varies with the version of Windows. Windows 9x and ME use a derivative of the original FORMAT program from the original DOS/Windows 3.1 operating system. Windows NT, 2000, and XP use a newer program called Disk Administrator, which does what FORMAT does and more.

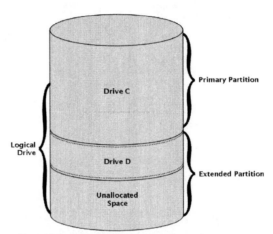

Figure 3.1: A simple partitioning scheme from a DOS/Windows viewpoint.

Partitioning a disk drive with Linux is similar to partitioning it in Windows. A program called **fdisk** creates the partitions. As with Windows, the raw partitions must be formatted before they can store data, although there are some exceptions to the rule. (For example, some DBMSs can write data to a raw partition.) Once the drive is partitioned, it needs to be formatted. For this task, Linux includes a program called **mke2fs** ("make ext2 file system") that performs the equivalent function of fdisk.

Linux and Windows diverge greatly, however, when it comes to managing partitions. Linux doesn't refer to partitions, or physical devices, with drive letters. There is no "A:" to represent the floppy drive or "C:" to denote the first hard drive or partition. Instead, the Linux file system is based on an *inverted tree structure*, typically drawn in a diagram with the root directory (indicated by a forward slash, /) at the top. Windows also uses this inverted tree structure, but does so by drive or partition, and with a backslash (\) instead of a forward slash for the root. Hence, there is a root directory on each floppy disk (A:\) and on each physical hard drive or partition (C:\, D:\, etc.). Linux, on the other hand, has only one root directory, and every file, subdirectory, partition, or physical device appears in the tree subordinate to the root.

Figure 3.2 shows a single hard drive divided into three partitions by Linux: one contains the actual kernel (/boot), one is used for swap space (virtual memory to be used in lieu of true physical memory), and one contains everything else (/). Notice that the drive and partitions appear multiple times in the directory tree in Figure 3.2. In the **/dev** (devices) directory, for example, the entire hard drive is referred to as **/dev/hda**, and the individual partitions are **/dev/hda1**, **/dev/hda2**, **/dev/hda5**, and **/dev/hda6**.

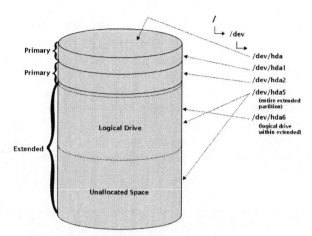

Figure 3.2:A Linux-eye view of a partitioned hard drive.

The mappings between the drive, partitions, and entries in **/dev** are done automatically during system startup. This mapping assumes that the drive is the master drive on the primary IDE channel. If it were the slave drive on the primary IDE channel, it would be **/dev/hdb**. The references to the primary and secondary drives on the secondary IDE channel would be **/dev/hdc** and **/dev/hdd**, respectively. In either case, an IDE CD-ROM drive would appear as one of these drives. And the floppy drive? If it were the standard 1.44 Mb floppy (which, to Windows, would be "A:"), you'd find it as **/dev/fd0**.

You might be wondering why **hda** partitions three and four have been skipped in the sequence. The reason is that only two of the four primary partitions have been created. The first is **/dev/hda1** and the second is **/dev/hda2**, which has been marked as an extended partition and encompasses the remainder of the drive. Any logical partitions created within an extended partition will be numbered beginning with five, thus creating the missing partition numbers.

Now that you have some idea of how Linux maps the physical drives and partitions, let's see how it refers to them whenever data is to be written to or read. To make the partition accessible, the **mount** command must be issued. This command associates a partition with a specific directory, grafting it into the directory tree on a directory called a *mount point*. This can be done manually, or automatically at system startup by adding entries into a configuration file called **/etc/fstab**.

In Figure 3.2, the second partition has been dedicated to swap space, and therefore does not appear anywhere other than in **/dev**. The other two partitions, however, have been grafted into the tree structure. Partition 1 has been mounted in the Linux file system as **/boot**, which is read as "the directory named *boot* appearing under the root directory." Partition 3 is mounted simply as **/**, the root partition. In the directory hierarchy, **/boot** and **/dev** are both subordinate to **/**.

If you are familiar with the Windows naming convention, you might find the Linux convention somewhat disconcerting. Once you become accustomed to it, however, you'll find it not only natural, but also much more flexible—even elegant. (For more about disk partitioning, refer to "An Introduction to Disk Partitions" in the appendix of the *Official Red Hat Linux Reference Guide.*)

There is one restriction when dealing with the contents of **/boot**. Most PCs have trouble booting operating systems where the kernel (stored in **/boot**) falls outside of the first 1,024 cylinders of the disk drive. With this in mind, it's best to create first a small (20 Mb or so) partition to serve as the partition containing **/boot**. This will ensure that the PC will be able to successfully load the kernel when the time comes.

The simple three-part partitioning strategy discussed in this section is the one recommended by Red Hat, primarily because it is fairly simple to understand. The next section discusses an alternative that is more complicated, but provides better flexibility. In this strategy, the disk partitioning and formatting is done during the installation of Red Hat, and you will not be required to manually invoke either **fdisk** or **mke2fs**. Instead, the graphical installer will handle these details for you, insulating you from the decidedly user-unfriendly **fdisk** program by replacing it with the kinder, gentler Disk Druid. If you ever need to do any partitioning on an active system, however, you will need to learn the mechanics of **fdisk**, since Disk Druid is available only during system installation. Once your system is up and running, you can read more about **fdisk** by accessing its **man** page (discussed in chapter 4).

Planning Your Backup and Recovery Strategy

One aspect of configuring any system is considering the ramifications if the worst happens and that shiny, new disk drive decides to quit. (Actually, the question isn't *if* the drive will quit, but rather *when* it will quit.) How are you going to get your system operating again? Even if you should happen across that one-in-a-million drive that possesses the secret to immortality, you will eventually want to upgrade the operating system to a newer level as your needs change or when helpful new functions are added to Linux. Planning a strategy for recovery or upgrade is much easier before you start the installation. Furthermore, the layout of a Linux system allows your plan for recovery to work for upgrading as well. Let's look at some of the factors you should consider when planning your system.

Have you ever noticed how many recovery and backup tools are available for the Windows platform? An entire industry has been built around these functions to compensate for what we believe are serious flaws in Windows' design. First on the list of big mistakes would have to be the concept of the *system registry*. This is a binary file that Windows uses to store configuration information about itself. Everything you've ever configured on your system has affected the system registry. Lose or corrupt that file, and you and your system are down for the count. The only way to make manual edits to the registry is with one of the Microsoft-supplied programs REGEDIT or REGEDT32. However, both of these require the Windows GUI to operate. So, if your system fails to boot, you are out of luck. To make matters worse, Microsoft has provided application program interfaces (APIs) to allow software authors to use the registry for the same purpose. If that file gets corrupted, but by some miracle your system still starts, your applications might not work like they used to. What a deal! You get two opportunities to lobotomize your system for the price of one.

Another flaw in Windows is the way application software and operating system software are segregated—or rather, *not* segregated. In fact, it appears as if Windows goes out of its way to ensure that application software gets mingled with operating system software. Load any application software on your system, and you really can't be sure which pieces got placed where on your hard drive. Sure, if the software's authors chose to use the standard Windows InstallShield Wizard, you can uninstall an application easily enough, most of the time. If you want to back up and restore a specific application, though, things get more difficult.

The solution to these problems has traditionally been to reinstall a failing application—or worse, the entire operating system and all of the applications. Granted, the latest versions of Windows seem to address these problems. A simpler design in the first place, though, might have obviated the need.

Not surprisingly, we believe that Linux has this simpler design. To begin with, Linux has no registry in which all configuration information is stored. All configuration files on a Linux system are stored individually, by program, in text files. Thus, they are easily identifiable and can be edited by any of the available text editors, such as those that run from a text console, like vi. This is a handy feature should you ever have to modify a configuration file from a command line, and it's the only option you'll have if you boot into single-user mode or from a recovery disk or CD. In addition, you can save each configuration file individually prior to making any changes. So, you always have the capability to immediately fall back to a previous configuration should things go awry with your experiments.

The only Red Hat Linux feature that is similar to the Windows registry is the *Red Hat Package Manager* (*RPM*) database. This is used during the installation of software bundles, packaged via RPM, to keep track of the software that has been installed on the system. Later, it can assist in the removal of specific packages, ensuring that their removal will not affect the correct operation of software remaining on the system. It will also be used whenever you install additional software to ensure that packages upon which the software depends are already available on the system or are in the list to be loaded. Because the RPM database is used only for keeping a software inventory, its corruption will not affect normal system operations. Its corruption will be problematic only when additional software is loaded via RPM. Unlike the Windows registry, though, the RPM database can be rebuilt, should it ever become corrupted.

To keep the system software from mixing with the operating system software, Red Hat and other Linux vendors support the *File System Hierarchy Standard* (*FHS*). The purpose of the FHS is to provide a standard definition of the names, locations, and purposes of certain files and directories. The collaborative document that describes FHS can be found at *www.pathname.com/fhs*.

We'll hold off on a complete description of the various Linux directories until chapter 4. For now, we'll concentrate on the following directories, which contain programs and data that do not necessarily come with your Red Hat distribution:

1. **/usr/local**—This is the location set aside by FHS for the administrator (you) to install software that you've obtained independently and wish to install.

2. **/opt**—This serves the same purpose as **/usr/local**. This is where we recommend that you place static software, such as StarOffice, the Tomcat servlet container, and the Java Development Kit.

3. **/home**—This is where the user's personal directory is placed. For example, a user named "Dewey" would have **/home/dewey** as his home directory.

If the Red Hat recommendations are followed, all of these directories will be on the same partition as the root directory. This isn't necessarily bad; for many people, it will be how their systems get configured. Consider what happens, however, if these three directories are placed on separate partitions. These directories contain programs and data that are basically independent of whatever distribution of Linux you load. So, if they are on separate partitions, they can be left untouched whenever the current distribution of Linux is replaced with a newer or entirely different version.

As mentioned earlier, one of the steps performed by the Red Hat installer is the execution of **mke2fs** to format the disk partitions prior to their actual use. A system that already contains formatted partitions will result in the installation program offering you the choice as to whether each existing partition will get formatted, with certain restrictions. (Obviously, you don't have a choice if the partition is not formatted with a file system compatible with your Linux distribution.) If the installer is querying you about one of those partitions, you simply indicate that you wish to leave it intact. The result is that all of the extraneous programs you've collected, as well as your user's data, will be available once your system is back up.

Indeed, Red Hat does have an installation option that gives the opportunity to upgrade your system from one version of its distribution to another. In our opinion, though, it's much better simply to install a fresh copy of a new distribution instead of upgrading an older one. This ensures that any oversights in Red Hat's installation program will not come back to haunt you later. After all, writing a program to upgrade a system is much more difficult than writing one to install a fresh system, since the former requires that you account for existing software and configurations.

Our recommendation for partitioning a drive is shown in Figure 3.3. We have extended Red Hat's standard three-partition scheme with partitions for **/usr/local**, **/opt**, and **/home**. Before you can commit to using this partitioning scheme, though, you must decide if your hard drive is large enough for it. Creating separate partitions for **/home**, **/opt**, and **/usr/local** is extremely flexible, but if your hard drive is too small, you'll undoubtedly end up making one partition too large (with lots of free space), at the expense of another partition, which will invariably run out of space.

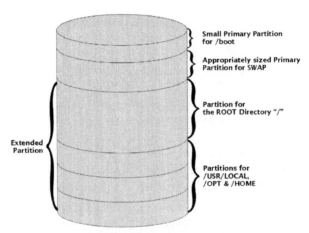

Figure 3.3: A disk partitioned for maximum flexibility.

To help you make this determination, refer to Table 3.1. This table is the output of the **du** command, which estimates used file space. The actual computer represented by this table is configured as both a workstation and a server on a company's intranet, so it contains most of the packages available from the Red Hat installation on both the workstation and server installations, as well as the IBM JDK, the StarOffice productivity suite, and lots of additional software documentation and hardware manuals.

Table 3.1: Output of the *du* command showing one server's partitioning.					
Filesystem	1k-block s	Used	Available	Use%	Mounted on
/dev/sda5	248895	132021	104024	56%	/
/dev/sda1	23302	8700	13399	40%	/boot
/dev/sda9	8262036	7101708	740632	91%	/home
/dev/sda7	1035660	4524	978528	1%	/tmp
/dev/sda10	814292	546184	259836	68%	/opt
/dev/sda2	2071416	1762524	203668	90%	/usr
/dev/sda8	4134900	971156	2953696	25%	/usr/local
/dev/sda6	521748	77300	417944	16%	/var

As you can see, the total space used for the partitions containing **/**, **/usr**, and **/var** is less than 2 Gb, while the partitions for **/home**, **/usr/local**, and **/opt** use over 5Gb! Don't panic—on this specific machine, one particular file in a user's home directory is 2Gb itself. You probably won't have a file that large on your machine, so your requirements will be more modest.

It comes down to this: If the machine you're using has a hard drive that is 4 Gb or smaller, use the three-partition scheme. You give up some flexibility with this smaller drive, but you probably won't run out of disk space for a while. If your drive is larger than 9 Gb, it's easy to add more partitions. If your system is between those two extremes, this decision will require some thought on your part. Keep in mind that **/home** should be dedicated to your user's personal programs and data, **/opt** is for static software acquired from somewhere other than the Red Hat distribution, and **/usr/local** has the same purpose as **/opt**.

Having discussed partitioning, we are ready to talk a bit about backup. The program you choose for backing up your system is up to you. Several commercial examples are included on the Red Hat Powertools CD, but the old standby is a program called **tar**, which is short for "tape archive." A how-to on the use of this program isn't appropriate in a chapter on installation, but we will mention that you don't need to back up your entire system. After all, you already have a backup for the system—the installation CDs. What you need to back up are the directories just discussed, as well as **/etc**, which contains all of the text-based configuration files, and perhaps certain subdirectories of **/var**, depending on where your application software, such as a database, has been configured to place its files. The documentation provided with the application should indicate where it places information and should be the guide for your total backup strategy.

Occasionally, you'll come upon a computer that fails to boot properly once Linux is installed. This usually occurs on older equipment because of the way the BIOS reports the geometry of the hard drive, but even new equipment sometimes has trouble getting started. To protect yourself from this problem, you need to create a boot diskette. At some point toward the end of the installation, you'll be asked if you wish to create one. Although it might be tempting to save a few minutes by declining the offer, we recommend that you do yourself a favor and perform the operation. Almost any problem with your installation can be fixed simply enough when the system is up. If you can't even get the system started, though, then you'll be kicking yourself because you didn't create the diskette. Just do it.

Installing, Configuring, and Testing

After you have read *The Official Red Hat Linux x86 Installation Guide* and have digested our comments pertaining to partitioning and recovery, you are ready to start installing Linux. Although it is possible to perform an installation across a network via FTP, NFS (Network File System), or HTTP, we make the assumption that you have the installation CDs and are going to be performing a local installation from a CD-ROM drive in your computer.

If your computer is capable of booting from CD, you are all set. If not, you'll have to create an installation diskette. To do that, take the *Install CD #1* and a blank 1.44 Mb floppy diskette to another computer that is running DOS or Windows. Insert the CD into the CD-ROM drive and, at a command line, type the items shown in bold:

```
C:\> d:  (This assumes that your CD-ROM drive is drive D:.)
D:\> cd \dosutils
D:\dosutils> rawrite
Enter disk image source file name: ..\images\boot.img
Enter target diskette drive: a:
Please insert a formatted diskette into drive A: and press -ENTER- : [ENTER]
d:\dosutils> (The diskette is now created.)
```

The file **boot.img** is a byte-for-byte copy of a 1.44 Mb Red Hat installation diskette. The **rawrite** program reads that file and restores it to another floppy, creating a duplicate of the diskette. (If you are using another Linux or UNIX computer to create it, use the **dd** program instead of **rawrite** to accomplish the same thing.)

At this point, you may begin the installation program. Power on your computer and insert *Install CD #1* into the CD drive. If your computer cannot boot from the CD, insert the installation diskette you just created. In either case, press the Reset button, and you will soon see the screen shown in Figure 3.4. This screen allows you to select a text-based or graphical installation, along with other options that you can ignore for now. (If you are inquisitive, you might want to press F2 and read the information on the general boot help screen. You may do likewise with the F3 through F5 keys. There is quite a bit of information on these screens that you might find useful should things not go as planned with your installation.)

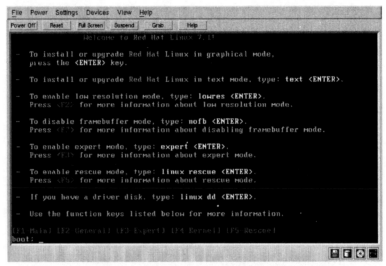

Figure 3.4:The initial screen presented by the Red Hat Installation CD.

Once you've assimilated the information presented on the help screens, press Enter to begin the installation program. The first screen that will require input from you is the Language Selection screen. If your computer supports graphics, you will be in the graphical installer, which you can identify by the inclusion of the "Man in the Red Hat" image in the upper-left corner. If your machine doesn't support graphical installation, you will be in the text-based installation program. The main difference between the two is the location of the help text. With the graphical installer, the pertinent help text is on the left side of the screen, with the options appearing at the right. With the text-based installer, the help text is available by pressing F1.

Additional information about the state of the installation script is available to you on other *virtual consoles*, so called because the Linux system treats them as separate devices without there being actual hardware to support them. To switch between virtual consoles, use the key combination Ctrl-Alt-F*n,* where *n* is a number between one and seven. If you are using the graphical installer, the installation dialog occurs on virtual console 7. The text-based installer uses virtual console 1. Others include virtual console 3, the installation log; virtual console 4, system-related messages; and virtual console 5, other messages. To see the installation log, press the key combination Ctrl-Alt-F3 from either installer. Press Ctrl-Alt-F7 to return to the graphical installer, or Ctrl-Alt-F1 for the text-based installer.

It is highly recommended that you take the time to read the help presented on each of the installation dialog screens to guide you on your selections. Red Hat will preselect options wherever possible, and, whenever it can it, offer a suggestion as to what your response should be.

These Are Your Options...

The next screen presented to you is the Install Options screen. Here, you can select the type of installation you intend to perform. If Red Hat finds a preexisting Red Hat installation, it will automatically select the option to upgrade. Since we assume that you're starting with a clean disk, the install option should be selected already, as well as the workstation type, which is fine for most installations.

If you read the help text provided on the Install Options screen, you'll note that the workstation and laptop options are similar, and permit Linux to be installed on a system that already has another operating system installed, assuming that you have some free, unpartitioned space on your hard drive. The software installed during a workstation/laptop installation is primarily what would be employed by a single user, including the X Window system. Both of these options partition your drive as mentioned earlier, with space for swap, **/boot**, and everything else as root (/).

The server installation option installs software that would be used by an Internet server, including the Apache Web server and the PostgreSQL database management system. Conspicuously missing is the X Window system, a reasonable option for a server, since it frequently runs without a monitor.

> **Note:** The server installation assumes that the entire system is to be used for a Linux server. It will delete all software from all drives connected to your system, regardless of operating system, and configure the drives for its own use. If you ever decide to do a server installation, be sure to keep this in mind.

The final installation option, "custom system," allows you to select how you want the drive(s) partitioned as well as which packages you want installed. We assume that you are installing Linux on a system that will be used as both a server (so others can connect to your system) and a workstation (where you'll design your Web site and connect to other Web servers). The custom system option provides the means to create such a system, so ensure that Custom System is selected, and click Next.

If the hard drive installed in your system has been wiped clean, you'll get an error message stating that the partition table is corrupt and needs to be initialized. Click OK and continue. In any case, you'll arrive at the Disk Partitioning screen. Once again, take the time to read the help information. Select the option to "manually partition with Disk Druid," and click Next.

The next screen, Partitions, is divided into three parts. At the left is the omnipresent help. On the upper right is a list of any partitions you have already created, along with their mount points and types. At the bottom right is a list of the hard drive(s) installed on your system and the percentage of space used on each. For this exercise, we'll assume that you have only one drive installed.

Begin partitioning the drive by clicking Add. You'll be supplied with a dialog box that requests the following:

- The mount point for the partition
- The size of the partition
- Whether Disk Druid should use the remainder of the drive for this partition

- The kind of partition you are creating

- The drives available on your machine

Using the drop-down arrow on the Mount Point box, and select **/boot** to indicate that you're creating the partition for **/boot**. Next, enter **16** into the Size (Megs) box to indicate that it should be 16 Mb (which is the size Red Hat creates in workstation or system installations). Ensure that the "Use remaining space?" check box is unchecked, since you don't want a single partition mounted on **/boot**! The correct partition type is Linux native, which should already be selected. Finally, if your machine has only one hard drive, then **hda** (or **sda**, if it's a SCSI machine) will already be selected. If not, select it, and deselect any of the other drives. Double-check your work, and when you're satisfied, click OK.

The partition you just created will appear in the upper right. Do not be concerned if the number under the Requested heading differs from that under the Actual heading. This is caused by the geometry of your hard drive. Disk Druid will find the closest size that will allow the partition to end on a cylinder boundary.

Next, you need to create a swap partition. Interestingly enough, Red Hat creates a 64 Mb swap partition if you select automatic partitioning on a custom system, workstation, or laptop installation. If you select a server installation, it creates a 256 Mb swap partition. Red Hat's own *Installation Guide* isn't very helpful in answering the question of what size you should use for the swap partition because it diverges from what the installation program will create (a "Do what I say, not what I do" scenario).

The traditional answer is calculated by this formula: multiply the physical memory in the machine by two. Thus, a machine with 128 Mb of RAM would have a 256 Mb swap partition. Adding to the confusion, however, are the latest reports that the new 2.4 version of the kernel is more aggressive in its use of swap space. Our recommendation is to use 256 Mb for swapping if you have a hard drive large enough to accommodate it; otherwise, use the RAM-times-two formula. In any event, don't make it larger than 512 Mb. Later, you'll be able to see what the results of your selection are, and if necessary, you can add additional swap space.

To create the swap partition, click Add as before, but this time, leave the mount point blank. Insert **256** (or your chosen size) in the Size box; then, using the drop-down box, select Linux Swap for your partition type, and click OK.

Now you have a big decision to make: Do you incorporate everything else into the root partition, or do you separate the pieces? If you choose former, you can finish up your partitioning by clicking Add, selecting **/** as the mount point, and then checking the "Use remaining space?" option. Disk Druid will allocate the remainder of your drive to the root partition, and you can continue the installation by clicking Next.

Otherwise, create each additional partition in the same way as the **/boot** partition was created (changing the mount point to something appropriate, of course). Click Add, select the mount point, and ensure that the partition type is marked Linux Native. When you've added all of the partitions that you need, continue the installation by clicking Next.

The following screen will allow you to choose the partitions to format. Since we assume that you're installing on an empty drive, you'll want to format each of the partitions. Red Hat has conveniently preselected all of the partitions you've created. An additional option, located at the bottom of the screen, is available to check for bad blocks while formatting. Modern drives check for bad blocks themselves, mapping them to spare blocks kept for this purpose, so having Linux do this is somewhat redundant. The only thing that it will cost you, should you choose to do it, though, is a little time during the format.

Next on the agenda is the *LILO configuration*. LILO is short for "Linux Loader." A complete description of its purpose is in chapter 4. Once again, if you've installed to an empty drive, Red Hat will have thoughtfully selected everything for you. Note the check mark next to Create Boot Diskette. The help text indicates that you should create it if you are not installing LILO on the master boot record or are not installing it at all. To reiterate: Create it in any case. Once you've reviewed everything here, click Next.

> **Note:** If you aren't installing to an empty disk, be sure to read the help text on the LILO Configuration screen, since a mistake here could cause a failure with any other operating systems that are sharing this drive.

If your machine has a network card installed, you'll get a Network Configuration screen. On it is the option to configure networking via DHCP or, if you uncheck that option, the ability to manually configure your networking card. We are unable to make this determination for you; you'll need to consult with your technical support for the appropriate information.

New to Red Hat (as of 7.1) is the Firewall Configuration screen. The ability to add a firewall has been part of Linux for a long time, but it required the user to configure it manually. The 2.4 kernel, however, has a much-improved version of the firewalling software, so in an attempt to improve out-of-the-box security, Red Hat has chosen to configure it as part of the installation. Network security and firewalls are beyond the scope of this book, but you basically have two choices. The first is to create no firewall at all, which is probably not the best choice unless your machine will be on a corporate intranet that is already inside a firewall. The other choice is to select the medium-security firewall, then select Customize to allow incoming Web connections, so that others may connect to your Web server. Once again, read the associated help text provided on this screen to determine the best choice for you.

The next screen, Language Support Selection, allows you to add additional languages to the base language you chose when the installation program started. After checking any that you want, click Next.

Following language support is the Time Zone Selection screen. In our opinion, you should set the hardware clock within your PC to use Greenwich Mean Time (GMT, the time in Greenwich, England, through which the 0° longitudinal line passes), also known as Universal Time Coordinated (UTC). Next, select the time zone in which your computer will maintain time. Using this method, you'll never have to reset your computer's clock when the time changes due to Daylight Savings Time. Linux will automatically make the conversion between local time and UTC, so the whole thing becomes a "set it and forget it" proposition. Given that a Linux box is expected to run non-stop for a long time (sometimes for more than a year), it's nice to have this feature available.

Now you're coming down the home stretch. You should be looking at an Account Configuration screen, divided into two sections. The first is a place to enter the password for the root user, which you'll duplicate in the Confirm box to ensure that you made no typographical errors. The second is a place for you to configure a regular system user.

Why would you want to create another user if you're the only one who will be using this machine? Because it is a horrible idea to run normal operations as the root user. Root is the almighty being of this computer, and a request to delete everything from the root partition (/) would be honored without question. Linux inherits from its UNIX parent the idea that, if you asked for it, you must want it. By creating another user account that lacks the capability to trash your system accidentally, you protect yourself from yourself. If you choose to ignore this advice, that's fine—just don't say we didn't warn you.

To create an account for yourself, fill in an account name (to save yourself some aggravation later, use only lowercase letters for all account names), enter the password twice (to confirm it), and (optionally) enter the full name of the account holder. Then click Add. When you see the new account listed on the screen, you're ready to continue to add additional users, or click Next to continue to the next screen.

Unless otherwise instructed, you'll want to ensure that "Enable MD5 passwords" and "Enable shadow password" are checked on the Authentication Configuration screen. Then, click Next.

You're almost done. Your next stop is at the Selecting Package Groups screen, where you'll select the packages that Linux will install on your system. In addition to the packages preselected by Red Hat, you'll want to select the following:

- Graphics Manipulation—So that you can get "the Gimp," an Adobe PhotoShop work-alike that will be helpful in creating graphics for your Web site.

- Games—You've got to have some diversions!

- SQL Server—In order to load the PostgreSQL DBMS onto your system. Most Web sites that provide dynamic content have some kind of database from which they pull information for display.

- WWW Web Server—To give you the Apache Web server.

- Development—To put the compilers onto your system. You might need these when you start loading software that comes in source form only. On an actual server, you'd omit these so that potential hackers wouldn't have tools conveniently provided for them, but on your development machine, they will be handy.

- Utilities—For useful tools to use while administering your machine.

Once you've selected these items, click Next, which will drop you into the X Configuration screen. Hopefully, the installer will have correctly identified the video card within your machine. If so, click Next again to pick your monitor. If you can't find your particular monitor, try to find one similar to it. Once you've done that, the installer will allow you to test the settings you've selected.

If you've done everything properly, you'll see a box with "Can you see this message?" on the screen. Be sure to select Yes if you were successful. At the bottom of the same screen is a choice of login types: text or graphical. Red Hat assumes that you want a graphical login, but in our experience, it is much more prudent to select text-based logins. Once you've logged in, you can start the X Window system manually. By setting yourself for text logins, you give yourself the best of both worlds; if anything goes awry with your X Window settings, you'll have an easier time starting your system. Besides, why waste system resources running X when you've logged off, and all your system is doing is acting as a server to the network?

Drum roll, please! You're at the About to Install screen, the final one that requires your intervention. No changes have been made to your hard disk yet; the installer has only been gathering information. If you have any qualms about the selections that you've made, click the Back button and make any necessary changes. When you're ready to commit, click Next, and the installation will begin.

At some point, the system will ask you for the second installation CD. Just follow the instructions it provides for this task, as well as the request to remove the floppy diskette from the drive (the one you used to create a boot diskette) prior to the reboot of your system. Once the system has restarted, you'll be presented with a request to sign on. Your installation has been successful!

What? You say that the computer rebooted and the letters "LI" appeared on the screen, but now things have ground to a halt? You've just encountered the problem mentioned earlier—the BIOS is improperly reporting the geometry of the drive. The permanent solution to the problem can be found in the documentation for LILO (**/usr/share/doc/lilo...**). For the short term, though, just insert the boot diskette (that we were adamant you create) and press the Reset button. Your machine should boot from the floppy and then start successfully, and you'll be rewarded with the sign-on screen.

Installation After-the-Fact

Although your system is ready for use, some documentation that you may find helpful has been omitted, so we'll take care of that now. Specifically, you're going to install the Red Hat FAQ, various HOWTOs, and the Red Hat manuals. To do that, you'll need the Red Hat Package Manager. Although this is a command-line tool, you'll be using the GUI front-end to it, which is called Gnome RPM.

To start, you'll need to log onto your system as the root user, to have the authority to install software. Once you've installed the documentation packages, sign off and then sign back on into the normal user account you created earlier. Once you're signed on as a mere mortal, you're welcome to play with all of the new toys on your system.

> **Note:** Remember that root is the omnipotent user profile, holding the power of life and death over your system. Do not do any experimentation while signed on as the root user, or you might find yourself reinstalling Linux.

Here is the text-based login:

```
Red Hat Linux release 7.1 (Seawolf)
Kernel 2.4.2-2 on an (your CPU type here)

(Your machine name here) login: MyLOGIN (the account you created)[ENTER]
Password: MyPassword[ENTER]
```

Note that the password will not be echoed to the screen as you type, but it is being entered. Furthermore, both the username and the password are case sensitive, so *password* isn't the same as *PASSWORD*. Enter the password exactly as you created it earlier, including case.

Once you've successfully signed on, you'll be presented with the following:

```
Last login: some date and time here from some terminal name.
[root@machine /root]#
```

The pound sign (#) indicates that you are signed on with omnipotent powers and that you should be very careful. To start the X Window system, enter the command **startx** and press Enter. Your X server will start, and you'll be presented with the main desktop, a Gnome Hints window (which you can close by clicking the Close button), and a warning that "you are running the Gnome File Manager as root." (Are you getting the idea how powerful root is by now?) Dismiss this warning (but heed it!) by clicking OK.

Next, insert the CD-ROM labeled "Linux Documentation" into the CD-ROM drive. You'll be presented with the GNU Midnight Commander, which is the Linux version of the Windows (NT) Explorer. The screen will display the contents of the CD, which you'll notice has been mounted automatically for you as **/mnt/cdrom**. Close Midnight Commander by clicking the X in the upper-right corner of the window. Now, click the "Gnome Foot" at the bottom left of the screen, move the pointer to Programs, then to the right to System, then right again, and click GnoRPM. This starts the Gnome RPM program. Click Documentation, and you should have the screen shown in Figure 3.5.

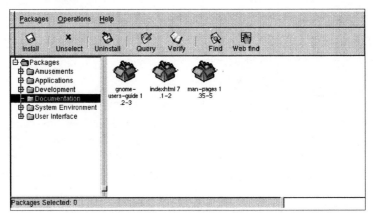

Figure 3.5:The Gnome RPM (gnorpm) graphical interface to Red Hat's rpm program.

The items in the right-hand box are packages that have already been installed. You want to add to that list, so click Install, and then Expand Tree. This will give you a detailed list of all of the installable packages on this CD. Select each of the packages in the following list by checking the box located to the right of each package, as shown in Figure 3.6:

- faq-7.1-1, Frequently Asked Questions

- howto-7.1-1, the Linux HOWTO directory

- rhl-cg-en-7.1, the Red Hat Customization Guide

- rhl-gsg-en-7.1-1, Red Hat Getting Started Guide

- rhl-ig-x86-en-7.1-1, the Red Hat x86 Installation Guide

- rhl-rg-en-7.1-1, the Red Hat Reference Guide

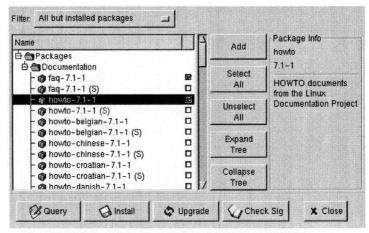

Figure 3.6:The documentation packages selected for installation.

Once these items are selected, click Install. When the packages are installed, close the installation window. If everything worked correctly, you should see the screen in Figure 3.7.

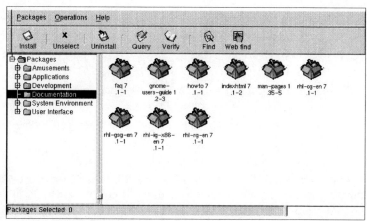

Figure 3.7:GnoRPM displaying the current installed documentation packages.

Although it might be tempting to see what else Gnome RPM does, this could be hazardous while signed on as root. Instead, close Gnome RPM by clicking the X in the upper-right corner of the window. Sign off of the system by clicking the Gnome Foot, and then click Log Out. You'll be prompted to confirm the log out. Ensure that Logout is selected under Action, and then click Yes.

You've logged out of X, but you still need to log off the system. At the command-line prompt, type **exit** and press Enter. You should be back at the sign-on screen.

Updating Your System

Once your distribution is loaded, you're ready to go, right? Well, not quite. Like any software, Linux is constantly in a state of change. The kernel and application software are always being enhanced with additional features, and bugs in the current code are being squashed. The latest version of Red Hat is fairly stable right out of the box, which might make you hesitate to install any upgrades, but the updates made to the software to improve security should push you toward keeping up-to-date. This is particularly true for the server you are currently configuring.

We discussed earlier the importance of acquiring the updates to Red Hat and pointed you to the appropriate Web site where updates and instructions are available (*www.redhat.com/errata*), so we won't give you detailed instructions here. In any case, the method you'll use to update your system depends on many factors. If you purchased a retail version of Red Hat, you can use the **up2date** program to retrieve and apply the updates. You'll need to read about it in Red Hat's documents.

To update your system by hand, go to the Red Hat Web site and retrieve the update RPMs. While you are there, read and print the update instructions for each package. The process is quite simple. You download an RPM, and, once it's on your system, you use the **rpm** program to install the package. Specific instructions are available with each package on Red Hat's site. Here is a quick summary of the **rpm** options used for updating a package:

1. **rpm -Fvh** *package_name.rpm* "freshens" an already installed package. If you attempt to use this command on any package that isn't installed, nothing will happen.

2. **rpm -Uvh** *package_name.rpm* updates or installs a package. If the package is not installed already, it will be installed. If it is installed already, older versions of the software will be replaced by the newer version.

3. **rpm -ivh** *package_name.rpm* installs a package. This option is typically used when updating a kernel package, since it allows the older version of the kernel to remain. Should anything go wrong with the newer version, you can always boot the older version.

Assume, for example, that you have a package on your system called **foo**. To see what version of **foo** is currently installed, type the command **rpm -q foo**. You should get a response like "foo-1.4.5-10." Assuming that a new package has become available, say "foo-1.5.0-1.rpm," you'd download it and type the command **rpm -Uvh foo-1.5.0-1.rpm**. Once the package has been installed, the command **rpm -q foo** would return "foo-1.5.0-1," indicating that the update was successful.

Chapter Summary

This chapter outlined the steps required to install Linux. It emphasized preparation, with the focus on creating a system that is flexible and can be easily upgraded or reconfigured. Good system administration requires that the system software be kept up-to-date to ensure the latest security upgrades and enhancements are in place. To ensure a smooth installation, nothing beats reading the documentation prior to installation. And no system is complete without a boot diskette.

End of Chapter Review

Key Terms

Boot diskette	LILO	Swap space
boot.img	Logical partition	tar
DBMS	Partition	Three-partitioning
Desktop workstation	Partition table	UDMA-100
disk druid	Primary partition	UDMA-33
EIDE	Root directory	UDMA-66
EIDE UDMA-100	Root partition	Ultra-160 SCSI
Extended partition	RPM	Virtual console
fdisk (mke2fs)	SCSI	x86 platform
FHS	Server	
GMT	SMP	
IDE	Swap partition	

Review Questions

1. List two undesirable consequences that may occur as a result of poor planning for a server installation.

2. What is the name of the command that allows you to access a partition?

3. The Red Hat Package Manager (RPM) is useful for what purpose?

4. Why do the authors recommend installing a fresh copy of a new distribution versus upgrading a previous version of that distribution?

5. Why is it necessary to create at least one normal user during a Linux install?

Programming Assignment

Exercise: Install Linux

1. Follow the Red Hat install prompts.

2. Use the suggestions in the chapter for selecting options during the Red Hat install.

3. [Optional] Load Linux on another machine.

4

Linux Configuration and Startup

The Linux lifecycle is composed of four phases:

- Booting or starting up Linux

- Logging on

- Using Linux applications

- When necessary for system maintenance, shutting down the system

This chapter covers all four of these phases.

Starting Up

The term *booting the system* was borrowed from the saying "pulling yourself up by your bootstraps," which refers to someone getting going without any help from anyone else. Picture some cowboy out on the prairie knocked unconscious after being thrown by a horse—with no help available, he has to pull himself up and get going again. *Bootstrapping* your computer is basically the same thing. The bootstrap of Linux, and most other operating systems, is a small file contained either on a floppy disk or on the first sector of your system's primary hard drive, known as the Master Boot Record, or *MBR*.

Your computer's hardware contains a little piece of software called the *BIOS* (Binary Input/Output System) that is hard-wired to your system's board. When you power on your system, the BIOS looks for the startup file on your system's floppy or primary drive. A Linux startup diskette contains a compressed version of the Linux kernel. Once loaded into memory, the kernel decompresses itself and starts executing.

Many Linux systems use *LILO* (Linux Loader) to control the boot process. LILO is installed on the MBR of your primary hard drive. Figure 4.1 show the LILO configuration file (**/etc/lilo.conf**) from a particular laptop. As mentioned in chapter 3, the Red Hat installation will configure LILO for you, but it's a good idea to understand what the various sections of **lilo.conf** accomplish. The first three statements of the file set up the basic parameters for Linux. The **boot** statement sets the name of the device where LILO should install itself in the MBR, **/dev/hda** in this system's case. Note that **hda** is the Linux name of a physical device, not a logical partition such as **hda2**. The **install** statement names the file containing the boot sector to use on the MBR, and the **map** statement specifies the map file that LILO creates when installed.

```
# basic parameters
boot=/dev/hda
install=/boot/boot.b
map=/boot/boot.b

# Boot option: Linux Version 2.4
image=/boot/vmlinuz-2.4.2-2
    label=linux
    read-only
    root=/dev/hda5

# Boot option: NeTraverse's Win4Lin kernel
image = /boot/win4lin
    label = win4lin
    root = /dev/hda5

# section for Windows/2000
other=/dev/hda1
    optional
    label=dos

# boot-time options
append="mem=512m"
```

Figure 4.1: The lilo.conf file supports boot-time options for multiple operating systems.

The next three sections of the LILO configuration file in Figure 4.1 qualify three operating-system options. LILO supports the optional booting of various operating systems. At boot time on this example system, you could select to run Linux version 2.4, a custom version of Linux by NeTraverse called Win4Lin (that supports running the Windows 98 operating system in a Linux process), or Windows 2000.

The last statement of the **lilo.conf** file in Figure 4.1 is a boot-time option. There are a dozen or so possible boot-time options, but this one qualifies that the laptop has 512 Mb of main memory.

Messages will be displayed while your system is booting, but there are so many that you might miss important error messages. So, after the boot process is complete, review all the messages in the log file **/var/log/messages**.

Note: If you modify **lilo.conf**, you must run the **/sbin/lilo** command while you are signed on as root to place the configuration options into the boot process.

Until Linux came around, IBM's iSeries only supported one operating system, OS/400. As a result, the iSeries did not have a generic process for loading and installing operating systems. Also, the iSeries runs Linux as a secondary operating system in a partition, with OS/400 always running in the primary partition.

To start up Linux on an iSeries machine, you load the kernel into the partition, initialize it, and link to the root file system. You do this with OS/400's Create Network Server Description command (CRTNWSD).

Initialization

After device drivers are installed by the boot process, the **init** program (located under the **/sbin** directory in Red Hat) is executed. This program starts or stops various Linux applications during system startup or shutdown. The processing completed by the **init** program is controlled by a special file called **inittab**, shown in Figure 4.2 (located under the **/etc** directory in Red Hat). Like **lilo.conf**, the Red Hat installation will configure **inittab** for you, but it is still a good idea to understand how it drives the processing of the **init** program.

```
#
# inittab       This file describes how the INIT process should set up
#               the system in a certain run-level.
#
# Author:       Miquel van Smoorenburg, <miquels@drinkel.nl.mugnet.org>
#               Modified for RHS Linux by Marc Ewing and Donnie Barnes
#

# Default runlevel. The runlevels used by RHS are:
#   0 - halt (Do NOT set initdefault to this)
#   1 - Single user mode
#   2 - Multiuser, without NFS (The same as 3, if you do not have networking)
#   3 - Full multiuser mode
#   4 - unused
#   5 - X11
#   6 - reboot (Do NOT set initdefault to this)
#
id:3:initdefault:

# System initialization.
si::sysinit:/etc/rc.d/rc.sysinit

l0:0:wait:/etc/rc.d/rc 0
l1:1:wait:/etc/rc.d/rc 1
l2:2:wait:/etc/rc.d/rc 2
l3:3:wait:/etc/rc.d/rc 3
l4:4:wait:/etc/rc.d/rc 4
l5:5:wait:/etc/rc.d/rc 5
l6:6:wait:/etc/rc.d/rc 6

# Things to run in every runlevel.
ud::once:/sbin/update

# Trap CTRL-ALT-DELETE
ca::ctrlaltdel:/sbin/shutdown -t3 -r now

# When our UPS tells us power has failed, assume we have a few minutes
# of power left.  Schedule a shutdown for 2 minutes from now.
# This does, of course, assume you have powerd installed and your
# UPS connected and working correctly.
pf::powerfail:/sbin/shutdown -f -h +2 "Power Failure; System Shutting Down"

# If power was restored before the shutdown kicked in, cancel it.
pr:12345:powerokwait:/sbin/shutdown -c "Power Restored; Shutdown Cancelled"
```

*Figure 4.2: The **inittab** file controls the initialization sequence of Red Hat Linux (part 1 of 2).*

```
# Run gettys in standard runlevels
1:2345:respawn:/sbin/mingetty tty1
2:2345:respawn:/sbin/mingetty tty2
3:2345:respawn:/sbin/mingetty tty3
4:2345:respawn:/sbin/mingetty tty4
5:2345:respawn:/sbin/mingetty tty5
6:2345:respawn:/sbin/mingetty tty6

# Run xdm in runlevel 5
# xdm is now a separate service
x:5:respawn:/etc/X11/prefdm -nodaemon
pptp:35:respawn:/usr/sbin/pptpd -f # pptpd-0.9.9-1
```

*Figure 4.2: The **inittab** file controls the initialization sequence of Red Hat Linux (part 2 of 2).*

The **inittab** file follows a format that is initially very difficult to understand. Each line conforms to the following format:

```
code:runlevels:action:command
```

The code is a unique one- or two-character sequence that identifies the specific entry in the **inittab** file. The runlevel indicates whether that entry is to be used during the execution of the **init** command. For instance, runlevel 0 executes the processes required to do a hard halt, runlevel 3 executes processes required to enable Linux multiuser mode, and runlevel 6 qualifies reboot processes to run. The **inittab** file has one line that identifies the default runlevel. In Figure 4.2, runlevel 3 is to be used unless otherwise qualified with the execution of the **init** program, such as during the boot process.

You can manually run the **init** program by invoking it with the runlevel as a parameter. For instance, to shut down your system, you could use the following command as the root user:

```
init 6
```

The **si::sysinit:/etc/rc.d/rc.sysinit** entry that follows the default runlevel entry causes a script called **rc.sysinit** to execute. This script does such things as checking and mounting file systems, enabling main memory for disk swapping, and synchronizing the Linux system clock with the platform's hardware clock. Following the execution of the **rc.sysinit** script, a script called **rc** is executed with a parameter that qualifies the runlevel.

On Red Hat, the **rc** script then executes scripts that exist in directories qualified, again, by the runlevel. For instance, when the **init** program executes with runlevel 3, the **inittab** file causes the **rc** script to turn around and run the scripts located in a directory called **/etc/rc.d/rc3.d**. Red Hat's rc3.d script executes all the scripts that are prefixed with a *K* before it executes the ones that are prefixed with an *S*. The *K* scripts kill, or shut down, processes that might already be executing, and the *S* scripts start processes. The two digits following the *K* or *S* control the execution order of the scripts.

On Red Hat, because the various runlevels start or stop the same processes, the common scripts are in a directory called **/etc/rc.d/init.d**, while symbolic links to those scripts are in the various rc*X*.d runlevel directories. To give you an example of how this works, consider a Red Hat 7.1 system where PostgreSQL should start when the system boots. While the **rc3.d** directory contains a link to the **/etc/rc.d/**

init.d/postgresql script called **K12postgresql**, it does not contain a link to **/etc/rc.d/init.d/postgresql** preceded by an *S*. When Red Hat was installed, it placed the link in **rc3.d** that would shut down PostgreSQL, in case the user happened to start PostgreSQL manually and forgot about it on Linux shutdown.

To have **rc3.d** automatically start PostgreSQL, you would simply have to create a link to **etc/rc.d/init.d/postgresql** called **S12postgresql** (where the *12* could be any two-digit number), with the following command:

```
ln /etc/rc.d/init.d/postgresql S12postgresql
```

Even though the **rc** scripts run as a separate process, the **init** program waits until they finish executing because the **rc** entries in the **inittab** file explicitly say to wait. After the **rc** scripts complete, the **init** program executes the rest of the entries in the **inittab** file. We'll skip most of them, as they are self-explanatory. However, take a look at the six **/etc/mingetty** scripts. These script executions start up six virtual consoles, which means you can sign on six different times as six different people on the single system console. To toggle between virtual consoles, press Ctrl-Alt followed by the number of the console you wish to see.

The only other **inittab** entry worth mentioning is this:

```
ca::ctrlaltdel:/sbin/shutdown -t3 -r now
```

This entry causes Linux to be able to capture the Ctrl-Alt-Delete keystroke combination and gently shut down the system.

Customizing Startup

A better way of causing PostgreSQL to start up, rather than adding the link in the **rc3.d** directory, is to modify the special script called **/etc/rc.d/rc.local**. Each of the **rcN.d** directories contains a link called **S99local** that points to a file called **/etc/rc.d/rc.local**. Because 99 is the largest possible number, a script called **rc.local** will always be executed last. So, instead of creating the link called **S12postgresql**, you could place the following entry in the **rc.local** script:

```
/etc/rc.d/init.d/postgresql start
```

There are two advantages to this approach:

• It places all your startup modifications in one script file.

• You can be sure that your custom processes are started after all the default processes are initialized.

Signing On

The root user is the omnipotent profile of Linux, also know as the *super user*. When Linux is installed, you are prompted for the password for the root user. Part of the Linux install is to also create a less powerful user. As discussed in chapter 3, Linux security is set up so that all the files on the system have three levels of authorization: user (or owner), user group, and users who are neither the owner nor part of the authorized user group. The root user, being all-powerful, has access to all files. For security purposes, you should use the root sign-on only when it is necessary.

To make it easier to use the root sign-on, Linux provides the **su** command (for "super user"). If you are logged in as a user other than root, but you need root privileges, enter the **su** command, which prompts for the root user's password. You can then execute commands that require root privileges. Be sure, however, to use the **exit** command to return to your alter-ego of a normal user with no super (and potential dangerous) powers. You can also use the **su** command while you're logged in as root to temporarily assume the role of a normal user. In that case, the command requires the user name. For instance, to temporarily run as user **bill** while logged in as root, you'd use this:

```
su bill
```

Running Linux Commands

The Linux logon screen program is known as the *bash shell*. Once you've logged into Linux, you can invoke thousands of commands from bash. Chapter 12 covers bash in detail, while this section bootstraps, so to speak, your knowledge of bash and Linux commands in general. The bash prompt defaults to your user name, the host name of your system, the current directory, and a dollar sign ($) if you are logged in as a normal user, or a pound sign (#) if you are logged in as root.

From the bash prompt, you are ready to begin mastery of Linux. Linux commands follow a common structure:

```
command option(s) argument(s)
```

Many commands, however, execute without requiring options or arguments. A starter set of Linux commands is shown in Table 4.1. The **cd** command can be used to move around the various directories of your file system. When you use **cd**, you can use either *relative* or *absolute* addressing. Absolute addressing means specifying the full directory location by preceding the directory name with a slash (/). For instance, to change the current directory to **/usr/local** you'd use the following command:

```
cd /usr/local
```

Relative addressing is used when you change your directory using a qualifier that is relative to your current directory. For instance, while you're in the **/usr/local** directory, if you wanted to move up one directory and down to **/usr/bin**, you'd use the following command:

```
cd ../bin
```

You can go up several directories by using a series of ../../. A single dot rather than two dots indicates the current directory.

Table 4.1: A Starter Set of Linux Commands

Command	Description
cd	Change the current directory.
pwd	Print the working directory.
ls	List all the files, directories, and links in the current or qualified directory.
cp	Copy a file.
mv	Move or rename a file.
less	Display the contents of a file one screen at a time.
man	Display documentation about a command.
apropos	List all commands that have the string argument qualified by the apropos command in their man page description.

Through a combination of **cd**, **ls**, **cp**, and **mv**, you should be able to control and maintain the files on your system. The **less** command provides a quick way to view the contents of text files, one screen at a time. An example of this command is to view the system log file **/var/log/messages**:

```
less /var/log/messages
```

The Home and End keys can be used to move to the first or last page of the file being displayed, while the PageUp and PageDown keys allow you to move one page at a time. To exit the **less** utility, press the q key.

There is a lot more power to the commands you've seen so far. To find out about them, use **man** followed by the name of the command you wish to read more about, like this:

```
man less
```

The display of **man** works just like **less**, so when you are done reading, press q to exit.

Linux keeps a history of commands, which can be retrieved, one line at a time, with the Up arrow key. That's handy if you want to execute a series of similar commands. Once you retrieve a command, you can use the Home, End, Backspace, and Left and Right arrow keys to edit it.

Of the thousands of commands in Linux, you'll end up remembering your favorites. Sometimes, though, you'll need to do something for which you can't remember the command. That's what the **apropos** command is for. Simply specify a keyword you'd expect to be on the manpage for the command.

DOS Comparisons

The bash shell is one of many shells, such as the C shell, K shell, and Q shell. Even Microsoft's DOS command screen is a shell, although limited when compared to UNIX versions. If you are already comfortable using the commands available in the rather limited DOS shell, Table 4.2 will help you move to a real shell.

Table 4.2: DOS to Linux Commands	
DOS Command(s)	**Linux Command(s)**
ATTRIB	chmod
CD	cd
CHKDSK	df, du
DELTREE	rm –R
DIR	ls –l
DOSKEY	Built-in arrow key
EDIT,NOTEPAD,WORDPAD	pico, vi, and KDE and Gnome editors
EXTRACT	tar
FC	cmp, tiff
FDISK	fdisk
FIND	find
FORMAT	fdformat
MORE	more, less
MOVE	mv
SORT	sort
START	at,bg
TYPE	cat
XCOPY	cp
WINZIP	tar, zip, gzip

Standard Linux Directories

As you move around your Linux system, you begin to see a rather complex directory structure. Table 4.3 describes what is contained in the more important Linux directories. Perhaps the most important directory is the **/home** directory because the user-specific directories exist under it. When a user is added to the system, a directory is automatically created under **/home** that has the same name as the user. When you log in, your current directory is automatically set to your home directory. As you accumulate personal files, they should be placed under your home directory. For more granular control of your projects, it's a good idea to create directories underneath your home directory to organize your files.

Another important directory is **/opt**. This is where you should place additional applications, such as JDKs, Sun's StarOffice, and IBM's WebSphere. Some Linux experts argue that you should place such applications under **/usr/local**. It's a matter of taste, but we feel that, since **/opt** stands for "optional," that's where optional applications should go. It is perhaps more important to be consistent about where you put your applications than whether they go in **/opt** or **/usr/local**. Pick one and stick with it.

Table 4.3: Standard Linux Directories

Linux Directory	Description
/bin	Essential Linux commands
/usr/bin	Commands that didn't make the cut for the main /bin directory
/usr/sbin	Commands typically only run by the super user for system administration
/boot	Commands and utilities required during the boot process
/etc	Files used by subsystems such as file servers, window controllers, and mail
/var	Administration logging files
/usr/lib	Standard Linux modules
/usr/local	Programs that have been added locally by the system administrator
/etc/skel	Sample startup files that can be placed in the home directories of new users
/opt	Optional applications added to the system
/home	User-specific directories are contained under /home

Editing Text Files

So far, this chapter has introduced two configuration files: **lilo.conf** and **inittab**. Both of these are simple text files that can be edited with any one of the variety of text editors available with Linux. All Linux configuration settings are done with text files, so it's time to learn how to use several of the editors: vi, pico, and gedit.

The vi Editor

The de facto editor of UNIX is vi ("visual interface"). Although it is not the easiest editor to use, you need to become comfortable with its basics because every UNIX or Linux system you might ever touch will have it. Also, many other Linux utilities adopt vi features. For instance, **man** and **less** support its powerful searching capabilities.

To start it, enter the **vi** command followed by the name of the file you want to edit. If the file doesn't exist, vi will create it for you. For example, the following creates a file called **vi-test** in the user's home directory:

```
$ vi vi-test
```

Figure 4.3 shows the resulting screen in a terminal session window. It you try to enter text at this point, however, you'll find that nothing happens. That's because vi works in three modes: input mode, command mode, and ex mode. The vi editor opens in command mode, which allows you to enter a number of mostly single-letter commands. For example, **i** (in lowercase) changes the mode from command to input.

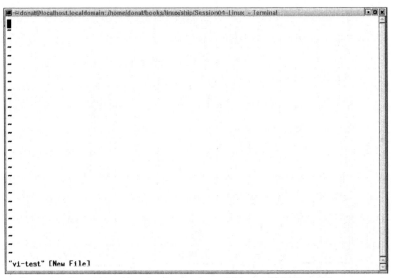

Figure 4.3: The vi (visual interface) editor is available on all UNIX and Linux systems.

While in input mode, you can type away to your heart's content, as shown in Figure 4.4. (The **—INSERT—** indicator pops up to remind you what mode you are in.) As you would expect, the Enter key starts a new line, and the Backspace and Delete keys remove text. Try as you might, though, you can't delete or copy a whole line of text. To do that, you have to go back into command mode by pressing the Escape key. (The **—INSERT—** indicator disappears.) To delete a line, use the **dd** command. To undo the deletion, use the **p** command.

Figure 4.4: The vi editor has three modes: insert, command, and ex.

To exit vi, you have to first go into ex mode by typing a colon while in command mode. From ex mode, you can exit with the **q** command. However, if you've modified the file, **q** will generate the following error message:

```
No write since last change (use ! to override).
```

With that error, vi goes back into command mode, so to exit without saving your modifications, type the colon followed by the **q** command and, like the message says, an exclamation mark:

```
:q!
```

To exit vi and save the modifications, go into ex mode with the colon, enter the **w** command to write, **q** to quit, and press Enter. If, while editing, you want to simple save your latest changes, go into ex mode with the colon, enter the **w** command, and press Enter.

The vi editor has many more capabilities. However, we'll cover only one more here—searching—with a real-world example. In the summer of 2001, we were getting ready to give a presentation with a new laptop that supported a resolution of 1600 * 1200. The projector, however, only supported a maximum resolution of 1024 * 768, so we needed to quickly modify our Linux graphical environment to use a resolution of 1024 * 768. Linux's graphical configuration file, **XF86Config**, is typically located in the **/etc/X11** directory. To edit that file, we started vi, qualifying the **XF86Config** file. To quickly find the 1600-*-1200 resolution setting, we used the search command, which is a slash (*/*):

```
/1600
```

The vi editor found the first occurrence of 1600 on a line that said "Identifier Generic Laptop Display Panel 1600x1400." That wasn't the right line, so to search for the same string again, we entered just the slash, by itself. The result still wasn't right, so we used the slash command again, to display the screen in Figure 4.5. Going into input mode with the **i** command, we added a pound symbol (#) in front of the Modes line to comment-out the original setting, pressed the End key followed by Enter to add a new line, and added this:

```
Modes "1024x768"
```

Then, we exited vi by going into command mode with the Escape key, ex mode with a colon, entering the **w** and **q** commands (to write and quit), and pressing Enter. After starting up the Linux GUI, the presentation went flawlessly (even if it was a little boring).

```
donat@localhost.localdomain: /home/donat/books/linux/ship/Session04-Linux - Terminal
           VertRefresh 60
#          Option "dpms"
EndSection

Section "Device"
           Identifier "My Video Card"
           Driver "nvidia"
           BoardName "Unknown"
           Option "NvAGP" "3"
       BusID       "PCI:1:0:0"
       Option "BackingStore" "On"
EndSection

Section "Device"
           Identifier "Linux Frame Buffer"
           Driver "fbdev"
           BoardName "Unknown"
       Option "BackingStore" "On"
EndSection

Section "Screen"
           Identifier "Screen0"
           Device "My Video Card"
           Monitor "Generic Laptop Display Panel 1600x1200"
           DefaultDepth 24
           Subsection "Display"
                   Depth 24
                   Modes "1600x1200"
/1600
```

Figure 4.5: The slash (/) command is used in vi to quickly search for a string.

Here are a few other things to be aware of when searching in vi:

- While the slash command searches forward, the question mark searches backward. Searching backward works just like searching forward; type the question mark followed by a string, or type a question mark by itself to search backward using the last search string.

- The search capabilities in vi support UNIX-style regular expressions. That might not mean much to you right now, but as you become more comfortable with Linux, you'll become exposed to the power of regular expressions. For example, the following search command looks for any string that starts with *M* or *m*, followed by an *o*, any lowercase character, and an *s* followed by and an *e*:

```
/[M|m]o[a-z]se
```

The gedit and pico Editors

If you find the modal interface of vi a little daunting, you might try pico or gedit. The pico editor runs in a terminal session, as shown in Figure 4.6. Its user interface is fairly intuitive, with the bottom two lines of the editor displaying the most commonly used commands, such as Ctrl-O to save a file, Ctrl-X to exit, and the all-important Ctrl-G to list help.

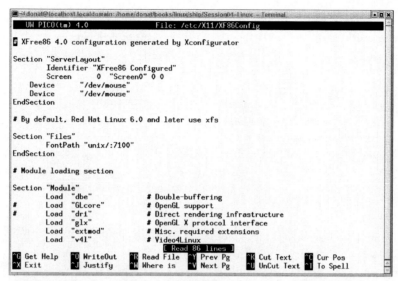

Figure 4.6: The pico editor, available with most Linux distributions, is easier to use than vi.

The gedit editor uses a graphical interface, as shown in Figure 4.7. With gedit, you have the user interface that you've come to expect from computer applications, complete with dropdown menus, popup windows, plugin capabilities, and hot keys. The problem with gedit, though, is that it requires a graphical environment, and Linux does not have one. Fortunately, many GUIs are available for Linux, with Gnome and KDE being the most popular. In the installation instructions in chapter 3, you loaded the Gnome environment. The gedit editor is actually part of Gnome.

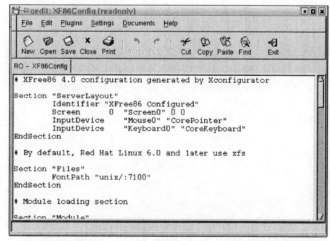

Figure 4.7: Gnome's gedit is a text editor with a graphical interface.

The X Files

Until gedit, none of the utilities in this chapter required a graphical user interface (GUI). When most people think GUI, they think Microsoft Windows. Microsoft, however, did not invent the window metaphor. They got that idea from Apple, and Steven Jobs (the creator of Apple) got the idea from the Palo Alto Research center. Windowed GUIs, then, were around before Windows.

The graphical environment for UNIX systems is formally known as the *X Window System* and informally as *X Windows* or simply *X*. It grew out of a 1980s MIT project called Project Athena. In 1984, the Apple Macintosh was released, sporting a windowed GUI. The Macintosh GUI, however, depended on specific hardware, while X is hardware-independent. One powerful feature of X is that, because it was developed using the client/server architecture, multiple workstations can connect to a single UNIX machine. In fact, until Linux came around, workstations known as X *terminals*, which didn't have stand-alone capabilities, were used to connect to UNIX servers. When Linus Torvalds started developing Linux, one of his first goals was to be able to connect to the University of Helsinki's UNIX systems from his Intel-based machine instead of an X terminal.

Earlier in this chapter, the discussion of the vi editor mentions a file call **XF86Config** that exists in the **/etc/X11** directory. The current version of X Windows (as of the summer of 2001) is X11R6.4. Linux uses a complete implementation of X Windows called XFree86. Even though the *86* in XFree86 refers to the Intel x86 product line that Linus Torvalds first developed Linux to run on, XFree86 runs on Alpha, MicroSPARC, PowerPC, and other architectures. Through the **/etc/X11/X86Config** file, XFree86 knows how to interface with the peculiarities of your workstation's monitor. Typically, the installation process of most Linux distributions, such as Red Hat, appropriately configures X Windows.

Whether you are using X Windows on a stand-alone workstation or connected to a UNIX/Linux server machine, it still functions under the client/server architecture. X Windows has a server program that handles requests from clients. Those clients may be from networked workstations or from the same machine that is running the X server. The look and feel of your X Windows interface is controlled by another client-based program called the *windows manager*. The three most prevalent windows managers are FWM, KWM, and Enlightenment.

Desktops

The actual graphical interface is handled, not by the windows manager, but by a desktop application. Like most things in the open-source world, you can pick from a variety desktops, but the two leading ones are the K Desktop Environment (KDE, *www.kde.org*) and Gnome (*www.gnome.org*). Both KDE and Gnome are freely available and bundled with most Linux distributions. Of the two, however, only Gnome is open-source. In the spirit of open-source (perhaps also because KDE is more like Microsoft Windows), the installation steps in chapter 3 asked you to load Gnome.

Unless, during the installation of Linux, you requested to have your selected desktop automatically start up, you'll need to use the **gdm** command to start Gnome desktop (or **kdm** to start KDE). The desktop will request your user name and password, and then present a desktop similar to the one in Figure 4.8 (which shows a few applications already open, to make it look a little more interesting).

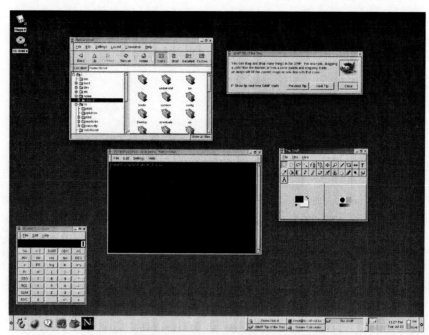

Figure 4.8: Gnome is one of the many powerful desktop environments available for Linux.

Logging Out

To finish this chapter's discussion of the Linux system lifecycle, you need to know how to end Linux. Perhaps the most technical way is to use the **init** command, qualifying the option of zero. You might recall from the **inittab** discussion earlier in this chapter that the zero option shuts down the system. Similarly, to shut down and force an immediate restart, you could pass option six to the **init** program. There are, however, two easier ways to shut down: use the logout option of your desktop or simply press the Ctrl-Alt-Delete key sequence. In the **inittab** file, this sequence is mapped to a command called **shutdown**, so you have yet another way to end Linux: invoke the **shutdown** command. This command has some sophisticated options, such as specifying the number of seconds to wait before shutting down, qualifying a warning message to be sent to all connected users, and specifying an option to restart the system immediately after Linux shuts down.

Chapter Summary

In this chapter, you were introduced to the system lifecycle of Linux. You learned how Linux bootstraps itself with LILO, how the application services are started with the **init** program (controlled by the **inittab** file), and how to customize what applications are automatically started. Next, you saw how to sign on to the system as the root, or super user, and as a normal user. Then, you were introduced to a basic set of Linux commands (with their DOS equivalents), to the standard directory structure of Linux, and where to put new applications and personal files.

Several text editors were covered: vi, pico, and Gnome's gedit. Since gedit requires a graphical user interface, you were presented with X Windows, windows managers, and the desktop environments KDE and Gnome. Finally, you learned several options for shutting down Linux.

End of Chapter Review

Key Terms

Absolute addressing	LILO	runlevel
bash shell	Master Boot Record	System boot
BIOS	pico	vi
Desktop application	rc.local script	Windows manager
gedit	rc.sysnit script	X Window System
init program	Regular expressions	XF86Config
inittab file	Relative addressing	XFree86

Review Questions

1. Why is a computer's BIOS so important?

2. List three tasks the **rc.sysinit** script accomplishes.

3. Describe the difference between relative and absolute addressing.

4. What command allows you to find the name of a command you're having trouble with remembering?

5. Describe what is meant by client/server with regard to X.

Programming Assignment

Exercise 1: Get Comfortable with vi

1. Create a file in your home directory:

   ```
   cd ~  or  cd /home/username
   vi practicevi.txt
   ```

2. Add several lines of text:

   a) Type **i** to enter insert mode.

   b) Type a line of text, press Enter, and repeat.

   c) Press the Escape key to return to command mode.

3. Save the file:

   ```
   Type :w (for "write").
   ```

4. Exit vi:

Type **:q** (for "quit")

5. Edit the file again:

vi practicevi.txt

6. Exit vi again:

    a) Type **i** to enter insert mode.

    b) Type a line of text, press Enter.

    c) Type **:q**, which reports an error saying to use the exclamation point.

    d) Type **:q!** (quit/force).

7. Modify the first line of text:

    a) Move the cursor to the first line.

    b) Type **i** to enter insert mode.

    c) Modify the text.

    d) Press the Escape key to return to command mode.

8. Exit vi:

    :q!

9. Edit the file again:

    vi practicevi.txt

10. Delete the second line:

    a) Place the cursor on the second line.

    b) Type **dd**.

11. Copy line 1 several times:

    a) Place the cursor on the first line.

    b) Type **yy** (the "yank" key).

    c) Type **p** several times (the "paste" key).

Exercise 2: Browse Your Linux File System

Use the various commands listed in Table 4.1 from a terminal session to perform the following steps.

1. Change your current directory to your home directory.

2. List all the files.

3. Display the documentation for the **ls** command.

   Hint: That particular command, like many others, controls the screen until you press **q** to quit (just as you do in vi).
   ---

4. List all the files in long format.

5. Dump the contents of the **.bash_history** file to the console once with the **cat** command, then again with the **more** command, and then with the **less** command.

6. Print (to the screen) your current working directory.

7. Change your current working directory to one of the standard Linux directories shown in Table 4.3.

   a) Print the new current working directory.

   b) List the contents of that directory.

   c) Drill down through some of that directory's subdirectories, printing the current working directory and listing its files as you go.

8. Repeat step 7 for several other standard Linux directories.

9. Search for the "appropriate" command for off-line printing.

10. List the contents of your user's **.bash_history** file to the printer. Be sure to return to your home directory first. (If you don't have a printer available, copy **.bash_history** to a diskette.)

Exercise 3: Modify the Startup Configuration

1. If PostgreSQL does not start up automatically, change the startup routines so that it does. Use your editor of choice, such as vi or gedit, to modify the appropriate configuration files.

2. If PostgreSQL already starts up automatically, change the startup routines so that it does not.

5

Documentation

Nowhere does the axiom "knowledge is power" apply better than in the Linux world, since the full power of the operating system is unleashed only to those with the knowledge to use it. The trouble is, the information you need to unlock this power is found in a hodge-podge of places and formats, a reminder that Linux is the result of a decade of development by many different people. Not only that, but Linux inherits vagaries from 25 years of UNIX and its variations. The biggest hurdle to mastering Linux, then, is figuring out where to find the documentation.

This chapter is devoted to helping you through this rite of initiation. Starting with the simplest form of documentation available, the text file, it works up to the state-of-the-art help systems currently employed by Red Hat Linux.

Lowest Common Denominator

One nicety we all take for granted in modern software is online help. Without it, software is immediately judged amateurish and incomplete, regardless of how good it might be. Today's help systems, with their hyperlinks, graphics, and search engines, are not a new idea; instead, they are the result of the evolution of the computer itself.

In "ancient" times (before the GUI, but after computers crawled out of the primordial ooze of wiring panels and punched cards), users communicated with their computers through dumb terminals. The earliest were teletypewriters, where every character was printed on paper. It was nice to have the complete transcript of a session that these terminals provided, but their speed was appallingly slow (some as slow as 11 characters per second), and their appetite for paper was huge.

Video display terminals (VDTs) were an immediate improvement over teletypewriters. They were usually faster and consumed no expendables, but they, too, were limited to displaying lines of text. It should come as no surprise, then, that the original means to document systems was through simple text files. Any text editor was sufficient to create one of these files, though most authors now embed *Standard Generalized Markup Language* (*SGML*) tags into their documentation so that the final output isn't limited strictly to text. Furthermore, no special software is required to view text documentation; the utilities that come standard with any Linux distribution are sufficient.

Let's take a moment to examine some text documentation that comes with Red Hat Linux. To begin, log onto your system as a normal user, and start the X Window system with the **startx** command. Open a terminal emulation session by clicking on the terminal icon at the bottom of the screen, and maximize the window. At the command prompt, type the following command:

```
cd /usr/share/doc
```

This changes your current directory to the one where Red Hat stores the text documentation for the software you've loaded, in addition to other types of documentation (discussed later in this chapter).

Now that you're in the correct directory, issue the list command, **ls**. You'll see a rather large listing of the directories under this directory. For the most part, each directory is named for the version of the program it documents. So, a directory called "**aProgram-1.3**" would contain documentation for version 1.3 of aProgram.

The directory of particular interest right now is **HOWTO**, which, as you probably have surmised, contains various how-to documents. Many of these are outdated, superseded by updates in the software they describe, but they are nonetheless useful, if for no other reason than to give you an idea of what's being accomplished for you by the configuration utilities. Issue the command **cd HOWTO**, and then once again issue the command **ls**. The list of files displayed are in text format, viewable using a text editor or programs such as **more** or **less**. If you scan the list, you'll see some fairly interesting documentation. Before Red Hat and other companies started to write software to ease system configuration, these documents provided the information required for a system administrator (that's you) to accomplish specific tasks.

The first how-to you should examine is HOWTO-INDEX, by issuing this command:

```
less HOWTO-INDEX
```

You'll be presented with the first page of the document. You can page down through the document by pressing the spacebar. Once past the first page, you can page back up by pressing the B key. A full set of navigation instructions can be obtained by pressing the H key (for help). When you have read HOWTO-INDEX, exit **less** by pressing the Q key. Be sure to browse through the other files you see; there's some excellent reading available.

In the Beginning, Geeks Created Man

And the programmers looked upon the text documentation they had created. And they thought, "It is good. But we can make it better." So, they put their heads together and decided to add the following features:

- The capability to search the documentation for a particular string. Sure, text-based documentation can be searched with tools such as **grep**, but it isn't an elegant solution.

- The capability to categorize the documentation into a meaningful hierarchy. This can be accomplished through the judicious use of directory names, but that requires everyone to agree on the location of the directories. It is also difficult to do if you want to include the next feature....

- The capability to work for any software, not only what is included with the operating system. If users create their own software and would like to use the same documentation method as the operating system, they should be able to do it. This same feature would also enable the documentation system to be cross-platform, or at least be useful across the various dialects of UNIX.

The result of the programmers' work is the document format known as the *manpage*. Each manpage is divided into several parts: *Name*, *Synopsis*, *Description*, *Options*, *Files*, *See Also*, *Bugs*, and *Author*. The command to view a manpage is simply **man** *manpage*, where *manpage* refers to a specific help file. These files are typically named the same as the commands that they document.

How does **man** satisfy the programmers' specifications? The first requirement was that the documentation be searchable, and manpages are searchable by using the command line option **-k**. For example, the following line tells **man** to search for "Search This" in the description section of each manpage, and then display the name and description of each manpage where the string is found:

```
man -k "Search This"
```

The second requirement was that the documentation be stored in a hierarchy. Manpages are segregated into nine sections, divided as follows:

1. Executable programs or shell commands

2. System calls (functions provided by the kernel)

3. Library calls (functions provided by the system libraries)

4. Special files

5. File formats and conventions

6. Games

7. Macro packages and conventions

8. System administration and commands

9. Nonstandard kernel routines

Your call to **man** can include the section in which you wish it to look for the manpage. So, if two manpages have the same name, as would be the case for a program called "foo" and a file called "foo," and you want the manpage for the foo program, you'd issue this command:

```
man 1 foo
```

The final requirement was that the documentation system be viable for any software, not just system software. This is accomplished by the use of the **manpath** environmental variable. This environmental variable is used by **man** to determine where it should look for the various manpages. If users install software that comes with manpages, or write their own manpages, they can manipulate **manpath** or declare it on the command line with the **man** command. The last part of this requirement was that the documentation be cross-dialect, and **man** is. It is the elder statesman among documentation strategies, available on all UNIX-like systems, including Linux.

View the manpage for **man** by issuing the following at a command prompt:

```
man man
```

You will be presented with the first screen of the manpage. Note that **man** is classified in section 1 (executable programs or shell commands). You can determine this by observing the numeral that appears between the parentheses after the name of the page. Paging through the manpage is done in the same manner as for in the **less** command: use the spacebar to page forward, the B key to page back, and the Q key to quit.

Using Info for Information

As nice as the manpages are, they do suffer from one serious inadequacy: they have no inherent navigation system. With manpages, you are forced to page through the screens sequentially or (at best) use the search facility. By now, everyone is used to hyperlink systems, where you can jump from one part of the documentation to another. The aforementioned programmers, having looked upon manpages and decided that they were better than text documents but could stand some improvement, created another document type: the *info format*.

The info format distinguishes itself from the manpage format by being broken down into pieces known as *nodes*, extending the functionality of a manpage by including navigational capabilities. You can jump from one node to another, select nodes from a menu of nodes and, if the author was clever, take advantage of cross-references. Before you issue the command to get into the info tutorial, keep in mind that info software was written to work on a video display terminal, not a GUI. Thus, it might seem a bit primitive to a person used to GUIs. To a person used to a VDT, however, it is quite an improvement. That said, issue the following command and take the time to read through the tutorial:

```
info info
```

It will only take a few minutes of your time, but it will be time well-spent.

You might be wondering how to determine which document type has been used to document a particular piece of software. The decision between the two formats is up to the author. Some purists prefer the manpage format and wouldn't be caught dead writing anything else. Others like the info format and use it exclusively. So, how do you know whether to use **info** or **man**? Fortunately, the authors of **info** considered this issue and took the path of least resistance: If you issue the command **info foo** and info can't find foo as an info page, it assumes it must be a manpage and displays that instead. Obviously, a manpage viewed through **info** won't have the same navigational abilities as a true info page, but you can at least use a single tool to read both. The converse of this is not true. If you issue the command **man foo** and foo is an info page, you'll get an error from **man** that states "No man page for foo."

Gnome Help Browser

We admit that you might be underwhelmed by **man** and **info** for documentation. After all, both of those programs are older than many of the readers of this book. If you have never used a computer system that didn't have a GUI, **man** and **info** might seem somewhat archaic and counterproductive. There is another alternative available through Gnome. The Gnome tool bar has an icon for the Gnome Help Browser. (It's a question mark surrounded by a comic-strip talk bubble.) When you click this icon, you'll be presented with the Gnome Help Browser window, shown in Figure 5.1.

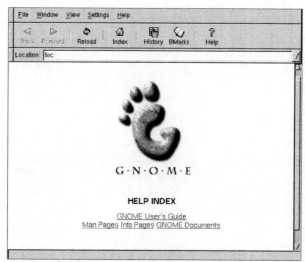

Figure 5.1:The Gnome Help Browser.

Besides the Gnome documents, the Help Index links to "Man Pages" and "Info Pages." These are exactly the same pages that are available through **man** and **info**. You should be perfectly comfortable with the Gnome Help Browser if you've ever been on the Internet, since it is essentially a Web browser. Behind the scenes, the manpages and info pages are converted to HTML, and then fed to the browser.

Just Browsing, Thanks

Speaking of browsing, quite a bit of documentation is now being produced in HTML format, the language of the Worldwide Web. Chapter 3 covers installing the documentation for Red Hat Linux 7.1. To access that documentation, click the links Gnome Foot->Programs->Documentation.

Once there, you'll have two options: Official Red Hat Linux, which contains the Reference, Installation, and Customization guides; and Linux Community, which contains the Linux HOWTOs and related FAQs. The HOWTOs were mentioned earlier in this chapter. When viewed through these links, however, they will be loaded into your browser, even though they are not marked up with HTML. So, in addition to **more** and **less**, you have your browser to view text-based documentation.

> **Note:** To view a text file from the command line, issue the command **netscape- communicator file:/directory/list/file.txt**, where */directory/list/file.txt* is the full path and file name. If the file is in your current directory, issue the command **netscape-communicator file:$(pwd)/file.txt**. The bash shell will expand **$(pwd)** into the current directory.

If you are new to Red Hat Linux, you'll probably have a greater interest in the various Red Hat Linux manuals. Click Gnome Foot->Programs->Documentation->Official Red Hat Linux->Red Hat Linux Reference Guide. This will cause the *Official Red Hat Linux Reference Guide* to be loaded into the Netscape browser. When this appears, pay close attention to the table of contents, specifically the link to "Finding Appropriate Documentation." Under the heading "New to Linux," you'll find a link to "Documentation for First-Time Linux Users." This link takes you to a page that lists specific resources you'll find useful. Be sure to take the time to familiarize yourself with the reference guide.

One other thing concerning HTML documentation: you aren't necessarily out of luck if you want to display an HTML file but you aren't using a GUI. A text-based browser, *Lynx*, is included with your Red Hat distribution and should be installed on your system. To read a document using this tool, issue the command **lynx file:/***directory/list/file.txt***, where */directory/list/file.txt* is the full path and file name.

Super Doc Site

The ultimate source for Linux documentation is the *Linux Documentation Project* (*LDP*), at *www.linuxdoc.org*. The LDP is staffed by volunteers who have committed their free time to ensure that thorough, useful documentation is available for Linux. The existence of this project demonstrates the variety of skills that are donated to the open-source movement. Although many LDP volunteers are technical people, some are not software authors at all. Instead, their forte is technical writing. These individuals write the prose that becomes the documentation you read. Perhaps you'll decide to contribute to this project as you become more skilled with Linux.

If you have access to the Internet, you can go to the LDP site to investigate what's available. To start off, all of the HOWTO documents discussed in this chapter are there. So are the FAQs and manpages from the Red Hat CDs. All three of these groups of documents tend to be more up-to-date than those included on the Red Hat CDs (since the site is updated, while the CDs are static).

In addition to HOWTOs, FAQs, and manpages, there are two other types of documents you might want to look at on the LDP. The first are the *guides*. These are significantly longer than typical HOWTOs, so they are given their own category. The other item of interest is a link to an online Linux e-zine, *Linux Gazette*. The *Gazette* is published monthly, and is free. The LDP mirrors the *Gazette* and has all back issues available, in addition to the current one. This resource is worthy of your attention because it is so well written and informative.

Other Common Formats

Although text, manpages, info pages, and HTML are the most common document types with which you will work, there are two others: the *Portable Document Format* (*PDF*) and PostScript. So that you have a document of each type with which to work, issue the following commands from a command line:

```
man -t man > man.ps
ps2pdf man.ps man.pdf
```

The first command instructs **man** to output the manpage for itself in PostScript format and direct the output to the file **man.ps**. The second command runs a program that takes as input the PostScript file you just created, and outputs a PDF version.

The Portable Document Format was created by Adobe. Its main advantage is that a PDF document will look the same whether you view it on your computer or print it to a printer. (The final proofs of articles we write for a particular technical magazine are sent in PDF format—the fidelity is that good.) PDF files are used frequently for storing images of hardware and software manuals. If you go to a vendor's Web site to retrieve a copy of the manual for that old widget you recently acquired, chances are that the file will be in PDF.

Viewing a PDF file requires a program specifically written for that purpose. Red Hat includes one, **xpdf**, that you invoke from a command line by issuing the command **xpdf** *filename.pdf.* (Although not required, files in PDF format usually have the extension **.pdf.**) Let's view the PDF version of the **man** manpage. At a command line, type the following:

```
xpdf man.pdf
```

You should see the manpage in the **xpdf** window, as shown in Figure 5.2. Notice that you can use the scroll bar at the right to move the page up and down, if your screen isn't large enough to display the entire page. At the bottom of the window are controls to page forward and backward, to skip to the first or last page, and to zoom in or out. You can also search the PDF file for a particular string by clicking on the binocular icon. PDF files can also be viewed using a program called **ghostview** (discussed later), included with Red Hat.

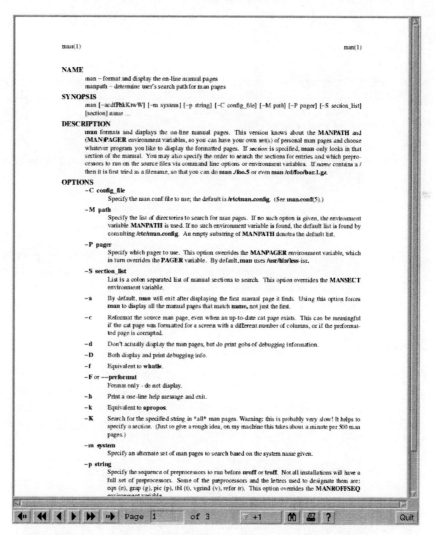

Figure 5.2: The man page for man, converted to Portable Document Format.

Although not included on the Red Hat distribution because of licensing issues, Adobe itself provides a free PDF viewer, called the Acrobat Reader, which runs on Linux. To obtain it, point your browser to *www.adobe.com* and follow the instructions for downloading Acrobat Reader. Once the file is downloaded, you'll need to untar (decompress) it by issuing the following command:

```
tar -xzf linux-ar-405.tar.gz
```

This will create a directory called **ILINXR.install** in which you'll find a document called **INSTGUID.TXT**. How to read it is an exercise left for the reader (we always wanted to say that), but here's a hint: it's a text document. You'll need to install Acrobat Reader as the super user, so be sure to issue the command **su** before you begin the installation, then type **exit** to return to your normal user profile.

The last common document format is the Adobe PostScript format. You might have already heard the term "PostScript" in the context of a printer, so you might be somewhat confused with the concept of a file in PostScript format. Actually, PostScript is a programming language that was created for rendering documents. A PostScript-capable printer is capable of executing the instructions presented to it in a PostScript file. By convention, PostScript files end with the extension **.ps**. Earlier in this chapter, you used **man** to create a PostScript version of its manpage. Issue the following command to see what's going on behind the scenes:

```
more man.ps
```

A PostScript rendering engine recognizes a PostScript file by the string **%!PS-Adobe-x.x** in the first line. The "x.x" is the version of the language used within the file. Since the PostScript version of the manpage isn't all that interesting to view in its native format, let's see what it looks like rendered. Exit **more** by pressing the Q key, and then issue this command:

```
ghostview man.ps
```

The **ghostview** program uses another program, **gs**, to render PostScript or PDF files and present the result on the screen. Like **xpdf**, **ghostview** provides the obligatory navigation icons with which you can page through the document. To exit **ghostview**, click the **X** in the upper-right corner of the window.

Chapter Summary

One of the fundamental skills that you must master on your way to becoming a Linux guru is learning where to find the documentation. With the long history that Linux has inherited comes an equally long list of methods to store thoughts and instructions. The ancient art of text-based documentation has been improved upon with the advent of manpages, info pages, PDF files, and HTML, but it has never been completely superceded.

End of Chapter Review

Key Terms

Gnome Help Browser	Linux Documentation Project	PDF
Ghostview	Lynx	Portable Document Format
HOWTO	Man	PostScript
HOWTO-INDEX	Manpage	Standard Generalized Markup
ls	Manpath	
LDP	Nodes	

Review Questions

1. Help-text authors now embed SGML tags into their documentation. What does SGML mean?

2. The **ls** command provides which function?

3. Manpages are each divided into several parts that are labeled: Name, Synopsis, Description, Options, Files, _____, Bugs, and Author.

4. How does the info format distinguish itself from the manpage?

5. What is Lynx?

Programming Assignment

Exercise 1: Explore the Standard Linux Documentation Directory

1. Use the **less** command to look at the HOWTO-INDEX file.

2. Use the **less** command to look at various HOWTO files, such as those for Apache and PostgreSQL

Exercise 2: Read UNIX Manpages

1. Look at the manpage for the **httpd** command and write a short summary of its various sections ("Synopsis," "Description," "Options," "Files," and "See Also").

2. Look at the manpage for the **man** command and write a short summary of its sections.

3. Use the manpage search option to find references to the word *dump*.

4. Use the **info** command to find information about the info format. Using its hyperlink capabilities, research how to use **info** and write a descriptive summary.

Exercise 3: Use HTML Browsers

1. Use Netscape to browse the HTML docs available for PostgreSQL.

2. Use the Lynx browser to browse PostgreSQL's HTML documentation.

Exercise 4: Explore the Linux Documentation Project

1. Browse HOWTO documents at the LDP Web site.

2. Browse FAQs at the LDP Web site.

3. Read the most recent issue of the *Linux Gazette*, and comment on some recent Linux news.

Exercise 5: Understand Documentation Conversion

1. Convert the manpage for the **httpd** command to PostScript and PDF formats.

2. Open the generated PostScript file using a PostScript reader.

3. Open the generated PDF file in a PDF reader.

6

An Introduction to the Web

The Internet was around for over 10 years before the Web was crafted on top of it. Tim Berners-Lee created the Web while he was an employee at the European Laboratory of Particle Physics (CERN). CERN is a research center where scientists from all over the world slam particles together in a special machine and analyze the results. These scientists then extrapolate complex theories from the reactions of these particles.

Although we don't profess to understand even the simplest of CERN's theories, we do understand the Web architecture that Berners-Lee created. The Web is an elegant solution to a big problem that the CERN scientists had: how to exchange information. The scientists all used different computer systems, making it extremely difficult to share information. CERN's computer systems were already connected via the Internet, but they lacked a common interface. Berners-Lee invented a standard information exchange protocol called *Hypertext Transfer Protocol* (*HTTP*). The idea was that an Internet server program would transfer HTTP packets on request to client programs. An HTTP packet would contain text-based information embedded within tags that described the presentation attributes of that information: *Hypertext Markup Language* (*HTML*). HTTP client applications, today known as Web browsers, would accept the HTTP packets, parse the HTML, and present the text-based information.

In 1993, the National Center for Supercomputing Applications (NCSA) at the University of Illinois created the first industrial-strength Web browser, called Mosaic. One of Mosaic's developers, Marc Andreessen, who had coded support for graphical images in Mosaic, foresaw the potential of the Web. In 1994, his new company, Netscape Communications Corporation, release Navigator. Where Berners-Lee brought information exchange to scientists and computer experts, Andreessen brought it to anyone who had a personal computer.

Applets

While the Web was under development, Sun Microsystems was developing a small, object-oriented language called Oak, which was designed to transfer code to small appliances, like a toaster. The small appliance would require a "virtual" operating system (a virtual machine) that could interpret and execute dynamically transferred chunks of code. Sun's Oak language was a technical success, but it was shelved because Sun's marketing department realized that the world was not ready to pay the surcharge for appliances that contained virtual machines. In other words, nobody would pay $350 for a toaster. (Coincidentally, people are paying $350 for smart appliances today, when you consider the success of PDAs.)

When the Web started to flourish, Sun realized that a Web browser was basically just a small appliance. Sun partnered with Netscape, and Netscape's Navigator was bundled with a virtual machine. Because Sun found out that there was a trademark for Oak, it had to come up with a new name. Sun lore tells about coming up with the name "Java" while in a coffee shop, but a more practical explanation is that it is an acronym for "Just Another Virtual Assembler." In any case, the marriage of Java and Web browser was a huge success.

The early success of Java soon evaporated, however, because it was based on applets. The name "applet" itself means "little application," and how many business programmers develop "little" applications? Applets just took too long to download from the Web server to a Web browser. In fact, Java would have died were it not for the introduction of server-side Java with servlets and JavaServer Pages. Chapter 7 covers servlets and JavaServer Pages. This chapter explains HTTP and HTML.

HTTP: The Protocol of the Web

A basic understanding of Hypertext Transfer Protocol is necessary to developing server-side Java applications. The first thing you need to understand is that the Web is a *stateless protocol*. Other Internet protocols, such as FTP, are *stateful*. When you use FTP, you sign on, and the FTP server maintains a persistent connection to the FTP client. If you change the directory or set an option, that FTP setting stays in effect throughout your session. With HTTP, however, each browser request requires a new connection to the server.

Consider a URL such as "http://www.WidgetsRUs.com/sales/itemlist.html" entered by a user into a Web browser. The protocol is qualified by "http:"; the TCP/IP address of the server machine is qualified by the domain name "www.WidgetsRUs.com"; and the file name is qualified by "/sales/itemlist.html." The Web server that is sitting on the TCP/IP address qualified by accepts the HTTP request and establishes a TCP/IP connection. The server locates the itemlist.html file and sends an HTTP response back to the client, which contains the contents of the requested HTML file. Then, the server terminates the connection. If the user immediately makes another request, the Web server makes a completely new connection. This means that your application's state (such as file cursors, data structures, and program variable) is not maintained between user requests. HTTP, therefore, is a stateless protocol.

Clearly, there must be a way around this. Otherwise, you'd never be able to visit a Web site like www.amazon.com, open a shopping cart, fill your cart with books, and confirm your order by entering your credit card information. Sun's Servlet API has a solution: the HttpSession object. The HttpSession object maintains the application state between user requests.

Client Request

Client HTTP requests come in two basic forms: **GET** and **POST**. A **GET** request is sent to the server when a user types a URL into a browser or clicks a hyperlink. The browser builds an HTTP packet that contains, at a minimum, the request method or command type, the name of the object that the user is requesting, the HTTP version, the product name of the browser, and the list of file types that the browser can handle:

```
GET /login HTTP/1.0
User-Agent: Mozilla/4.02 [en] (Win95; I)
Accept: image/gif, image/jpeg, text/html, */*
```

Meanwhile, the domain name (or IP address), the qualifier for the request object, and the user input parameter (if any) are passed as what is known as the *query string*:

```
http://www.mc.com/servlet/login?user=don&pass=secret
```

Again, the "http:" portion of the URL says that it is using the Hypertext Transfer Protocol. The domain name of the server is "//www.mc.com portion" (although this could also be an IP address). The "/servlet" portion is the qualifier for the requested object, and "/login" is the name of the requested object. The question mark indicates that a query string follows, and the equal sign begins a key/value pair for a user request parameter. The ampersand then shows the start of a new key/value parameter pair. In the example, the parameters are the user name "don," and the password "secret" (which isn't, now).

This brings up the (justifiable) concern about sending information such as passwords as free text across the Internet. To avoid this, use **POST** instead of **GET**. An HTTP **POST** request embeds all the parameters to the HTTP packet, instead of sending them as part of the URL. Then, as long as you have Secure Sockets Layer configured on your server, all the data in the HTTP packet is encrypted by the browser and decrypted by the server. Explicitly specifying **POST** is covered later in this chapter.

The Response

The earliest Web servers served merely static HTML and images. When a user requests a static HTML page, the *qualifier* portion of the request is used as the path to the HTML file on the host. For example, if the request was for "http://www.WidgetsRUs.com/html/HelloWorld.html," the Web server would simply open the file called HelloWorld.html in the directory called html, and then stuff the contents of that file into an HTTP response packet. That response packet is fairly easy to build, as you can see in Figure 6.1. The packet starts by specifying which version of HTTP it contains (in this case, 1.0), followed by the HTTP status code. Status codes are used to tell the client (the browser) whether the request was successfully filled. A summary of HTTP status codes is shown in Table 6.1.

```
HTTP/1.0 200 OK
Server: Little Web Server
Content-type: text/html
Content-length: 133

<HTML><BODY>Hello World</BODY></HTML>
```

Figure 6.1: An HTTP packet contains header information along with an embedded file, typically HTML, that is the HTTP server's response to the browsing client's request.

Table 6.1: HTTP Status Codes

Error	Description
1xx	Informational. HTTP/1.0 does not define any, but HTTP/1.1 does.
2xx	Successful. The request was received, understood, and accepted.
3xx	Redirection. The server requests that the Web client redirect to another URL.
4xx	Client error. The request was improperly formatted or cannot be fulfilled.
5xx	Server error. There was a valid request that the server cannot fulfill.

You have probably noticed that the HTTP response packet in Figure 6.1 contains not only the complete contents of the HelloWorld.html file, but also a few extra lines that further describe the response. Those extra lines contain *HTTP headers*. The server header tells the browser the name of the HTTP server that handled its request. The content type header specifies that the embedded content contains text-based HTML, while the content-length headers gives the total length of the file. There are more HTTP headers than server, content length, and content type; a few of the more interesting ones are listed in Table 6.2.

Table 6.2: HTTP Headers that Enable Sophisticated Internet Applications

Header	Description
Allow	Tells the client which HTTP methods are supported, such as get, post, and head.
Expires	The date when the HTML becomes invalid.
Pragma	A general-purpose field commonly used to specify "no cache."
If-Modified-Since	Returns the file to the client only if modified since a date.
Last-Modified	The date when the file was last modified.
Location	The directory of the server-based file.
Referer	The address of the file that linked to this file.
Set-Cookie	Application-specific information, often used to maintain state across a stateless protocol.
User-Agent	The name and version of the HTTP client.

Where's My Package?

When the Web first became ubiquitous, every company had to have a Web site. Many of them quickly slapped one together by converting their marketing material to HTML and images. This type of Web information is known as *brochureware* because it is nothing more than your standard advertising information, except that it is on the Web. To get a return on their investment in a Web site, however, companies need *dynamic information*—information retrieved from powerful corporate relational databases using an application programming language.

For a simple example of dynamic information retrieved via the Web, see the Federal Express site at *www.fedex.com*. From any Web browser, you can enter your package identifier to find out where your package is at any given time. User input comes from HTML forms, such as the one in Figure 6.2. The code for this form is shown in Figure 6.3. An HTML form tag contains an **ACTION** option with which you specify the program that is coded to process the form's input. A Web server passes the user's form request to this host program. The host program then dynamically builds the HTTP response, which it subsequently returns to the HTTP server.

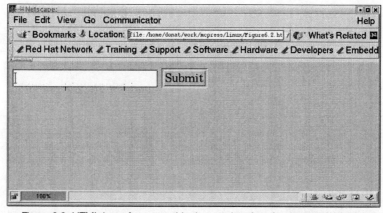

Figure 6.2: HTML input forms provide the user interface for dynamic Web sites.

```
<HTML>
<BODY>
<FORM
  ACTION="/servlet/PackageFind"
  METHOD="POST">
<INPUT TYPE="TEXT" NAME="packageNumber">
<INPUT TYPE="SUBMIT" NAME="Submit" VALUE="Submit">
</FORM>
</BODY>
</HTML>
```

Figure 6.3: An HTML input form qualifies the server program that is to respond to the user request.

In the early 1990s, HTTP servers were extended using Common Gateway Interface (CGI) to respond to user requests with dynamically created HTML content. Today, however, the best option is to use Java servlets. How does a Web server know when to invoke a Java servlet instead of simply returning static HTML? The Web server looks for the string **/servlet** in its qualifier. If it's anything else, the server will use the qualifier as the directory path for the HTML file. When the qualifier contains **/servlet**, your server will hand the request over to a servlet engine (such as IBM's WebSphere) for processing. You can also configure your Web server to support CGI. In that case, when the Web server sees the **/cgi-bin** URL qualifier, it passes the request on to a CGI plug-in that invokes a legacy program.

"Need to Know" HTML

There are dozens of books available on HTML, but most of them are half-a-foot thick and cover far more HTML than a business programmer needs to know. Buy one of those books, but don't read it cover-to-cover; instead, use it as a reference book. The next several pages quickly cover just the minimal HTML you need to know to present and accept information via a Web browser. You can let an HTML developer "pretty up" your forms later. Better yet, you can simply run your HTML files through a visual editor such as Microsoft's FrontPage or IBM's WebSphere Studio.

There are two parts to the HTML covered here: the basic tags for formatting information, and the tags required to build input forms.

Basic Tags

HTML is comprised of sets of tags that describe how to present the data contained within those tags. An HTML file is wrapped by **<HTML>** and **</HTML>** tags. The data to be displayed is wrapped by **<BODY>** and **</BODY>**. The following, for instance, is a minimal HTML file:

```
<HTML><BODY>Minimal HTML file</BODY></HTML>
```

Normally, however, an HTML file includes global settings, such as the title within the **<HEAD>** tag:

```
<HEAD><TITLE>Minimal HTML</TITLE></HEAD>
```

Web browsers will automatically wrap text. If you want an explicit line break, however, you can use the break tag, **
** (which, unlike the other tags you've seen so far, is not part of a pair).

Text headings are identified with **<Hx>** tags that display the headings in decreasing font size. The following HTML, for instance, presents the screen in Figure 6.4:

```
<HTML><BODY>
<H1>One:</H1><H2>Two:</H2><H3>Three:</H3>
</BODY></HTML>
```

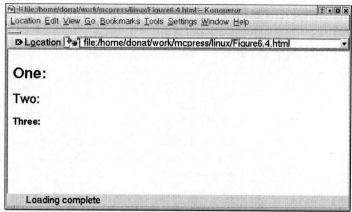

Figure 6.4: Text contained within <Hx>..</Hx> tags is displayed in decreasing font sizes.

The HTML in Figure 6.5 shows a few other tags that center text, present an image, insert a hyperlink, create a numbered list, and create a bulleted list. As shown in Figure 6.6, the **<CENTER>..</CENTER>** pair of tags simply centers the text it contains. The **<IMG>** tag is used to present a graphic (normally a GIF or JPG file). The **<A>** (anchor) presents a hypertext link to a Web site, where "Click here for cool stuff" is the hyperlink.

A numbered list is identified with the **<OL>..</OL>** (ordered list) pair of tags, while a bulleted list is identified with **<UL>..</UL>** (unordered list). Each list element in both the ordered and unordered list is identified with an **<LI>** (list item) tag (without a closing tag).

```
<HTML>
<BODY>
<CENTER>Centered Text</CENTER>
<BR>
<IMG SRC="Java400.gif">
<BR><BR>
<a href="http://www.ibm.com/">
    Click here for cool stuff</a>
<BR>
<OL>
  <LI>one
  <LI>two
</OL>
  <LI>first
  <LI>second
</UL>
</BODY>
</HTML>
```

Figure 6.5: A combination of some simple HTML tags can be used to develop an interactive Web page.

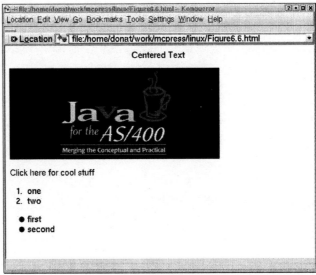

Figure 6.6: Images, lists, and hyperlinks are often used to spice up a Web page.

Images

The **<IMG>** tag qualified with the **SRC** option, as used in Figure 6.5, presents an image that exists in the same directory as the HTML itself. Although you can find a lot of images on the Web, you will soon need to develop your own. Linux has a well-known open-source utility for creating images: the Gimp (which stands for "GNU Image Manipulation Program" or "General Image Manipulation Program"). The Gimp, which is functionally comparable to Adobe's Photoshop, is a GUI-driven utility that allows you to draw your own images or perform screen captures.

Another powerful image utility is **gqview**. The **gqview** utility presents an easy-to-use tree view of your Linux directory. From the tree view, you can pick the image you wish to display. Further, you can select one of four standard Linux image utilities—the Gimp, Electric Eyes, XV, and Xpaint—with which to modify that image.

Form Precedes Function

While we believe that business programmers need not know much about how to make HTML "pretty," we strongly believe they need to know how to develop HTML input forms. A single input form, comparable to a display file's record format, is described within a pair of **<FORM>..</FORM>** tags. The following code snippet from Figure 6.2 presents the simple input panel shown in Figure 6.3:

```
<FORM ACTION="/servlet/myServlet" METHOD="POST">
  <INPUT TYPE="text" NAME="TextField">
  <INPUT TYPE="SUBMIT" NAME="Submit" VALUE="Submit">
</FORM>
```

The **<FORM>** tag has two options: **ACTION** and **METHOD**. The **ACTION** option qualifies the name of the server-side application program that is to process the form's input data. The **METHOD** option specifies whether the input data is passed as part of the URL (with **GET**) or within the HTTP packet (with **POST**).

The form contains two input fields: one typed as **text** and one typed as **submit**. The use of **text** is fairly obvious, and you've probably already guessed that **submit** is used to present a button that, when pressed, causes the input data to be sent to the server.

HTML forms can contain a variety of input types, such as text fields, radio buttons, check boxes, dropdown lists, and hidden fields. Figure 6.7 shows an HTML file called **Panel.html**, which contains each of these input types. Figure 6.8 show how **Panel.html** looks in KDE's Konqueror Web browser.

```html
<HTML>
<HEAD>
<TITLE>Example HTML Panel</TITLE>
</HEAD>
<BODY>
<CENTER><H1>Example HTML Panel Design</H1></CENTER>
<CENTER><H3>Please complete the following skill survey</H3></CENTER>
<FORM ACTION="/servlet/PanelServlet" METHOD="GET">
<BR>
<B>Name:</B>
<INPUT TYPE="text" NAME="name" SIZE=25 MAXLENGTH=25>
<BR><BR>
<B>I know the following computer languages</B> :
<BR><BR>
<INPUT TYPE="checkbox" NAME="rpg" VALUE="RPG">RPG
<INPUT TYPE="checkbox" NAME="cobol" VALUE="COBOL">COBOL
<INPUT TYPE="checkbox" NAME="java" VALUE="Java">Java
<INPUT TYPE="checkbox" NAME="vb" VALUE="Visual Basic">Visual Basic
<INPUT TYPE="checkbox" NAME="cpp" VALUE="C++">C++
<BR><BR>
<B>I have been programming for:</B>
<BR><BR>
<INPUT TYPE="radio" NAME="exp" VALUE="<5">less than 5 years
<INPUT TYPE="radio" NAME="exp" VALUE="5-10">5 to 10 years
<INPUT TYPE="radio" NAME="exp" VALUE="10-15">10 to 15 years
<INPUT TYPE="radio" NAME="exp" VALUE=">15">15 or more years
<BR><BR>
<B>My titles is</B>:
<BR><BR>
<SELECT NAME="prof">
<OPTION VALUE="Programmer Analyst" SELECTED="SELECTED">Programmer
Analyst</OPTION>
<OPTION VALUE="Systems Manager">Systems Manager</OPTION>
<OPTION VALUE="Senior Programmer">Senior Programmer</OPTION>
<OPTION VALUE="Web Master">Web Master</OPTION>
</SELECT>
<BR>
<HR>
<CENTER>
<INPUT TYPE="SUBMIT" NAME="Submit" VALUE="Submit">
<INPUT TYPE="RESET" NAME="Reset" VALUE="Reset">
</CENTER>
<INPUT TYPE="HIDDEN" NAME="hiddenField" VALUE="secret">
</FORM>
</BODY>
</HTML>
```

Figure 6.7: HTML forms effectively replace DDS screen record formats.

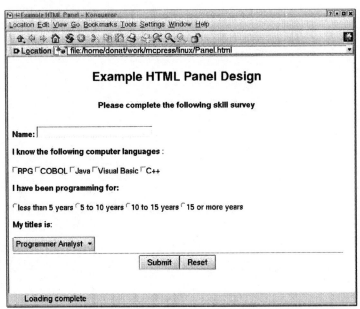

Figure 6.8: HTML forms can be displayed in any Web browser such as KDE's Konqueror.

Text Fields

Of the input types in Figure 6.7, the text field is the easiest to describe:

```
<INPUT TYPE="text" NAME="name" SIZE=25 MAXLENGTH=25>
```

The **TYPE** option declares the input as text; **NAME** creates what amounts to a variable name; **SIZE** declares the number of characters viewable on the browser panel; and **MAXLENGTH** declares the maximum number of characters that can be entered in that text field. Notice that the prompt for the input field, **<B>Name:</B>**, precedes the input declaration. (The **<B>Name:</B>** tags just signify bold.)

Check Boxes

The first check box in Figure 6.7 defines the input field as a check box with a variable name of **RPG**:

```
<INPUT TYPE="checkbox" NAME="rpg" VALUE="RPG">RPG
```

Unlike the text field, the checkbox field has its value explicitly specified as **"RPG"**. Check boxes are Boolean values. In this example, a user clicks it to indicate that he or she has RPG programming experience. If the user does not click the check box, the RPG input field isn't even sent to the server. If the user does click the check box, the input field identified with the variable name of **RPG** is sent to the server with the value of **"RPG"**.

Radio Buttons

Use radio buttons instead of check boxes when you have a group of options whose Boolean values are mutually exclusive. All of the radio buttons in Figure 6.7 have the same variable name, **exp**. Because they all have the same name, the user can only select one of them. The value specified for the selected radio button is sent to the server. You can explicitly check one of your radio buttons (or check boxes, for that matter) by simply placing **CHECKED** in the input statement:

```
<INPUT TYPE="radio" NAME="exp" VALUE="<5" CHECKED>
```

Dropdown Lists

Dropdown lists (also called "select lists") make it easy for a user to quickly select an item. Whenever a user's input has to match a specific list of values, use a select list. You should not, for instance, force the user to enter the two-letter abbreviation for a state, only to respond that the particular abbreviation is invalid.

The **<SELECT>** tag in Figure 6.7 uses the **NAME** option to identify the variable **"prof"**. The select list is populated with options. The **<OPTION>** tag always has a value specified. Before the closing **</OPTION>** tag, the display value is specified. An option for a select list of states, for instance, might have the state code as the value, but the state spelled out for display:

```
<OPTION VALUE="VA">Virginia</OPTION>
```

The Submit Button

The submit button was mentioned earlier, but one trick we want to mention here is how to simulate function keys with HTML submit buttons. In legacy midrange and mainframe applications, function keys are used to tell the application program how to process the screen input data. If you'd like the same facility in an HTML form, just specify several submit fields. The following two submit buttons, for instance, add an item to an order or cancel the order, respectively:

```
<INPUT TYPE="SUBMIT" NAME="Submit" VALUE="Add Item">
<INPUT TYPE="SUBMIT" NAME="Submit" VALUE="Cancel Order">
```

Notice that both of the variable names for the submit buttons are the same because the user can only select one of them. The value associated with that button is passed to the server program, which can then use predicate logic based on that value to change the execution of the code path.

Take a look at the input tag that follows the tag for the submit button in Figure 6.7. It has the input type of **RESET**. When the user selects the reset button, all the values in the form are reset to their original values, the forms stays active in the browser, and nothing is sent to the server.

One last, powerful input field remains to be described: the hidden field. Just like subfile hidden fields, HMTL form hidden field are not displayed to the user. They are explicitly for use by the server program. Typically, hidden fields are used in HTML forms to maintain application state, but you can use them for any reason you wish. Just keep in mind that the HTML form still needs to be sent over the Internet, so don't overuse them.

HTML, the New User Interface

The "psuedo-GUI" of HTML is good enough for users. It has all the required features of a full-blown GUI, such as a desktop metaphor. With HTML, if you need a popup window, you simply insert a hyperlink that makes another browser session open. If a user wants several HTML-based applications running at one time, he or she simply opens additional browser windows. As you've seen, HTML also has check boxes, radio buttons, and dropdown lists.

Yes, the full GUI of an applet or client/server application is more sophisticated, but the extra programming required to handle window events adds considerable programming effort to both development and maintenance. It is far easier to use HTML as the user interface, with Java servlets to handle the input, perform the business logic, and respond to the user, than to develop true GUI applications.

End of Chapter Review

Key Terms

Applets	HTTP	Stateful Protocol
Common Gateway Interface	HTTP Headers	Stateless Protocol
Dynamic Information Retrieval	HttpSession Object	Web
Get	Java	
HTML	Post	
HTML Tags	Secured Sockets Layer	

Review Questions

1. JAVA is generally accepted to be an acronym for what term?

2. Define the term "applet."

3. A _____ request is sent to the server when a user keys a URL into his browser or when he clicks a hyperlink.

4. How does a Web server know when to invoke a Java servlet instead of simply returning static HTML?

5. Define the term "HTML tag."

Programming Assignment

Exercise 1: Understand HTTP

1. From a terminal session, use the telnet utility to perform an HTTP **GET** request for the file **index.html** from *www.ibm.com*:

```
$ telnet www.ibm.com 80
$ get /index.html
```

2. Notice how the connection was closed. HTTP connections always close after the response was sent back to the requesting client.

3. Using the PageUp key, review the HTML file returned from IBM's Web site.

   A. Notice the opening HTML tag.

   B. What HTTP status code was returned?

4. Request the same file from IBM again, but this time, say you are using HTTP version 1.0:

```
$ telnet www.ibm.com 80
$ get /index.html HTTP/1.0
```

5. Review the first dozen or so lines returned by IBM's Web server. This time, because you said to use HTTP version 1.0, IBM returned a set of HTTP document headers. From this information, answer the following questions:

   a) What HTTP server is IBM using?

   b) What type of data is contained in the HTTP packet?

   c) When was **index.html** last updated?

   d) How many bytes of data were returned to your telnet request?

Exercise 2: Create an HTML Page

1. Create the HTML file shown in Figure 6.7, and name it **Panel.html**.

2. Access the HTML file from Netscape Navigator.

3. Add additional input fields to the form:

   a) Add another text field.

   b) Add another set of radio buttons.

   c) Add another select list.

   d) Add another set of check boxes.

   e) Add another submit button that displays the word Delete.

7

Server-side Java

Java is a programming introduced by Sun Microsystems in 1996. It was originally used for creating browser-based applications known as *applets*. Users, however, quickly tired of the slow download times associated with Java applets. In 1998, Sun introduced the servlet specification. Today, the predominant use for Java is in server-side applications.

Java has become the ubiquitous language of network computing for many reasons. Here are a few of the more important ones:

- *Object orientation*—Java is an OO (object-oriented) language that improves reliability and reusability of code. Many computer languages today are OO, including C++ and SmallTalk. Even legacy languages like COBOL are evolving into OO-capable languages. One of the benefits of Java is that it was designed from the beginning as an object-oriented language, so it strongly enforces OO rules.

- *Small executables*—Java generates very small executables, which means it is well-suited to an environment where application code needs to be downloaded from the server to a client machine.

- *Security*—Java programs execute within the Java virtual machine (JVM) instead of the native mode of the client operating system. Therefore, Java cannot corrupt memory outside its process space. For example, a Java program that runs in a Web browser cannot access anything that the client machine doesn't grant it access to. This kind of Java program (an applet) can't even perform file I/O.

- *Machine-independence*—Since Java code runs through a JVM, and JVMs are available on most computers (through browsers or natively through the operation system), you write your Java code once, for all platforms.

- *Simplicity*—Although similar to C++, Java is simpler. Many of the complexities of C++ have been removed. For example, in Java, you don't need to be concerned about memory allocation and deallocation, and you don't have to work with pointers. While this allows for portability, the downside is that Java programs are interpreted, so they run more slowly than native executable code. A technique known as *Just-in-Time compilation (JiT)*, however, can improve a Java program's performance. When a Java program is received by a client computer, the JiT compiler converts it into a native program.

How Java Works

When you compile a Java program, the compiler does not create an executable program for the particular architecture of the machine on which you're compiling. Instead, the Java compiler creates what is known as *Java byte codes*. These byte codes are instructions that a Java virtual machine understands and executes. JVMs became available in Netscape Navigator 2.0 and Microsoft Internet Explorer 3.0. All major computer operating systems also offer JVMs.

There are three types of Java programs:

- *Applets* are programs written to run in a Web browser. Applets are actually launched from an HTML document through special embedded HTML statements.

- *Applications*, unlike Java applets, do not run from a Web browser. Instead, they run on the computer like a native program. For example, the JVMs available for Linux allow you to run Java applications from a Linux command line.

- *Servlets* are run, not from a browser or from a command line, but from a Web application server, such as IBM's WebSphere or Apache's Tomcat.

To be able to compile a Java class, run a Java application, or run a Web application server, your computer will need a JVM installed. JVMs for Linux are available for free from Sun (*http://java.sun.com*), BlackDown (*www.blackdown.org*), and IBM (*www.ibm.com/developerworks/java*). If your system does not already have a JVM installed, the Sun download site has a Red Hat RPM, which provides the easiest installation. The download will be in binary format, with a name such as **j2sdk-1_3_1_01-linux-i386-rpm.bin**. To install the JVM, simply execute the binary while logged on as the root user:

```
. /<your download dir>/j2sdk-1_3_1_01-linux-i386-rpm.bin
```

We suggest placing your JDK under the standard Linux **/opt** directory. Once you install your Linux JVM, you will need to modify your **/etc/profile** file to add the **JAVA_HOME** environment variable and modify the **PATH** variable to point to the location Java's **bin** directory, for example:

```
export JAVA_HOME=/opt/jdk1.3
export PATH=$PATH:$JAVA_HOME/bin
```

To test that your JVM is installed properly, restart Gnome (or KDE), open a terminal, and enter the following command:

```
java -version
```

The terminal should display the currently installed version number of the JVM qualified in your **PATH** environment variable.

Java Statements

A Java statement can be a comment, a declaration, a control statement, or a block. Most Java statements end with a semicolon.

Comments

Comment statements do not end with a semicolon. There are two types of comments. The first type starts with two slashes (//), and the comment continues to the end of the statement. This type of comment is usually just one line long. For example, the first line of the following is a comment:

```
// add 1 to integer variable x
int x = 0;
x = x + 1;
```

This type of comment can also be added to an executable Java statement (which ends with a semicolon):

```
x = x +1; // add 1 to integer variable x
```

Use the second type of comment for multiple lines or blocks of comments. The comment starts with the /* characters and continues until the */ characters are encountered. This type makes it much easier to deal with blocks of statements:

```
/* This is a block of comment statements that continues line
   after line
   after line
   until here */
```

Declaration Statements

Declaration statements, as the name implies, declare something, such as a variable or a class. For example, the following declaration statement declares integer variable **x** and initializes it to the value of one.

```
int x = 1;
```

To add one to variable **x** and assign the value to **x**, you would use this statement:

```
x = x + 1;
```

As in RPG, variables in Java can be defined on the fly; they don't have to be defined at the beginning of the program. In the following example, the statement performs an assignment to variable **x** and defines it at the same time:

```
int x = x + 1;
```

Conditional Statements

Conditional statements are used for program flow control. There are basically four conditional statements: the **if** statement, the **while** loop (which can also function as a **do/until**), the **for** loop, and the **switch** statement.

Here is the basic structure of the **if** statement:

```
if (boolean expression) {
  // statement here
} else {
  // statements here
}
```

Here is an example of the **if** statement:

```
if(amount >= 100.00) {
  discount = .10;
} else {
  discount = .00;
}
```

There are two forms of the **while** loop. The first is similar to the DOW or DOWxx loop in RPG. The statement or block following the **while** is executed while the condition in the expression is true:

```
while (boolean expression) {
  // statements here
}
```

Here is an example of this kind of **while** statement:

```
int counter = 0;
while (counter <100) {
  counter = counter + 1;
}
```

The second form of the **while** loop is similar to an RPG DOU or DOUxx loop. The block of code is always executed at least once, and the loop continues until the condition is not true:

```
do {
  // statements here
} while (boolean expression)
```

Here is an example:

```
int counter = 0;
do {
  counter++;
} while (counter < 100)
```

The **for** loop is probably the most popular form of loop structure. You will see it used often in Java applications. Here is its basic structure:

```
for (expression1; boolean_expression; expression2) {
  // statements here
}
```

The **for** statement works like this:

1. Evaluate expression1.

2. Evaluate the boolean_expression.

   a. If it evaluates to true, execute the body of the FOR loop.

   b. If it evaluates to false, pass control to the statement after the FOR statement (or beyond the closing brace, if the statement is a block statement).

3. Evaluate expression2.

4. Repeat step 2.

In the following example, a **for** loop loads an array with the numbers zero through nine:

```
int numbers[] = new numbers[10];
for (int counter = 0; counter < 10; counter++) {
  numbers[counter] = counter;
}
```

The **switch** statement is used when you want to select one of many alternatives. For example, you could use a **switch** to process the selected option from a menu. The **switch** statement is similar to the RPG SELECT/WHEN/ENDSL operations. Figure 7.1 shows an example.

```
switch(expr)
{
  case constant_integer_expression1:
    // statements here
    break;
  case constant_integer_expression2:
    // statements here
    break;
  default;
    // statements here
}
```

Figure 7.1: Java's switch statement selects one of many options.

You might have noticed the braces contained within the group of statements in Figure 7.1. To apply a conditional **switch** to more than one statement, form a *statement block* with opening and closing braces. (Java statement blocks do not end with a semicolon.)

Often, blocks are associated with conditional statements. For example, in the Java code in Figure 7.2, the first statement block executes if **TotalSales** is greater than or equal to $10,0000; otherwise, the second block executes. For RPG programmers, it might be helpful to compare Figure 7.2 to the RPG equivalent, with IF, ELSE, and ENDIF operators.

```
if ( TotalSales >= 100000.00) {
  vacationDays = vacationDays + 2;
  bonus = 200.00;
} else {
  vacationDays = vacationDays + 1;
  bonus = 0.00;
}
```

Figure 7.2: Blocks of code within if clauses are demarcated with curly braces.

Data Types

The size of each variable type is an intrinsic part of the language. No matter what platform you are running Java on, the size of each data type is the same. This greatly improves the language's portability. There are eight variable types, shown in Table 7.1.

Type	Size in Bytes	Default Value	Range
Table 7.1: Java's Eight Primitive Data Types			
Integers (Non-fractional)			
int	4	0	-2,127,483,648 to 2,147,483,647
short	2	0	-32,768 to 32,767
long	8	0	-9,223,372,036,854,775,808 to 9,223,372,036,854,775,807
byte	1	0	-128 to 127
Floating-point (Numbers with Fractional Parts)			
float	4	0.0F	±3.40282347E+38
double	8	0	±1.79769312486231570E+308
char	2	'x0'	65,536 various characters
boolean	1	false	false or true

Declaring Variables

All variables must be declared before they are used. Java is case-sensitive, so the variable name **anum** is different from the variable **ANUM**. If you don't initialize a variable, a default value is assigned, as shown in Figure 7.3. You must declare the variable type when you define a variable.

```
// declare a variable named x as type integer
int x;

// declare variable name ch as character variable
char ch;

// declare an integer variable named y and initialize it to 1
int y = 1;

// declare a character variable named ch and initialize it to A
char ch = 'A';
```

Figure 7.3: Variables can be declared and initialized with the same statement.

Arithmetic Operators

The arithmetic operators for addition, subtraction, multiplication, and division are +, -, *, and /. Here are two examples of statements that use arithmetic operators:

```
linetotal = (qty * price) - discount;
percent = amounbotal + amount;
```

The **mod** (or remainder) operation is also supported, through the **%** character. For example, the following statement will assign the value of two to variable **x**:

```
x = 12 % 5;
```

There is no symbol for exponentiation. You must use the Java **pow** method of the math class (**Math.pow**). You will see an example of this in the sample mortgage program later in this chapter.

Unary Operators

There are four unary operators in Java: - (negation), ++ (increment), -- (decrement), and ~ (bitwise complement). The negation operator is simple. If you want to negate a value, you simply precede it with the negation character.

The increment and decrement operators can be used in two different ways. The first is pre-increment or -decrement, like this:

```
int counter = 1;
int totalcounter = ++counter; // totalcounter equals 2
```

Because the unary ++ operator precedes the variable **counter**, it is incremented before the value is assigned to **totalcounter**. If **counter** was equal to one prior to this operation, **totalcounter** equals two.

You can post-increment a variable by following the variable with the unary ++ operator:

```
int counter = 1;
int totalcounter = counter++; // totalcounter equals 1
```

In this example, if **counter** equals one before the operation, **totalcounter** also equals one because **counter** is not incremented until after the assignment is performed.

The bitwise operator (~) works on bit patterns, which is beyond an introductory chapter like this. If you need to know, see a Java book or your JDK's help text.

Relational and Boolean Operators

Since the equal sign (=) is used for assignment, double equal signs (==) are used to compare for an equal relationship. Use the != characters for "not equal."

Use < for less than, > for greater than, <= for less than or equal to, and >= for greater than or equal to. Java, like C, uses && for the **and** operator and ‖ for the **or** operator.

Arrays

An array is basically defined by specifying the type of data it will contain, the name of the array, and then the number of elements. For example, the following declaration defines an integer array called **IntArray** with 10 elements:

```
int[] IntArray = new int[10];
```

An array is actually an object, so you must use the **new** operator to explicitly create it. An array can also be defined with the brackets after the array name, like this:

```
int IntArray[] = new int[10];
```

However, placing the brackets before the array name is more common.

You reference the first element of an array in Java with a zero, the second element with a one, and so on. For example, the following statement prints the third element of the array:

```
System.out.println("The third element of IntArray = " + IntArray[2]);
```

In this example, the plus sign is a *concatenation symbol*. It concatenates the value in element 3 of **IntArray** to the character string preceding the plus sign.

Here's a snippet of code that loads an integer array of 10 elements with the numbers zero through nine:

```
for (int = 0; i < 10; i++) {
   IntArray[I] = i;
}
```

Strings

In Java, **String** does not refer to a data type; it refers to a class. A string is simply a sequence of characters. Declare a string as follows:

```
String CoName;
Declare and initialize a string like this.
String CoName = "Midrange";
```

You can concatenate a string with the plus sign. The following example concatenates a blank to **FirstName**, and then concatenates **LastName**:

```
FullName = FirstName + ' ' + LastName;
```

Unlike a Java array, you cannot change a specific character within a string. For example, you can't change the spelling of *Midranje* to *Midrange* by replacing the *j* with a *g*. However, you can modify the string by concatenating the characters you want to replace with the substring you want to keep. Assuming a string called **Name**, to change *Midranje* to *Midrange*, you could use the following statement:

```
Name = Name.substring(0,5) + "ge";
```

In Java, you invoke an object's method with the *.method* notation. In the above example, **substring** is a method of object **Name**. The first argument of the **substring** method (0) references the first position of the substring, and the second argument (5) specifies the ending position. In this case, the value of **substring** is *Midran*. Notice the first position of the substring is referenced with a zero, not a one, so the ending position is five, not six. As with Java arrays, strings start with zero.

Constants

In Java, you define constants for the entire class; you cannot define a local constant for a specific function (method) of the class. So, it stands to reason that you define constants prior to the main function. Use **static final** to declare a constant, as illustrated in Figure 7.4.

```
class Test
{
    static final double pie = 3.14159265;
    public static void main(String[] args)
    {
        System.out.println("Pie = " + pie);
    }
}
```

Figure 7.4: A Java application's main method is the entry point to the class.

In this example, the scope of **pie** is to this class only. To declare the **pie** constant as global, precede **static final** with **public** (i.e., **public static final**).

Literals

While a variable is a reference to data, a literal is a symbol or quantity that is itself the data. Java contains five types of literals: integer, numeric containing a decimal point or exponent, Boolean, character, and special character. Integer literals by default are 32-bit (four-byte), signed decimal numbers, similar to an **int** variable. Any integers greater than 2,147,483,647 are assumed to be long integers. You can force a number to be a long integer by ending with *l* or *L*. To force 31 to be a long integer, for example, specify **31L**.

Any numeric literal that contains a decimal point or an exponent is assumed to be a floating-point number, type **double**. An *f* or *F* can be appended to the end of a literal to force it to be a floating-point number (type **float**), while *d* or *D* forces it to be a floating-point number (type **double**).

Literals can be expressed in octal by preceding the number with a zero. For example, **037** would be an octal literal. A literal can also be expressed in hexadecimal by preceding the number with a *0x* or *0X*.

Java uses two Boolean literals: true and false. Boolean literals do not need to be defined. You simply specify one or the other literal, for example:

```
while(true) {
    //statements here
}
```

Character literals must be enclosed in single quotes, so ' ' is a space. You can also define a character literal with a Unicode value. In that case, a space would be defined as **'x20'**. Certain particularly useful special characters (including some nonprintable ones, like "new line" or "backspace") have their own special values, as shown in Table 7.2.

Table 7.2: Java Special Characters	
Special Character	**Literal**
New line	\n
ar0Horizontal tab	\t
Backspace	\b
Carriage return	\r
Form feed	\f
Single quote	\'
Double quote	\"
Backslash	\\

Compiling Java Programs

Each Java source file should contain the definition of one Java class. The Java source file should always have the same name (and capitalization) as the class that it contains, followed by the extension **.java**. For example, the Java class in Figure 7.4 would be contained in a single text file called **Test.java**. To create an executable version of that class, use the Java compile command, **javac**, followed by the name of the Java source file:

```
javac Test.java
```

As long as there were no errors, this compile would create a file called **Test.class**. The **Test.class** file is binary (nontextual) and is executed by the JVM. To test it, you would use the following command:

```
java Test
```

Note that the **.class** extension is not included when you run the file.

Host-based Applications

Java applets have fallen out of favor for Internet business applications. In 1997 and 1998, applets were all the rage because they delivered client-side applications over the Web. Web designers began using applets because they presented a graphical interface far superior to HTML, but they soon discovered that applets were fat clients; in fact, the code required to present that "superior" interface leaned toward obesity. Java servlets, on the other hand, are host-based. Servlets keep business logic on the server, and because the user interface for servlets is HTML, download speeds are not an issue. Some client-side logic might be required, but, more often than not, you can implement that client-side processing via a scripting language such as JavaScript.

Dynamic generation of HTML with Java servlets is the same strategy CGI programmers have used for several years. CGI allows you to associate a URL request with a host program that can be implemented using your language of choice. However, on most platforms, each time a URL invokes a CGI program, that program is restarted, incurring normal expenses of security checks, memory allocation, and file opens. Once the program completes the request by returning an HTML response containing dynamically constructed information, that program instance is purged. Each subsequent invocation of the CGI program imposes a program initialization penalty on the server. Java servlets, in contrast, are not purged; the servlet instance remains available to the Web server for invocation by multiple clients.

Legacy programmers are often reticent to believe that Java servlets outperform their C, RPG, COBOL, Pascal, or other third-generation language. Java servlets are able to outperform legacy languages as Web application drivers because of the thread-based architecture of Java. With languages like RPG and COBOL, a different program instance is required for each browser-based request (complete with their own job starts and database file opens). On the other hand, one instance of a Java servlet handles all client requests because it spawns a thread for each new request. A thread is essentially a subprocess that runs in the same address space as its spawning job. Because threads are in the same address space, they can share common resources, such as file opens.

Web Logic

Typically, a URL you enter in your Web browser refers to an HTML file within an explicit host directory: *http://yourDomain/home/level1/level2/SomeHtml.html*. The host simply sends the HTML file from the location specified back to the client. Often, for simplicity and security, the host configuration maps a "logical" directory name to the real directory name, decreasing the length of the URL and concealing the real host directory name. CGI implementations also use the concept of a logical directory by mapping directory name **cgi-bin** to a library of host CGI programs. When the HTTP server sees **cgi-bin**, it executes the program name that follows.

Web servers that support Java servlets hand over any request that have a directory qualifier of **/servlet** to a Web application server such as IBM's WebSphere or Apache's Tomcat. The Web application server, in turn, invokes the Java servlet qualified by **/servlet**.

The browser sends a URL request to the Web server in packets of information formatted according to the Hypertext Transfer Protocol (HTTP). (Note that HTTP servers and Web server are just two different names for the same service because HTTP is the low-level protocol of the Web.) When a Web browser sends HTTP requests to a Web server they can be one of two types: **GET** or **POST**.

When the Web server receives an HTTP **GET** request, the servlet engine invokes the **doGet** method of the Java servlet whose name was qualified in the **/servlet** portion of the URL. When the server receives an HTTP **POST** request, such as one sent from the entry form in Figure 7.5, the servlet engine invokes the **doPost** method of the servlet qualified by the **action** parameter of the HTML **<FORM>** tag. The HTML for Figure 7.5, for example, includes the following:

```
<FORM ACTION="/servlet/PanelServlet" METHOD="POST">
```

The PanelServlet example responds by simply listing the values entered by the user as shown in Figure 7.6.

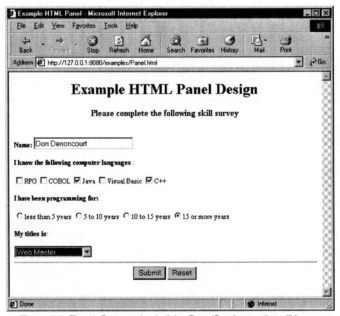

Figure 7.5: The doPost method of the PanelServlet servlet will be invoked when the user of this form clicks the Submit button.

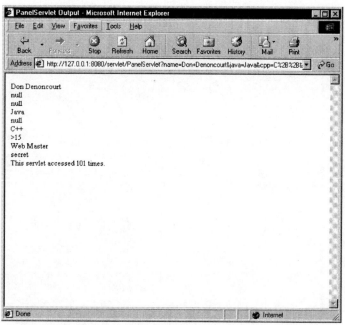

Figure 7.6: The servlet qualified in the HTML form's action tag handles the user request by dynamically constructing an HTML response.

The Servlet API

The examples shown in Figures 7.5 and 7.6 use the HTML file **Panel.html** and a Java servlet called "PanelServlet." The servlet is invoked by the URL request *http://127.0.0.1:8080/servlet/PanelServlet*. The PanelServlet servlet dynamically builds the HTML response.

The servlet is a Java class that is built on top of the generic HttpServlet class. HttpServlet provides code implementations for common services, two of which we've already mentioned: **doGet** and **doPost**. HttpServlet's implementations for **doGet** and **doPost** do nothing worthwhile. They're in HttpServlet as placeholders to assure the servlet engine that all servlets have these methods, by order of an object-oriented feature of Java called *inheritance*. This is important because the servlet engine calls the **doGet** or **doPost** methods based on what HTTP method type was qualified in the HTML form tag. One way to be sure your servlet has the appropriate method coded is to code a **doPost** that simply invokes the **doGet** method.

We like to use HTTP **GET** requests when we test, but HTTP **POST** requests for production. Using this simple trick, a servlet requires no changes when we change the HTML form's **method** option to **POST**.

The HttpServlet base class also has a method called **init**. The servlet engine invokes **init** the first time that servlet is requested. For servlets, you might want to code your **init** method to load a Java Database Connectivity (JDBC) driver and initialize a JDBC connection variable.

A Servlet for PANEL.HTML

Chapter 6 introduced HTML and, more explicitly, HTML forms. The PanelServlet example is coded to respond to the form discussed in chapter 6 (which, for your convenience, is shown in Figure 7.7).

```
<HTML>
<HEAD>
<TITLE>Example HTML Panel</TITLE>
</HEAD>
<BODY>
<CENTER><H1>Example HTML Panel Design</H1></CENTER>
<CENTER><H3>Please complete the following skill survey</H3></CENTER>
<FORM ACTION="/servlet/PanelServlet" METHOD="GET">
<BR>
<B>Name:</B>
<INPUT TYPE="text" NAME="name" SIZE=25 MAXLENGTH=25>
<BR><BR>
<B>I know the following computer languages</B> :
<BR><BR>
<INPUT TYPE="checkbox" NAME="rpg" VALUE="RPG">RPG
<INPUT TYPE="checkbox" NAME="cobol" VALUE="COBOL">COBOL
<INPUT TYPE="checkbox" NAME="java" VALUE="Java">Java
<INPUT TYPE="checkbox" NAME="vb" VALUE="Visual Basic">Visual Basic
<INPUT TYPE="checkbox" NAME="cpp" VALUE="C++">C++
<BR><BR>
<B>I have been programming for:</B>
<BR><BR>
<INPUT TYPE="radio" NAME="exp" VALUE="<5">less than 5 years
<INPUT TYPE="radio" NAME="exp" VALUE="5-10">5 to 10 years
<INPUT TYPE="radio" NAME="exp" VALUE="10-15">10 to 15 years
<INPUT TYPE="radio" NAME="exp" VALUE=">15">15 or more years
<BR><BR>
<B>My titles is</B>:
<BR><BR>
<SELECT NAME="prof">
<OPTION VALUE="Programmer Analyst" SELECTED="SELECTED">Programmer
Analyst</OPTION>
<OPTION VALUE="Systems Manager">Systems Manager</OPTION>
<OPTION VALUE="Senior Programmer">Senior Programmer</OPTION>
<OPTION VALUE="Web Master">Web Master</OPTION>
</SELECT>
<BR>
<HR>
<CENTER>
<INPUT TYPE="SUBMIT" NAME="Submit" VALUE="Submit">
<INPUT TYPE="RESET" NAME="Reset" VALUE="Reset">
</CENTER>
<INPUT TYPE="HIDDEN" NAME="hiddenField" VALUE="secret">
</FORM>
</BODY>
</HTML>
```

Figure 7.7: The Panel.html file contains an input form that uses a variety of HTML input fields to gather information from the user.

If you look at the HTML **<FORM>** tag in Figure 7.7, you'll see that its action qualifies PanelServlet as the server-side application that will handle the user request. Figure 7.8 shows the code for PanelServlet. It imports three packages: **java.io**, **javax.servlet**, and **javax.servlet.http**. The I/O package provides input and output stream files for the HTTP requests. The two **javax** packages are considered standard extensions to the Java language. All of your Java servlets will, at the very least, import these three packages.

```
import java.io.*;
import javax.servlet.*;
import javax.servlet.http.*;

public class PanelServlet extends HttpServlet
{
  Integer globalCount;

  public void init()
  throws ServletException
  {
     globalCount = new globalCount("100");
  }

  public void doGet(HttpServletRequest request,
                    HttpServletResponse response)
  throws ServletException, IOException
  {
    response.setContentType("text/html");
    PrintWriter out = new PrintWriter(response.getOutputStream());

    // retrieve user input from the HTML form
    String name = request.getParameter("name");
    String rpg = request.getParameter("rpg");
    String cobol = request.getParameter("cobol");
    String exp = request.getParameter("exp");
    String prof = request.getParameter("prof");
    String hide = request.getParameter("hiddenField");

    // increment global count
    int count = globalCount.intValue();
    count++;
    globalCount = new Integer(count);

    // generate HTML response
    out.println("<HTML>");
    out.println(
        "<HEAD><TITLE>PanelServlet Output</TITLE></HEAD>");
    out.println("<BODY>");
    out.println(name+"<BR>");
    out.println(rpg+"<BR>");
    out.println(cobol+"<BR>");
    out.println(exp+"<BR>");
    out.println(prof+"<BR>");
    out.println(hide+"<BR>");
    out.println("This servlet accessed "+count+" times.<BR>");
    out.println("</BODY>");
    out.println("</HTML>");
    out.close();

  }
  public void doPost(HttpServletRequest request,
                     HttpServletResponse response)
  throws ServletException, IOException
  {
    doGet(request, response);
  }
}
```

Figure 7.8: The PanelServlet Java class is coded to respond to the form in Panel.html.

The PanelServlet class extends the HttpServlet class. PanelServlet then declares its global fields—there is only one, **globalCount**. It is important to remember that the values of global fields (more appropriately called *instance fields*) are accessible to all Web browsing clients that invoke the same servlet, since one servlet instance handles all Web request. There could be a hundred different Web clients using this same servlet instance, and they'd all be referencing the same datum.

Instance or global variables are initialized in a special function called **init**. If your servlet contains an **init** function (it is not required), the function is automatically invoked by the Web server the first time your servlet is invoked. That same servlet instance is then used by all subsequent requests, so the **init** method will not be invoked again. PanelServlet's **init** method constructs an integer object, **globalCount**, which counts the number of times the servlet responds to a user request, initializing its value to 100. Your own real-world business servlets will probably instantiate things like JDBC connections and prepared statements in **init** functions.

Get or Post

The **doGet** function defined after the **init** function runs every user request. The **doGet** function has two parameters: **HttpServletRequest** and **HttpServletResponse**. The first parameter contains information about the request; the second contains the dynamically generated HTML response. Tables 7.3 and 7.4 show a subset of the functions available through HttpServletRequest and HttpServletResponse. It is worthwhile to study the Java documentation for these two classes, however, because they have some powerful capabilities. Both of them, for instance, have methods that make using HTTP cookies a breeze (which are typically used to maintain application state).

Table 7.3: HttpServletRequest Methods	
Method	**Description**
getCookies	Returns an array of cookie objects sent from the browser.
getMethod	Returns the HTTP request type, typically either a GET or a POST.
getHeader	Returns the value of HTTP headers.
getHeaderNames	Returns an array of all the HTTP headers included in the request.
getRemoteUser	Returns the user name, if the user has logged in using HTTP authentication.
getRemoteAddr	Returns the IP address of the user's Web browser.
getRequestURI	Returns the request URL without the request parameters.
getSession	Returns a handle to a special object variable that maintains the application state for a user.
getContentLength	Returns the total length of the user's request parameters.
getContentType	Returns the type of content sent from the user.
getQueryString	Returns a string containing all the user's request parameters.
getParameter	Returns the value of a specific request parameter.

Table 7.4: HttpServletResponse Methods	
Method	Description
addCookie	Adds textual data in the HTTP request, which the user's browser will subsequently add to its cookies repository.
encodeRedirectURL	Encodes the specified URL for use in the sendRedirect method.
encodeURL	Stuffs the session ID in the response URL.
sendError	Sends an error response to the client using the specified status code and a default message.
setHeader	Adds an HTTP response header with a given name and values.
setStatus	Sets the status code for the HTTP response.
getCharacterEncoding	Returns the name of the character set used for the MIME body sent by this response.
getOutputStream	Returns a handle to a data stream that can be used to write binary response data.
setContentLength	Sets the length of the content the server returns to the client.
setContentType	Sets the content type of the response the server sends to the client, such as text/html.

For right now, the most important function of the **request** HttpServletRequest variable is the **getParameter** function. This function retrieves input values from the HTML form. Before discussing HTML form parameters, we need to discuss the first two statements in PanelServlet's **doGet** function:

```
response.setContentType("text/html");
PrintWriter out = new PrintWriter(response.getOutputStream());
```

These are pretty much template code; any **doGet** function that you create should start with these two statements. Both of them use **response**, which is the HttpServletResponse variable. You can think of **response** as a handle to an HTML file containing the response to the user's request. The first statement, **response.setContentType("text/html")**, says that the HTTP response to the client will contain text-based HTML. The next statement receives a handle to the output stream. It's sort of like setting a record format in an RPG screen program. PanelServlet then uses the **out** variable to output an HTML response.

After setting the content type and retrieving a handle to the HTML output stream, the **doGet** function then retrieves the user's HTML form input. It does that by invoking the HttpServletRequest object's **getParameter** function. The code is fairly self-explanatory, in that all of the input fields from the HTML form are retrieved. What you might find odd is that if a user did not select one of the check boxes, the parameter is not available to the servlet. Whenever the **getParameter** function cannot find a parameter with the name qualified, **getParameter** returns a *null* (the Java term for nothing). If you misspell the variable name or use incorrect capitalization, the **getParameter** will also return a null.

Once all the values are retrieved, the **doGet** function increments the **globalCount** variable. The value of **globalCount** will be added to the dynamically constructed HTML response. The **out** variable's **println** function is used to output the obligatory tags, such as <HTML>, <HEAD>, <TITLE>, and <BODY>, before it starts to echo the user's values. Notice that the **println** function is passed the variable name and the HTML line break. The value for **globalCount** is then listed with the following statement:

```
out.println("This servlet accessed "+count+" times.<BR>");
```

The closing tags are added, and the output stream is closed.

Figure 7.5 shows a screen of entries to test PanelServlet. Note that I entered my name, selected Java and C++ as programming languages (personally, I'd rather not do RPG and COBOL anymore), said I had more than 15 years experience, and that I was a Web Master. When I clicked Submit, the following URL string was passed to my server:

```
http://127.0.0.1:8080/servlet/PanelServlet?name=Don+Denoncourt&java=Java&cpp=C%2B%2B&e
xp=%3E15&prof=Web+Master&Submit=Submit&hiddenField=secret
```

Let's break down that URL and look at the form parameters that it contains. The question mark that follows the qualification of PanelServlet identifies the beginning of what is called the *query string*. The query string is made of name/value pairs separated by ampersands. The first name/value pair is "name= Don+Denoncourt." **Panel.html**'s **name** text-input field will have a value of *Don Denoncourt*. (The plus sign is used as a placeholder for a space.)

There are no name/values pairs for RPG, COBOL, or Visual Basic because those check boxes were not selected on the form. The query string contains a value for **java** and then **cpp**. However, the value for **cpp** looks a bit odd: **C%2B%2B**. The **%2B%2B** simply represents the hexadecimal value of the plus sign, since a plus sign in a query string normally identifies a space. The browser recast the string **C++** to **C%2B%2B**. When PanelServlet reads the **cpp** parameter, the value returned will be **C++**.

The **exp** parameter also has a hexadecimal value to represent the greater-than symbol. The values for **prof**, **submit**, and the hidden field follow.

If **Panel.html**'s **<FORM>** tag had used **POST** rather than **GET**, the query string would not have been in the URL. Instead, it would have been embedded to the HTTP packet. We use the **GET** method while testing so we can clearly see the query string, but change to **POST** when the code is moved to production. Another helpful hint for testing is to hardcode a hyperlink to the Java servlet right on the HTML page—servlets don't always have to be invoked from a form.

When PanelServlet is invoked by the servlet engine of the Web server, it responds with the HTML page shown in Figure 7.6. Notice the line "This servlet accessed 101 times." If the **Panel.html** form was submitted again, the response would say, "This servlet accessed 102 times." That numerical value comes from PanelServlet's instance field, **globalCount**. The value for **globalCount** is available to all clients, and the **doGet** function increments it by one. If several clients are invoking PanelServet, they will each be using the same value for **globalCount** and causing it to increment because all clients share the instance fields of a servlet. As mentioned earlier, instance fields are typically used for things like JDBC connections—variables that are to be shared among all Web-browsing requestors.

A Servlet Development Environment

The PanelServlet classes can be installed and tested with IBM's WebSphere but, because the robust WebSphere product can be difficult to install and configure, we recommend that you install Tomcat (a simple servlet test environment) on your system. Tomcat is an all-Java Web application server, so it will run on any platform that has a JVM. You can get it from Apache's Jakarta Project Web site, *http://jakarta.apache.org*. Click the link to the latest release (currently 4.0.2), then the **/bin** link, and you'll be taken to a directory listing. At first, you may find the long list of files a little confusing. The only file required to get things rolling is the one that ends **.tar.gz**. Once you've downloaded it, log on as root and start the installation.

You'll need to decide where to place Tomcat. As mentioned in an earlier chapter, we recommend you place "optional" software in the **/opt** directory. Change your current directory to **/opt** with the **cd** command, and then issue the Linux extraction command, which will look similar to this:

```
tar -xzf <download directory>/jakarta-tomcat-4.0.2.tar.gz
```

This **tar** command will extract the file into the directory **/opt/jakarta-tomcat-4.0.2**. Since the Tomcat documentation refers to the installation directory as simply jakarta-tomcat, the following little command renames the directory so that the installation matches the docs:

```
mv jakarta-tomcat-4.0.2 jakarta-tomcat
```

The documentation is in the file **tomcat_ug.html** in the directory **/opt/jakarta-tomcat/doc/uguide** (assuming you are using the directory tree described here). Since it is in HTML format, you can open it in your browser.

The last step is to add an environment variable to **/etc/profile**, so that Tomcat can find itself:

```
export TOMCAT_HOME=/opt/jakarta-tomcat
```

To start Tomcat, simply change your terminal session's current directory to **/opt/jakarta-tomcat/bin**, and execute its startup script:

```
cd /opt/jakarta-tomcat/bin
sh startup.sh
```

Because Tomcat is an Internet server application, it runs a never-ending loop as it awaits TCP/IP requests. To test Tomcat, open Netscape and enter the following URL:

```
http://127.0.0.1:8080
```

You should see a Web page similar to the one in Figure 7.9.

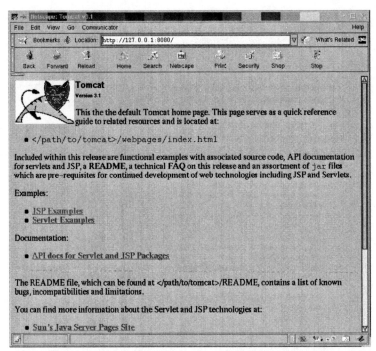

Figure 7.9: Tomcat ships with numerous examples of JavaServer Pages and servlets.

Tomcat Application Configuration

The easiest way to deploy PanelServlet and its **Panel.html** front-end to Tomcat is to copy the compiled Java servlet, **PanelServlet.class** to **/opt/jakarta-tomcat/webapps/ROOT/WEB-INF/classes**. Then, copy **Panel.html** into **/opt/jakarta-tomcat/webapps/ROOT/**. With the Tomcat server started, you should then be able to invoke PanelServlet from Netscape with the following URL request:

```
http://127.0.0.1:8080/Panel.html
```

If the PanelServlet application was production-quality, you would have created an application-specific directory under Tomcat's **webapp** directory, with a subdirectory structure standardized by Sun's Servlet 2.2 API. A Tomcat Web application appropriately called "examples" and found in **/usr/local/tomcat/webapps/examples** follows this standard.

Note that to be able to compile **PanelServlet.java**, you'll need to add Tomcat's **servlet.jar** file to your Java **CLASSPATH** environment variable and compile **PanelServlet.java** with your current directory being the one that contains the **PanelServlet.java** source file:

```
CLASSPATH=$CLASSPATH:/opt/jakarta-tomcat/lib/servlet.jar
javac PanelServet.java
```

JavaServer Pages

In a period of about 12 months after Sun Microsystems introduced the Servlet API, servlets became widely adopted as a standard for host-based Internet applications. Java servlets are essentially Java with embedded HTML. A JavaServer Pages (JSP), on the other hand, is essentially HTML with embedded Java.

Your JSP files are placed in the same directories as your HTML. Like HTML, they are qualified by users in a Web browser. The only difference is that the JSP file has an extension of **.jsp** rather than **.html**. When the Web server sees the **.jsp**, it passes the request on to a Web application server such as IBM's WebSphere or Apache's Tomcat.

The best way to learn how JSP works is to follow a simple example. The following line of text contains the complete HTML syntax from a file called **Minimal.html**:

```
<HTML><BODY>
Minimal HTML file
</BODY></HTML>
```

If you place this file in Tomcat's **/usr/local/tomcat/webapps/ROOT** deployment directory and request it from your Web browser with *http://127.0.0.1:8080/Minimal.html*, Tomcat simply sends that HTML text file down to the browser. If you rename **Minimal.html** to **Minimal.jsp**, however, the process works entirely differently.

When you request **Minimal.jsp**, the Web server sees the .jsp extension, creates a Java source file that contains the complete HTML and Java syntax of the JSP, and compiles it into a Java servlet. For example, when I entered *http://127.0.0.1:8080/Minimal.jsp* into my Netscape browser, Tomcat created the Java servlet source file shown in Figure 7.10, compiled it into a Java class called **Minimal_jsp_1.class**, and then executed that servlet. The servlet simply sent the dynamically generated HTML file with the string "Minimal HTML file" back to my Web browser.

```
public class _0002fMinimal_0002ejspMinimal_jsp_0 extends HttpJspBase {
    static {}
    public _0002fMinimal_0002ejspMinimal_jsp_0( ) { }
    private static boolean _jspx_inited = false;
    public final void _jspx_init() throws JasperException {}

    public void _jspService(HttpServletRequest request, HttpServletResponse
response)
        throws IOException, ServletException {

        JspFactory _jspxFactory = null;
        PageContext pageContext = null;
        HttpSession session = null;
        ServletContext application = null;
        ServletConfig config = null;
        JspWriter out = null;
        Object page = this;
        String _value = null;
        try {
            if (_jspx_inited == false) {
                _jspx_init();
                _jspx_inited = true;
            }
            _jspxFactory = JspFactory.getDefaultFactory();
            response.setContentType("text/html;charset=8859_1");
            pageContext = _jspxFactory.getPageContext(this, request, response,
                    "", true, 8192, true);
            application = pageContext.getServletContext();
            config = pageContext.getServletConfig();
            session = pageContext.getSession();
            out = pageContext.getOut();
            // HTML // begin [file="/Minimal.jsp";from=(0,0);to=(1,0)]
                out.write("<HTML><BODY>Minimal HTML file</BODY></HTML>\r\n");
            // end
        } catch (Exception ex) {
            if (out.getBufferSize() != 0)
                out.clearBuffer();
            pageContext.handlePageException(ex);
        } finally {
            out.flush();
            _jspxFactory.releasePageContext(pageContext);
        }
    }
}
```

Figure 7.10: The servlet code automatically generated by a Web application server is not meant to be modified.

Obviously, this compile process takes a considerable amount of time (perhaps a few seconds). The next time a client requests that same JSP file, however, the server will simply execute the servlet created earlier. Meanwhile, if a Web developer modifies the JSP file, the server will notice that the JSP has been changed, re-create the Java code, and compile a new servlet.

To see the real value of JSP technology, you need to understand more about JSP syntax. There are five types of Java syntax, as shown in Table 7.5.

Table 7.5: The Five Types of JSP Syntax	
JSP Syntax Type	**Examples**
Expression	<%= new java.util.Date()%>
Scriplet	<% for (int idx = 0; idx < 5; idx++) { %>
Directive	<%@ page import="java.util.*" %>
Declaration	<%! Connection con = null;%>
	<%! public Connection getConnection()
	{
	// method code implementation
	}
	%>
Comment	<%— comment not in HTML sent to browser —%>
	<!— comment will be in the HTML sent to client —>

Expressions

JSP *expressions* are one of the five types of Java code that can be contained in a JSP file. Consider this example:

```
<HTML><BODY>
Today's date <%=(new java.util.Date()).toLocaleString() %>
</BODY></HTML>
```

A JSP expression simple dumps the string representation of the object variable that follows the **<%=** tag into the dynamically generated HTML. When the JSP page shown is requested, the servlet automatically generated by the Web server will dynamically insert today's date into an HTML file. The dynamically constructed HTML file is sent to the requesting browser and presented to the user in the following format:

```
Today's date May 29, 2001 1:57:53 PM
```

Request and Response Objects

Because a JSP file ultimately becomes a Java servlet, the parameters that are sent to the standard functions of a servlet, **request** and **response**, can be used in the JSP. The following example uses the HttpServletRequest object variable called **request** to retrieve the name of the requesting Web browser:

```
<HTML><BODY>
<%= request.getHeader("User-Agent") %>
</HTML></BODY>
```

When I requested the JSP file containing this syntax from Internet Explorer, the browser displayed "Mozilla/4.0 (compatible; MSIE 4.0; Windows 95)," but when I requested it from Netscape Navigator, I saw "Mozilla/4.06 [en] (Win95; U ;Nav)."

The HttpServletRequest class provides encapsulated object-oriented access to all the information that could ever possibly be embedded in Web requests, such as HTTP cookies, HTTP headers, HTML form input, and HTTP query strings. Table 7.3 shows a list of the methods at your disposal from JSP's **request** variable.

Four other object variables are also available in the Java code of your JSP file: **response, session, out,** and **in**. The PrintWriter and BufferedReader classes of the **out** and **in** object variables are from the **java.io** package. The class of the **session** object variable is HttpSession; it is used to maintain the user state. The class of the **response** object variable is HttpServletResponse. It's sort of the opposite of HttpServletRequest; as you might guess, it encapsulates object-oriented access to any of the facilities available with an HTTP response that is to be sent back to the client. (Table 7.4 shows a list of the methods available to **response**.) Through the methods of the **request, response,** and **session** object variables, you will be able to do with ease what CGI programmers must struggle with.

Scriptlets

When more than one line of Java code is contained within the **<%** and **%>** tags, that section of code is known as a *scriptlet*. The Java syntax inserted between those tags can be as complex as you desire. The following example shows a Java **for** loop:

```
<HTML><body>
<%  for (int idx = 0; idx < 3; idx++ ) { %>
Current index is <%=idx%> <br>
<% } %>
</BODY></HTML>
```

The first scriptlet in this example starts the **for** loop with an opening curly brace, but the scriplet abruptly ends with the closing **%>**. The string "Current index is" is just good old HTML, but then a JSP expression is used to dump the value of the **idx** variable. Finally, the loop is terminated with a closing curly brace. The output of this simple JSP is as follows:

```
Current index is 0
Current index is 1
Current index is 2
```

Directives, Declarations, and Comments

JSP *directives* are identified by the at symbol (**<%@**). Directives are typically used to qualify the packages of Java classes you wish to use in your JSP. For instance, an earlier example fully qualified the Date object as **java.util.Date**. If you remove the **java.util** qualifier, the example JSP won't compile to a servlet. If you use a page import directive, however, the Date class need not be qualified:

```
<%@ page import="java.util.*" %>
<HTML><BODY>
Today's date <%=(new Date()).toLocaleString() %>
</BODY></HTML>
```

JSP *declarations* are identified by the exclamation point (**<%!**). Declarations are used to describe object variables that can be used in any of the Java code within a JSP file. All the browser-based requests for that same JSP share the values of the declared object variables. JDBC Connection objects are good candidates to be defined in a JSP declaration.

JSP *comments* are identified by a set of double hyphens (**<%—** and **—%>**). Use the comment type when you don't want the comment code to be included in the HTML sent to the browser. On the other hand, when you do want the comments to be shown in the generated HTML, use the standard HTML comment tags of (<!— and —>).

End of Chapter Review

Key Terms

Arrays	Get/Post	Strings
Comments	JavaServer Pages	Tomcat
Conditional statements	Object-oriented language	Unary operators
Constants	Operators	Variables
Data types	Scriptlets	WebSphere
Declaration statements	Servlets	

Review Questions

1. What are the advantages of using Java?

2. Explain Just-in-Time (JiT) compilation.

3. What are the three types of Java programs?

4. Where do servlets run?

5. What are JavaServer Pages?

Programming Assignment

Exercise 1: Code and Test Your First Java Application

1. Download the Sun JDK from *http://java.sun.com* and install it using directions in the chapter.

    a) Be sure to modify your path to contain the qualification of the JDK's **bin** directory.

    b) Be sure to set the **JAVA_HOME** environment variable to point to the JDK directory.

    c) Test for proper JDK installation:

    ```
    $ java -version
    ```

2. Enter the code in Figure 7.4 into a file called **Test.java**.

    a) Use the **javac** command to compile it:

    ```
    $ javac Test.java
    ```

    b) Once any potential errors are corrected, use the **java** command to test the application:

    ```
    $ java Test
    ```

Exercise 2: Install a Web Application Server

1. Following the directions in the chapter, install Tomcat.

2. Start Tomcat:

```
$ cd /opt/jakarta-tomcat/bin
$ sh startup.sh
```

3. From Netscape Navigator, request Tomcat's home page using the following URL:

```
http://127.0.0.1:8080
```

4. Walk through all of the links on Tomcat's home page to view the various technologies supported by server-side Java.

Exercise 3: Create Your First Java Servlet

1. Copy the **Panel.html** file created in exercise 2 of chapter 6 to the **tomcat/webapp/ROOT** directory.

2. Access **Panel.html** from Netscape Navigator served by Tomcat, using the following URL:

```
http://127.0.0.1:8080/Panel.html
```

3. Fill in the form, and click the Submit button. An error will be presented saying that the PanelServlet was not found or available. To fix that error, you'll have to deploy PanelServet.

4. Using your favorite Linux editor, create a file called **PanelServlet.java** and enter the Java source shown in Figure 7.8.

5. To compile the source, you'll have to set the **CLASSPATH** environment variable to point to the Java archive that contains the Servlet API Java classes:

```
$  CLASSPATH=$CLASSPATH:/opt/tomcat/lib/servlet.jar
```

6. Use the **javac** command to compile **PanelServlet.java**:

```
$  javac PanelServlet.java
```

7. Once any errors are corrected and the compile completes successfully, copy the Java executable, **PanelServlet.class**, to **/opt/tomcat/webapps/ROOT/WEB-INF/classes**:

```
$ cp PanelServlet.class /opt/tomcat/webapps/ROOT/WEB-INF/classes
```

8. Access **Panel.html** from Netscape Navigator served by Tomcat.

   a) Fill out the form and click Submit.

b) Notice that PanelServlet simply echoes the values keyed. A production servlet would do some more complex processing and relational database access.

Exercise 3: Create Your First JavaServer Page

1. Copy **Panel.html** to a new file in the same directory. Call it **Panel.jsp**.

2. List the contents of **tomcat/work/localhost_8080**.

3. Access **Panel.jsp**, which should look exactly like **Panel.html**:

```
http://127.0.0.1:8080/Panel.jsp
```

4. List the contents of **tomcat/work/localhost_8080** and take note of the new Java source file created by Tomcat's JSP compile process. (It will have *Panel* in its name.)

5. Use the **less** command to look at the Java source file. Look for the HTML tags from **Panel.jsp**.

6. Using your favorite Linux editor, edit **Panel.jsp** to add a JSP expression that outputs today's date:

```
Today's date <%=(new java.util.Date()).toLocaleString() %>
```

7. Access **Panel.jsp** again:

```
http://127.0.0.1:8080/Panel.jsp
```

8. List the contents of the new Java source file in Tomcat's **work/localhost_8080** directory and find the date code that you added to the JSP.

8

RDB, SQL, and JDBC

Relational databases (RDBs) are the predominant storage mechanism for business information. In this chapter, you learn what an RDB is, how to create and maintain an RDB using Structured Query Language (SQL) commands, and how to automate SQL in Java applications with Java Database Connectivity (JDBC).

You are probably already comfortable with the concept of a database, but you might be unfamiliar with the concept of a *relational* database. Basically, a relational database is a set of files that can be connected to form an additional, virtual file. Each database file contains fields that describe the attributes of a specific business entity. Files are populated with records that store information specific to real-world instances of business entities. RDBs refer to files as *tables*, fields as *columns*, and records as *rows*.

Consider the accounts-receivable database shown in Table 8.1. Its invoice table stores information about money payable to a company, its invoice detail table stores information about line items associated with an invoice, and its customer table stores information about each customer.

Table 8.1: A Simple Accounts-Receivable Database with Invoice, Invoice Detail, and Customer Database Files							
Invoice							
InvoiceNo	CustNo	InvoiceDate	CloseDate				
1234	981	11/10/1999					
Invoice Detail							
InvoiceNo	LineNo	Desc	Qty	Charge			
1234	1	Bolts	2	1.98			
1234	2	Washers	15	2.66			
Customer							
CustNo	LastName	Street	City	ZipCode	State	PhoneNo	
981	Denoncourt	5650 El Camino Real	Carlsbad	99999	CA	(800)477-5665	

Each table in a database has a *key*. A key is composed of one or more columns that uniquely describe the data contained in one row. That is, the key uniquely defines the row that represents a real-world business entity. For instance, the key for the customer table in Table 8.1 is the customer number; the key for the invoice table is the invoice number; and the key for the invoice detail table is the combination of invoice number and line number. These keys are known as *primary keys*, as they are used to retrieve specific rows.

In addition to primary keys, a table may also have one or more *foreign* keys. A column that is a foreign key in one table matches the primary key in another. For instance, the customer number in the invoice table is a foreign key that matches the customer table's primary key. Foreign keys store a table's relationship with another table—hence the term "relational" database. For example, in Table 8.1, the value of customer 981 from the invoice table's row is a foreign key that associates customer "Denoncourt" from Carlsbad, California. Proper maintenance of a database requires that the values for foreign keys correspond to the primary key in the related table. The RDB term for this requirement is known as *referential integrity*.

The foreign key relationships allow you to join related tables to form virtual tables. For instance, selected columns from the customer, invoice, and invoice detail tables can be joined to form the virtual table shown in Table 8.2. Note the redundant information in Table 8.2: the customer number, state, and invoice date columns are duplicated. Remember, however, Table 8.2 is a virtual table; it doesn't exist on a persistent storage device (disk). The information in the table was obtained by joining the records from the customer, invoice, and invoice detail tables based on their foreign-key and primary-key relationships.

A major benefit of RDBs is that you control redundant information. The information related to a customer is stored in one row. The information about an invoice is stored in another row. If information relating to one business entity were duplicated in the rows of various tables, the integrity of information would be difficult to maintain.

Table 8.2: A Virtual File Formed by Joining Files Using Their Key Relationships							
Invoice							
InvoiceNo	CustNo	LastName	State	LineNo	Desc	Qty	InvoiceDate
1234	981	Denoncourt	CA	1	Bolts	2	11/10/1999
1234	981	Denoncourt	CA	2	Washers	15	11/10/1999

Data Types

RDB tables (files) are defined to contain columns of specific data types. Table 8.3 shows the basic RDB data types supported in IBM's DB2 database management system. Note that business applications use the "numerically exact" data types of DECIMAL and NUMBER to store monetary values, since they enable fixed-point decimal precision. The "numerically approximate" data types of FLOAT, REAL, and DOUBLE are often used for scientific applications that require floating-point numbers. The Charge column in the invoice detail table, for instance, would be appropriately typed as a decimal number with a precision of nine and a decimal count of two: **DEC(9,2)**.

Data Type	Description
CHAR(n)	A fixed-length character string of *n* characters.
DECIMAL(p,s)	A decimal number with precision *p* and scale *s*. Precision is the total number of digits, and scale is the total number of digits to the right of the decimal point.
NUMERIC(p,s)	A synonym for DECIMAL.
INTEGER	A 32-bit integer.
SMALLINT	A 16-bit integer.
REAL	A 32-bit, single-precision, floating-point number.
DOUBLE	A 64-bit, double-precision number.
FLOAT	A synonym for DOUBLE.
DATE	Stores the year, month, and day.
TIME	Stores the hour, minute, and second.
TIMESTAMP	Stores the year, month, hour, minute, second, and microsecond.

Table 8.3: Basic DB2 SQL Data Types

Defining Your Database

Now that you know the basic theory behind relational database design, it's time to create a database. The standard method of designing (as well as manipulating and retrieving) relational data is to use SQL. SQL is a relatively simple language to learn because it uses a relatively small number of commands. To define tables, you use the **CREATE TABLE** command:

```
CREATE TABLE table name (column name data type [,?])
```

The following SQL commands create the invoice, invoice detail, and customer database tables:

```
CREATE TABLE invoice (InvoiceNo INT, CustNo INT, InvoiceDate DATE, CloseDate Date)
CREATE TABLE invoiceDetail (InvoiceNo INT,LineNo INT,Desc CHAR(50), Qty INT, Charge
DEC(9,2))
CREATE TABLE customer (CustNo INT, LastName CHAR(20), Street CHAR(20), City CHAR(15),
                ZipCode INT, State CHAR(2), PhoneNo CHAR (10))
```

Data can be inserted into a table immediately after it is created. However, before you see that, you need to learn how to build SQL indexes on top of SQL tables. An *index* is a special file that allows the RDB to quickly retrieve rows from a table. It is standard practice to create an index for each database table on its primary key. Indexes enhance database performance because they optimize retrieval based on the key of the index. Since the primary key of any table is the primary access mechanism, it stands to reason that you should create an index by each file's primary key. The SQL syntax to create an index is as follows:

```
CREATE [UNIQUE] INDEX index name ON table name (column name[,?])
```

Here are the SQL statements to create indexes over the three accounts-receivable tables:

```
CREATE UNIQUE INDEX invoice01 on invoice (InvoiceNo)
CREATE UNIQUE INDEX invoiceDetail01 on invoiceDetail (InvoiceNo, LineNo)
CREATE UNIQUE INDEX customer01 on customer (CustNo)
```

The **UNIQUE** keyword tells the RDB to disallow duplicate key values. If you create an index over another column (or columns) of a table where the key of that index is not unique, you would omit **UNIQUE**.

Populating the Database

Adding rows to a table is done with the SQL INSERT command:

```
INSERT INTO table name VALUES (value1[,?])
```

To add the rows displayed in the database in Table 8.1, you would use the following commands:

```
INSERT INTO customer
  VALUES(981, 'Denoncourt', '5650 El Camino Real', 'Carlsbad', 99999, 'CA',
'8004775665')
INSERT INTO invoice VALUES (1234, 981, '11-Nov-1999', NULL)
INSERT INTO invoiceDetail VALUES (1234, 1, 'Bolts', 2, 1.98)
INSERT INTO invoiceDetail VALUES (1234, 2, 'Washers', 15, 2.66)
```

The SQL keyword **NULL** means the value has explicitly not been set.

Querying the Database

Companies consider the information in their databases to be a corporate asset. Much of the value of a database comes from the ability of individuals and automated processes to query it so that a business process can act on the results of that query. For example, an automated process might print labels from information stored in a product catalog file so a company's marketing department can send mailers to all customers who ordered more that $100 worth of merchandise in the past year. A salesperson, on the other hand, might want to interactively view information about a specific customer along with all open orders for that customer.

RDB queries are requested via the SQL **SELECT** statement, in this format:

```
SELECT *|column name[,?] FROM table name;
```

A **SELECT** always includes the table name. It can explicitly qualify the columns to list in the query result, as in this example:

```
SELECT LastName, State, PhoneNo FROM customer
```

If your want to list all the columns of a table, you can use the asterisk wildcard in the **SELECT** statement:

```
SELECT * FROM customer
```

Rarely does a business process require a query that returns the entire contents of a table. Most queries contain what is known as a *predicate*. The predicate "pre-dictates" what rows are to be retrieved. Place your predicate in the SELECT statement's optional **WHERE** clause. For instance, to list all customers in the state of Montana, you would use the following query:

```
SELECT LastName, State, PhoneNo FROM customer WHERE State = 'MO'
```

Predicates can become extremely complex. There are a number of predicate forms: *relational*, *between*, *null*, *exists*, *like*, and *in*. This book covers only relational predicates. (For the use of other predicates, see a book on SQL.)

SQL predicates are written as algebraic expressions. In fact, SQL has its own brand of algebra, known as *relational algebra*. The relational predicates can use any of the relations shown in Table 8.4.

Table 8.4: Predicates Written as Algebraic Expressions	
Algebraic Relation	**Description**
=	Equal to
!= or	Not equal to
>	Greater than
!>	Not greater than
<	Less than
!<	Not less than
>=	Greater than or equal to
<=	Less than or equal to
and	Logical and
or	Logical or

Expression can include multiple ANDs and ORs, and parentheses can be used to order the evaluation of the expression. The following query, for instance, retrieves all of the customers who have a last name of "Denoncourt" and live in southern California:

```
SELECT *
   FROM customer
 WHERE LastName = 'Denoncourt'
     AND State = 'CA'
     AND (ZipCode = 11111 OR ZipCode = 99999)
```

Queries always return what is known as a *result set*. A result set is basically a virtual table; it is a file that exists in main memory, but not on a persistent storage device.

SQL queries are based on relational algebra. The relational algebra used in the **WHERE** clause of a **SELECT** statement is comprised of Boolean expressions that identify the subset rows contained within a table. Said another way, an SQL result set is the subset of rows that match the search criterion specified in the **WHERE** clause.

The Order By Clause

One other feature of the **SELECT** statement worth noting is the **ORDER BY** clause. This clause is used to sort the result set returned from a **SELECT**. The following statement, for instance, lists all customers by state:

```
SELECT *
  FROM customer
ORDER BY State
```

Joining Files

Because information is spread out among multiple tables, the **SELECT** statement allows you to query multiple tables in one statement. In relational algebra, this multitable query capability is known as a *join*. To join the results of two or more tables, you list them using the **FROM** clause. The **SELECT** statement can contain columns from any of the tables specified in **FROM**:

```
SELECT column name[,?] FROM table name, table name[,?] WHERE join predicate
```

The organization of the **WHERE** clause of an SQL join is extremely important. The predicate should start with the foreign-key relationship of the primary table to the secondary table (or tables). For instance, the virtual table shown in Table 8.2 was the result of joining all three of the files in the accounts-receivable database with the following **SELECT** statement:

```
SELECT invoice.InvoiceNo, customer.CustNo,
           customer.LastName, customer.State,
           invoiceDetail.LineNo, invoiceDetail.Desc,
           invoiceDetail.Qty, invoice.InvoiceDate
  FROM invoice, invoiceDetail, customer
 WHERE invoice.InvoiceNo = invoiceDetail.InvoiceNo
     AND invoice.CustNo      = customer.CustNo
```

In this join operation, the ambiguous column names (those used in multiple files) are qualified with the table name and a dot operator. For optimal performance, your **WHERE** clause should cut out as many rows as possible, early in your SQL statement's predicate.

Database Maintenance

So far, this chapter has covered how to create tables and indexes with SQL's **CREATE** statement, populate them with the **INSERT** statement, and query them with the **SELECT** statement. Next, you need to know how to modify rows in a table and how to delete rows, tables, and indexes.

SQL's **UPDATE** statement is used to change the values of columns in the rows of a table:

```
UPDATE table name SET column name = expression [,?]   [WHERE predicate]
```

If an update operation has no **WHERE** clause, all the rows of the table will be modified to the value specified in the **SET** clause. For this reason, most **UPDATE** operations should contain **WHERE** clauses. For example, the following statement changes the CloseDate column for a particular invoice:

```
UPDATE invoice
        SET CloseDate = '28-Nov-1999'
 WHERE InvoiceNo = 1234
```

Rows are removed from a table with the **DELETE** statement:

```
DELETE FROM table name WHERE predicate
```

It is good practice to test the predicate of an **UPDATE** or a **DELETE** statement by using it in a **SELECT** statement first.

Tables and indexes can be removed with the **DROP** statement:

```
DROP TABLE table name
DROP INDEX index name FROM table name
```

For instance, a customer table could be removed with the following:

```
DROP TABLE customer
```

Note, however, that this statement won't run for the customer table created earlier because that table has an index. Before you delete a table, all the indexes built over it must be removed. You would remove the customer table's index with the following statement:

```
DROP INDEX customer01 FROM customer
```

Using SQL in Java

In the mid-1980s, when client/server architectures were coming into vogue, SQL became a pervasive technology because of a technology called *Open Database Connect* (*ODBC*). Microsoft designed ODBC as a standard communications protocol to allow multiple languages to access relational data from any database (that had an ODBC driver). Microsoft's developers of ODBC wanted everyone to access the RDBs of midrange and mainframe servers, as well as Microsoft's SQL servers, from a Microsoft workstation. They were pretty darn successful. Today, all the major RDBs have ODBC drivers, and most PC-based languages have APIs to those ODBC drivers.

The Java designers at Sun Microsystems looked at ODBC and decided, rather than providing a Java API to ODBC, to improve and simplify ODBC. The result is *JDBC*, or *Java Database Connectivity*. The designers at Sun did a great job. JDBC is powerful, yet easy to learn and use.

The JDBC API was based on ODBC, although its developers simplified the interface and streamlined processing. Initially, however, the only JDBC drivers available used ODBC drivers in the background to connect with your RDB of choice. You used the default JDBC driver that was (and still is) shipped with the Java Development Kit (JDK). That driver is known as a *JDBC-to-ODBC driver* because it requires an ODBC driver.

The problem with JDBC-to-ODBC drivers is that your applications run slowly because you are essentially using two middleware products. RDB vendors quickly saw the potential for Java, however, and developed "100% pure" JDBC drivers that did not require the use of ODBC drivers. Many of those JDBC drivers were faster than their ODBC counterparts, and most RDB vendors made their JDBC drivers available for free. Eventually, for optimal performance, RDB vendors created what are known as *native JDBC drivers*. These drivers were implemented to use the architecture of the RDB's native platform, rather than the interpreted cross-platform Java language. The iSeries, for instance, has both a 100% pure JDBC driver for cross-platform client access to DB2/400, and a native JDBC driver for host-based access to DB2/400. The AS/400 Toolbox for Java (*www.iseries.ibm.com/toolbox/downloads.htm*) contains the 100% pure JDBC driver. The AS/400 Developer Kit for Java (OS/400 license program 5769-JV1) contains the native AS/400 JDBC driver.

The JDBC API

JDBC has four components:

- Driver manager
- Host connection
- SQL statement
- Result set

Components in Java are classes. (Remember that, as yet, discussion has not turned to IBM's Java Toolbox for the AS/400.) These four components, and the associated JDBC utility classes, are standard JDBC classes and—in theory—conform to the JDBC standard published by Sun. However, your JDBC Java code could access DB2/400 one day, and the next day, after one of those nasty mergers, access Oracle or Ingres.

The following JDBC classes encapsulate the features of the corresponding JDBC components:

- DriverManager
- Connection
- Statement
- ResultSet

The DriverManager class tells the Java Virtual Machine (JVM) which driver you are using. The following specifies the AS/400 Toolbox for Java's 100% pure JDBC driver:

```
Class.forName("com.ibm.as400.access.AS400JDBCDriver");
```

The Connection class connects to the platform where your relational database resides. To obtain a connection object, use the DriverManager's **getConnection** method:

```
Connection con =
   DriverManager.getConnection (
      "jdbc:as400://your400DomainOrIP", "user", "password");
```

The first parameter of **getConnection** has three sections: protocol, subprotocol, and data source name. The protocol is always **jdbc**, but the subprotocol varies with each JDBC driver. (By the way, you have already used protocols, in URLs. The URL *http://www.mcpressonline.com* has a protocol of http, no subprotocol, and a domain name of *www.mcpressonline.com*.) For the 100% pure JDBC driver available from the AS/400 Toolkit for Java, the subprotocol is **as400**. For the native JDBC driver from the AS/400 Developer Kit, however, it's **db2**. The data source name is simply the domain name or IP address of your AS/400. The second and third parameters of **getConnection** are the user's name and password.

The JDBC Statement class executes the SQL statement mentioned earlier. A Statement object is obtained from the Connection object:

```
Statement stmt = con.createStatement();
```

The Statement object has two powerful methods for the execution of SQL statements: **executeQuery** and **executeUpdate**. The **executeQuery** method accepts an SQL **SELECT** statement as a string, asks the RDB to execute that query, and then returns the set of records from the query. That set of records is returned in the JDBC ResultSet object. For example, the following Java statement returns all the records from the **invdtl** file, since no **WHERE** clause is specified:

```
ResultSet rs =
   stmt.executeQuery(
      "SELECT * FROM invdlt");
```

Set Processing

To iterate through the set of records contained in the ResultSet object, use the ResultSet's **next** method. You can think of **next** as manipulating a file cursor (except it's actually a set cursor). When the **next** method positions the cursor to the subsequent element of the set, you can then use the ResultSet's **getter** methods to retrieve the values of the fields of a particular record. The **getter** methods convert the data from the internal format of your RDB to Java objects. There is a **getter** method for every data type from DB2/400—too many to cover in detail here. For the most part, though, you will use **getString** for character fields, and **getBigDecimal** for packed and zoned values. Each **getter** method is overloaded to accept two options for parameters. The first option accepts a field name, and the second option accepts a number that represents the ordinal position of the field as it occurs in the SQL **SELECT** statement.

Data Modifications

As mentioned earlier, RDB modifications are done with SQL's **UPDATE** statements. The **UPDATE**, **INSERT**, and **DELETE** statements must be executed with JDBC Statement class's **executeUpdate** method. The following Java code executes an **UPDATE** statement:

```
stmt.executeUpdate(
    ""UPDATE invoice SET cust = "Agway" WHERE invno = 101");
```

An Example JDBC Servlet

The steps to access RDB data with JDBC are quite simple. The example application in Figure 8.1 illustrates the process. The explanation that follows steps through the use of the four main JDBC components.

```java
import java.io.*;
import javax.servlet.*;
import javax.servlet.http.*;

import java.sql.*;
import java.math.*;

public class JDBCBasics extends HttpServlet {
  Connection con = null;

  public void init () {
    try {
      Class.forName("com.ibm.as400.access.AS400JDBCDriver");
    } catch (ClassNotFoundException e) {
      System.out.println("JDBCBasics driver load error: "+e);
    }
    try {
      con = DriverManager.getConnection (
            "jdbc:as400://207.212.90.55",
            "denoncourt", "jiujitsu");
    } catch (SQLException e) {
      System.out.println("JDBCBasics SQL Connection error: "+ e);
    }
  }
  public void doGet(HttpServletRequest request,
                    HttpServletResponse response)
  throws ServletException, IOException
  {
    response.setContentType("text/html");
    PrintWriter out = new PrintWriter(response.getOutputStream());

    out.println("<html><body>");
    try {
      Statement stmt = con.createStatement();

      ResultSet rs = stmt.executeQuery (
        "SELECT CUSNUM, LSTNAM, INIT, STREET," +
        "       CITY, STATE, ZIPCOD, CDTLMT, " +
        "       CHGCOD, BALDUE, CDTDUE " +
        "FROM QIWS.QCUSTCDT");
      while (rs.next ()) {
        String cusnum =
            rs.getString(1);
        String cusnam =
            rs.getString("LSTNAM");
        BigDecimal baldue =
            rs.getBigDecimal(10, 2);
```

Figure 8.1: The four components of a JDBC example are easy to use (part 1 of 2).

```
            out.println(cusnum + " " +
                cusnam + " " + baldue+"<br>");
        }

    } catch (SQLException e) {
        out.println("SQL error : " + e);
    }

    try {
        Statement stmt = con.createStatement();
        stmt.executeUpdate(
            "UPDATE QIWS.QCUSTCDT " +
            "    SET CITY = 'Richmond', " +
            "        STATE = 'VA' " +
            " WHERE CUSNUM = 1234");
        out.println("update worked fine");
    } catch (SQLException e) {
        out.println("update error: "+ e);
    }

    out.println("</body></html>");
    out.close();
    }
}
```

Figure 8.1: The four components of a JDBC example are easy to use (part 2 of 2).

The JDBCBasics servlet's **init** method starts by loading the JDBC driver:

```
Class.forName("com.ibm.as400.access.AS400JDBCDriver");
```

Note that this code refers to a specific vendor's implementation of a JDBC driver. When you register the JDBC driver, you have to refer to an explicit one. This particular servlet uses a database that resides on OS/400. If you wanted to switch your relational database, you'd have to change this line to specify a JDBC driver that works with the new RDB. Also note that the driver name is a string, which means that it can be (and normally is) softcoded. (*Softcoding* refers to the technique of putting site-specific information in a text file that is retrieved at runtime by the application.)

The next step, after registering the driver, involves setting up a connection to the RDB's host. To do this, you specify a URL with the protocol of **jdbc** and a subprotocol of **as400** (for the AS/400), followed by the IP address or domain name of your AS/400 and the user profile and password:

```
Connection con = DriverManager.getConnection(
 "jdbc:as400://my400Domain", "Profile", "Password");
```

Setting the protocol to **jdbc** is similar to setting the protocol to **http** when you surf the Internet. There is, as yet, no subprotocol for the Hypertext Transfer Protocol (HTTP). The JDBC protocol, however, does require a subprotocol. OS/400's JDBC requires a subprotocol of **as400**. IBM's DB2 UDB for the Linux JDBC driver requires a subprotocol of **db2**. The JDBC driver for PostgreSQL, the open-source relational database, requires a subprotocol of **postgresql**. Note that if you softcode your JDBC driver name, you should also softcode the subprotocol.

As you learned in the last chapter, the **init** method of a servlet is called the first time the servlet is loaded. All subsequent requests to that servlet will not cause the **init** method to execute. The JDBC connection object created in the **init** method is a global variable that will be shared by all requestors. Each user's request to the JDBCBasics servlet will be handled with its **doGet** method.

After the obligatory statements for setting the content type, getting an output stream, and dumping out the opening HTML tags, the **doGet** method is ready to specify the SQL statement by creating a Statement object:

```
Statement stmt = con.createStatement();
```

This object is an interface class whose **executeQuery** function enables SQL statements to funnel through the JDBC driver to your host RDB:

```
ResultSet rs = stmt.executeQuery(
        "SELECT CUSNUM, LSTNAM, INIT, STREET," +
        "      CITY, STATE, ZIPCOD, CDTLMT, " +
        "      CHGCOD, BALDUE, CDTDUE " +
        "FROM QIWS.QCUSTCDT");
```

When that SQL query function completes, it returns a set of records in the form of a ResultSet object. Table 8.5 shows all the functions of the JDBC Statement class. One particularly noteworthy function, **executeUpdate**, is used for executing an SQL **INSERT**, **UPDATE**, or **DELETE** statement.

Table 8.5: Useful Functions in the Statement Class

Function	Description
cancel()	Enables a thread to cancel a statement being executed by another thread.
clearWarnings()	After this call, returns null until a new warning is reported for this Statement object.
close()	Immediately releases a Statement's database and JDBC resources instead of waiting for this to happen when it is automatically closed; desirable in many cases.
execute(String)	Executes an SQL statement that may return multiple results.
executeQuery(String)	Executes an SQL statement that returns a single result set.
executeUpdate(String)	Executes an SQL INSERT, UPDATE, or DELETE statement.
getMaxFieldSize()	Specifies (in bytes) the maximum amount of data returned for any column value; applies only to BINARY, VARBINARY, LONGVARBINARY, CHAR, VARCHAR, and LONGVARCHAR columns.
getMaxRows()	Specifies the maximum number of rows a result set can contain.
getMoreResults()	Moves to a statement's next result.
getQueryTimeout()	Limits the number of seconds the driver will wait for a statement to execute.
getResultSet()	Returns the current result as a result set.
getUpdateCount()	Returns the current result as an update count; if the result is a result set or there are no more results, -1 is returned.
getWarnings()	Returns the first warning reported by calls on this statement.
setCursorName(String)	Defines the SQL cursor name for use by subsequent Statement execute methods.
setEscapeProcessing(boolean)	Tells the driver to perform escape substitution before sending the SQL to the database, if escape scanning is on (the default).
setMaxFieldSize(int)	Limits the size of data (in bytes) that can be returned for any column value; applies only to BINARY, VARBINARY, LONGVARBINARY, CHAR, VARCHAR, and LONGVARCHAR fields.
setMaxRows(int)	Limits the number of rows that any result set can contain.
setQueryTimeout(int)	Specifies the number of seconds the driver will wait for a statement to execute.

To retrieve the records from the ResultSet object returned from the **executeQuery** function, you simply use the **next** function of that object. The example application invokes **next** within the clause of a **while** loop. That way, the application continues retrieving records until **next** returns a Boolean value of false:

```
while (rs.next())
```

The **next** function simply positions the pointer to a subsequent record in the ResultSet. To retrieve the values of that record, you have a little work to do; you must use one of the ResultSet's **get** functions to pull those values out of the record. Table 8.6 lists all of the **get** functions of the ResultSet class. They can be categorized into two groups: one in which you specify the ordinal number of the SQL statement's column position, and another in which you specify the field name:

```
String cusnum = rs.getString(1);
String lstnam = rs.getString("LSTNAM");
String baldue = rs.getString(10);
```

Table 8.6: ResultSet Class Functions Used to Retrieve Data

Function	Description
getBigDecimal(int)	Gets the value of a column in the current row as a java.lang.BigDecimal object.
getBigDecimal(String)	Gets the value of a column in the current row as a java.lang.BigDecimal object.
getBinaryStream(int)	Retrieves a column value as a stream of uninterpreted bytes, and then reads chunks from the stream.
getBinaryStream(String)	Retrieves a column value as a stream of uninterpreted bytes, and then reads chunks from the stream.
0getBoolean(int)	Gets the value of a column in the current row as a Java Boolean.
getBoolean(String)	Gets the value of a column in the current row as a Java Boolean.
getByte(int)	Gets the value of a column in the current row as a Java byte.
getByte(String)	Gets the value of a column in the current row as a Java byte.
getBytes(int)	Gets the value of a column in the current row as a Java byte array.
getBytes(String)	Gets the value of a column in the current row as a Java byte array.
getCursorName()	Gets the name of the SQL cursor used by this result set.
getDate(int)	Gets the value of a column in the current row as a java.sql.Date object.
getDate(String)	Gets the value of a column in the current row as a java.sql.Date object.
getDouble(int)	Gets the value of a column in the current row as a Java double.
getDouble(String)	Gets the value of a column in the current row as a Java double.
getFloat(int)	Gets the value of a column in the current row as a Java float.
getFloat(String)	Gets the value of a column in the current row as a Java float.
getInt(int)	Gets the value of a column in the current row as a Java int.
getInt(String)	Gets the value of a column in the current row as a Java int.
getLong(int)	Gets the value of a column in the current row as a Java long.
getLong(String)	Gets the value of a column in the current row as a Java long.
getMetaData()	Provides the number, types, and properties of a result set's columns.
getObject(int)	Gets the value of a column in the current row as a Java object.
getObject(String)	Gets the value of a column in the current row as a Java object.
getShort(int)	Gets the value of a column in the current row as a Java short.
getShort(String)	Gets the value of a column in the current row as a Java short.
getString(int)	Gets the value of a column in the current row as a Java string.
getString(String)	Gets the value of a column in the current row as a Java string.
getTime(int)	Gets the value of a column in the current row as a java.sql.Time object.
getTime(String)	Gets the value of a column in the current row as a java.sql.Time object.
getTimestamp(int)	Gets the value of a column in the current row as a java.sql.Timestamp object.

Because the example uses the **getString** functions, all of the values—even the numeric ones—are retrieved as strings. To get the zoned, six-digit, two-decimal values for **BALDUE**, you'd use one of the **getBigDecimal** functions:

```
BigDecimal baldue01 = rs.getBigDecimal(10);
BigDecimal baldue02 = rs.getBigDecimal("BALDUE");
```

The **getBigDecimal** function uses metadata (data about data) contained in the ResultSet object to find out the count of decimals to be set in the retrieved BigDecimal object. If you run the example JDBC application, you will obtain the simple list in Figure 8.2 showing customer number, name, and balance due.

```
846283 Alison   10.00
475938 Doe      250.00
938472 Henning  37.00
938485 Johnson  3987.50
839283 Jones    100.00
192837 Lee      489.50
389572 Stevens  58.75
693829 Thomas   0.00
397267 Tyron    0.00
392859 Vine     439.00
593029 Williams 25.00
update worked fine
```

Figure 8.2: Running the application from Figure 8.1 provides a list of customer numbers, names, and balances due from the records in the QCUSTCDT file.

Data Modifications

As mentioned earlier, RDB modifications are done with SQL's **UPDATE** statements. The **UPDATE**, **INSERT**, and **DELETE** statements must be executed with JDBC Statement class's **executeUpdate** method. The following Java code executes the **UPDATE** statement shown earlier:

```
stmt.executeUpdate(
     ""UPDATE invoice SET cust = "Agway" WHERE invno = 101");
```

Stuff Happens

Things don't always work, so your code must be prepared to handle potential problems. Most of the JDBC methods generate error objects called *SQL exceptions* when things go wrong. All of the JDBC method invocations had to be wrapped with Java **try** blocks. The **init** method's **try** blocks list errors using **System.out.println**, while the **doGet** method's **try** blocks list errors to the dynamically constructed HTML with **out.println**.

JSP Version

Figure 8.3 shows the JSP version of the JDBCBasics servlet.

```
<%@ page import="java.sql.*" %>
<%@ page import="java.math.*" %>

<%! Connection con = null; %>

<%! public Connection getConnection () {
    if (con != null) {
      return con;
    }
    try {
      Class.forName("com.ibm.as400.access.AS400JDBCDriver");
    } catch (ClassNotFoundException e) {
      System.out.println("JDBCBasics driver load error: "+e);
      return null;
    }
    try {
      con = DriverManager.getConnection (
            "jdbc:as400://207.212.90.55",
            "denoncourt", "jiujitsu");
    } catch (SQLException e) {
      System.out.println("JDBCBasics SQL Connection error: "+ e);
      return null;
    }
    return con;
  }
%>

<html><body>

<%
    con = getConnection();
    try {
      Statement stmt = con.createStatement();
      ResultSet rs = stmt.executeQuery (
        "SELECT CUSNUM, LSTNAM, INIT, STREET," +
        "       CITY, STATE, ZIPCOD, CDTLMT, " +
        "       CHGCOD, BALDUE, CDTDUE " +
        "FROM QIWS.QCUSTCDT");
      while (rs.next ()) {
        String cusnum =
            rs.getString(1);
        String cusnam =
            rs.getString("LSTNAM");
        BigDecimal baldue =
            rs.getBigDecimal(10, 2);
%>
        <%= cusnum %>   <%= cusnam %> <%= baldue %> <br>
<%    }
    } catch (SQLException e) {
%>
        SQL error :   <%= e %>
<%  } %>
</body></html>
```

Figure 8.3: JDBC can be accessed in JSPs.

It might be tempting to use JSP rather than servlets for development because the compile process is automated. However, production Web applications work better when complex code is kept in Java servlets and JavaServer Pages are used for the presentation layer.

End of Chapter Review

Key Terms

Data types	Join	Relational database
Driver manager	JSP	**SELECT**
Foreign keys	ODBC	Structured Query Language
INSERT	Primary keys	Set processing
JDBC	Referential integrity	**UPDATE**

Review Questions

1. What are the four components of JDBC?

2. What is a relational database?

3. What is a primary key?

4. What is a foreign key?

5. List three examples of data types in a database.

Programming Assignment

Exercise 1: Create a Database

1. Create order, order detail, and customer tables as outlined in the chapter. Add foreign key relationships where appropriate. If you are using PostgreSQL for your database, here are a few notes:

   a) Remember from chapter 5 that PostgreSQL documentation is available under the **/usr/share/doc** directory.

   b) The following starts PostgreSQL:

   ```
   # /etc/rc.d/init.d/postgresql start
   ```

   c) To set up a user for PostgreSQL, use the following steps:

      i. Log in as root,

      ii. Use the **su** command with **postgres** as the argument:

   ```
   # su postgres
   ```

      iii. Use the PosgreSQL **createuser** command qualified by the user name, and follow the prompts:

   ```
   # createuser username
   ```

      iv. Use the PosgreSQL **createdb** command qualified by the user name, and follow the prompts

   ```
   # createdb username
   ```

   d) Use the **psql** command to invoke an interactive SQL session.

2. Create indexes for each table over the table's primary key. Make sure to disallow duplicate keys.

3. Populate your database with several orders for each customer and several line items for each order.

4. Try adding a row that contains a duplication primary key. (If you created a unique index on that table, the DBMS will disallow the addition of a row that has the same key value as an existing row.)

Exercise 2: Display Database Information

Use the database created in exercise 1 to do the following:

1. List orders by customer.

2. List orders for a specific customer.

3. List an order and order detail for a specific customer.

Exercise 3: JDBC

1. Deploy the JDBCBasics example servlet in Figure 8.1 to Tomcat.

   a) Enter the code in a file called **JDBCBasics.java**.

   b) Run the following SQL statements to create and populate the table used in JDBCBasics:

```
CREATE TABLE QCUSTCDT (    CUSNUM NUMERIC(6, 0), LSTNAM CHAR(8), INIT CHAR(3),
            STREET CHAR(13),    CITY CHAR(6), STATE CHAR(2), ZIPCOD NUMERIC (5, 0),
            CDTLMT NUMERIC (4, 0),    CHGCOD NUMERIC (1,0), BALDUE DECIMAL (6, 2),
            CDTDUE NUMERIC (6, 2)  );
INSERT INTO QCUSTCDT VALUES( 938472,'Henning',  'G K','4859 Elm Ave ',
                                         'Dallas',  'TX', 75217, 5000, 1, 37.00, 0);
INSERT INTO QCUSTCDT VALUES( 839283,'Jones    ', 'B D','21B NW 135 St',
                                         'Clay ',  'NY', 13041,  400, 1, 100.00,0 );
INSERT INTO QCUSTCDT VALUES( 392859,'Vine     ', 'S S','PO Box 79    ',
                                         'Broton',  'VT',  5046,  700, 1, 439.00,0 );
```

   c) Make sure a **.jar** file that contains a JDBC driver for your selected database is available.

   PostgreSQL's is called **jdbc7.1-1.2.jar** (where 7.1 is the PostgreSQL version number, and 1.2 indicates that it support JDK 1.2). That file is normally located under **/usr/share/pgsql**. You might have to install it from the Red Hat installation CD or download it from one of the PostgreSQL Web sites.

   d) Modify the driver registered with **Class.forName** to be that of the database you are using

   e) Modify the subprotocol, IP, username, and password in the **getConnection** method call to qualify the appropriate JDBC driver, database server, and user.

   f) To compile the source, set the **CLASSPATH** environment variable to point to the Java archive that contains the Java Servlet API classes:

```
$  CLASSPATH=$CLASSPATH:/opt/tomcat/lib/servlet.jar
```

   g) Use the **javac** command to compile **PanelServlet.java**:

```
$  javac PanelServlet.java
```

h) Once any errors are corrected and the compile completes successfully, copy the Java executable, **JDBCBasics.class**, to **/opt/tomcat/webapps/ROOT/WEB-INF/classes**:

```
$ cp JDBCBasics.class /opt/tomcat/webapps/ROOT/WEB-INF/classes
```

i) Copy your JDBC driver's **.jar** file to the **WEB-INF/lib** directory (you might have to create the directory):

```
$ cp /usr/share/pgsql/jdbc7.1-1.2.jar /opt/tomcat/webapps/ROOT/WEB-INF/lib
```

2. Access the servlet from Netscape Navigator:

```
http://127.0.0.1:8080/servlet/JDBCBasics
```

3. Deploy the JSP example shown in Figure 8.3 to Tomcat.

a) Enter the source in a file under the **/opt/tomcat/webapps/ROOT/** directory.

9

The Apache Web Server

The Native Americans known as the Apaches once freely roamed the southwestern United States. Theirs was a society in which everyone had a voice in the direction of the tribe. Apaches lived efficiently off the land—land that they believed was not to be owned, but was there to be used by everyone. The spirit of the Apaches is alive and well today. It flourishes in cyberspace, where over half of all Web sites are hosted by Apache HTTP servers. Like the land inhabited by the Apaches, the Apache HTTP server is not owned by anyone. Companies and individuals have free access not only to the server itself, but also to its source code.

The Apache HTTP server is available for free download from *www.apache.org*. The **.org** extension to the domain name identifies the site as a nonprofit organization. Is the Apache HTTP server merely shareware, then, as Microsoft likes to suggest? No. It is a viable and robust Web server for both large and small Web sites. IBM's WebSphere application server, for instance, is designed as a plugin for the Apache HTTP server on all platforms.

To understand a little more about the Apache HTTP server, you need to look at its history. Until 1995, only a few Web servers were available, and the number-one Web server was the National Center for Super Computing Applications (NCSA) HTTP server. However, by early 1995, the NCSA server project began to stall. Not wanting the project to collapse, its users informally created a group that freely distributed code patches to the original server. The spirit of a new HTTP server began to evolve from what amounted to "a patch here and a patch there," and the Apache ("a patchy") HTTP server was born. Its creators were a collection of serious computer scientists who wanted an HTTP server that was powerful enough to meet their expanding requirements. These programmers formed a nonprofit organization called the Apache Group, and, in April 1995, the first version of the Apache HTTP server became available to the general public. By the end of 1996, Apache was the leading Web server in an increasingly competitive market.

You might be wondering why any individuals or organizations would devote their time and talents to improving a Web server without the promise of a return on their investment. First, you must understand that there is a return: an improved Web server. Second, organizations that extend the Apache HTTP server want to pay back the Apache organization by sharing their improvements with everyone. Third, there are bored developers who want to make a contribution to cyberspace and choose to do so by enhancing the most popular Web server in the world. (It looks pretty good on a résumé, too.)

Patches

The thought of "a patch here and a patch there" conjures up a pair of old jeans with haphazard patches on areas that weren't designed properly. Forget the term *patch* when thinking of Apache; the only significance of the word is to understand the history behind the Apache name. Instead, think of the term *module*. The design of the Apache HTTP server has been crafted well; it is not a haphazard set of fixes on top of old source. Apache has a base set of *core modules*, plus about a dozen other modules that are shipped as a standard part of the server. Table 9.1 shows the modules that Red Hat's 7.1 distribution loads when Apache is started with its default configuration settings.

Table 9.1: Apache Modules Included in the Default Configuration File	
Module	**Services Provided by the Module**
mod_vhost_alias	Allows virtual hosting with aliases.
mod_env	Passes environment variables to CGI and SSI (server-side include) scripts.
mod_log_config	Determines logging configuration.
mod_mime	Maps extensions to content types.
mod_negotiation	Allows selection based on Accept headers.
mod_status	Gives access to server status information.
mod_info	Gives access to configuration information.
mod_include	Provides support for SSIs.
mod_autoindex	Builds an HTML page containing an index of all accessible files.
mod_dir	Redirects requests for directives that do not include a trailing slash.
mod_cgi	Allows a higher-level language to dynamically build responses to HTTP requests.
mod_asis	Sends a document as it is, without HTTP headers.
mod_imap	Provides imagemap support.
mod_actions	Specifies CGI scripts to act as handlers for particular file types.
mod_speling	Corrects URL spelling based on file and directory names in the server file system.
mod_userdir	Selects resource directives by user name and a common prefix.
mod_alias	Maps one part of a file system to another.
mod_rewrite	Rewrites URLs using specified rules.
mod_access	Runs a CGI script based on MIME type or HTTP request method.
mod_auth	Provides basic HTTP authentication against text-based password files.
mod_auth_anon	Allows anonymous access to authenticated areas.
mod_auth_db	Provides HTTP authentication against a database.
mod_expires	Handles responses with expired HTTP headers.
mod_headers	Manipulates HTTP response headers.
mod_so	Loads modules at runtime.
mod_setenvif	Sets environment variables based on header fields in the request.

To use a module, you must specify the AddModule directive in a configuration file, qualifying the name of the module whose services you want to enable with your Apache server. Pretty clean. The base server is very small and fast, but easily extensible with standard modules to support such advanced features as Java servlets, Perl, FastCGI (a.k.a. persistent CGI), HTTP cookies, server-side includes, and Secured Sockets Layer.

The parade of modules doesn't stop there, however. The Apache HTTP server was designed to take full advantage of the power of modular programming, which resulted in an easily extensible and customizable server. Anyone can extend the Apache HTTP server by creating a custom Apache module.

Sometimes, after a particular custom module becomes heavily used and well regarded, the Apache Group will add it to the core set of modules included with the Apache download. Many frequently used and recommended third-party modules are also freely available from *http://modules.apache.org/.*

The Apache Code

The add-on Apache modules can be statically or dynamically bound to the HTTP server program. As mentioned, you dynamically bind an Apache module by specifying the AddModule directive and the module name in a configuration file. For speed, however, you can statically bind Apache modules to the Apache HTTP server by recompiling the server program. The server program is called **httpd** (which stands for "Hypertext Transfer Protocol Daemon"). You can think of **httpd** as a demon that hides in the background, waiting for requests from people trying to gain Web-based access to your host via TCP/IP and HTTP. The Apache HTTP server is delivered with the binary executable **httpd** program, the bindable modules, the complete C source code for **httpd**, and the C code for all of the standard Apache module extensions.

Apache Startup

The Apache Web server can be started by invoking the **httpd** command from a terminal session, but most distributions have a startup script that simplifies Apache. Red Hat's script is also called **httpd**, and it exists in the **/etc/rc.d/init.d/** directory. If you attempt to invoke the script without any options, you'll receive the following message:

```
$ /etc/rc.d/init.d/httpd
Usage: httpd {start|stop|restart|reload|condrestart|status}
```

This helpful message tells you the arguments required by the **httpd** script. The **status** option will tell you whether or not Apache is active, and the other options are obvious.

When Apache is started, it looks for the **httpd.conf** configuration file in **/etc/httpd/conf.** You might be a little overwhelmed the first time you look at that **httpd.conf**, so we've supplied a minimal version in Figure 9.1. Apache expects a particular directory structure:

- A **conf** directory for the **httpd.conf** file

- A directory called **htdocs** to hold the hypertext documents Apache is to serve

- A directory called **logs** to hold various pieces of information that Apache can be configured to log

```
            # httpd.conf Apache configuration file
            ServerRoot "/etc/httpd"

            Port 8888

            User nobody
            Group nobody

            ServerAdmin denonco@attglobal.net

            ServerName localhost

            DocumentRoot "/home/donat/www2/htdocs"

            LoadModule mime_module          modules/mod_mime.so
            LoadModule dir_module           modules/mod_dir.so

            AddModule mod_mime.c
            AddModule mod_dir.c

            TypesConfig /etc/mime.types

            DirectoryIndex tomcat.html
```

Figure 9.1: A minimal httpd.conf Apache configuration file enables basic Web serving.

Each of the lines in Figure 9.1 is known as a *directive* (except for the comment line, which is preceded by a pound symbol). The ServerRoot directive qualifies the directory that contains the Apache modules. The Port directive tells Apache to sit on the TCP/IP port number of 8888. (If this directive is omitted, the default HTTP port number of 80 is used.) The next two directives, User and Group, qualify the user profile that Apache will use to verify access to requested files. The user name of "nobody" sounds fake, but if you look at the **/etc/passwd** file (which lists all users for your system), you'll find user nobody listed. User nobody pretty much *is* a nobody in terms of accessing sensitive information on your machine. And that's the point. When remote users request files from your Apache HTTP server, they will only be able to access those files that user nobody has rights to.

The ServerAdmin directive simply qualifies the email address of the Web master, should a Web-browsing user wish to contact him or her. The ServerName directive qualifies the domain name of the server machine. Since this configuration is for test purposes only, it uses the special loop-back domain of **localhost**. The DocumentRoot directive qualifies the directory created earlier to hold the files to be served by this Apache instance.

Let's skip the LoadModule and AddModule directives for a moment, and move ahead to TypesConfig and DirectoryIndex. TypesConfig qualifies a file that maps HTTP content types to file extensions. It is through this file that Apache is able to set the appropriate HTTP content-type header sent to the browser. Table 9.2 shows a partial list of the **mime.types** file.

Table 9.2: A Partial List of the Default /etc/mimes.types File

HTTP Content Type	File Extension
application/pdf	.pdf
image/gif	.gif
image/ief	.ief
image/jpeg	.jpeg, .jpg, or .jpe
audio/x-realaudio	.ra
audio/x-wav	.wav
text/css	.css
text/xml	.xml
video/x-msvideo	.avi
text/html	.html or .htm

The last directive in this minimal **httpd.conf** file, DirectoryIndex, qualifies the name of the HTML file that Apache is to serve, should a Web-browsing user enter only the server name.

Now, back to the LoadModule and AddModule directives. The default **httpd.conf** file that exists in the **/etc/httpd/conf** directory contains numerous LoadModule and AddModule directives. However, the minimal example **httpd.conf** file only qualifies the **mod_mime** and **mod_dir** modules to be loaded and added. We had to add these because they enable the TypesConfig and DirectoryIndex directives. If you remove the LoadModule and AddModule directives (or comment them out by adding a pound symbol as the first character in their lines), and Apache will fail to start.

One problem with the minimal Apache configuration is that you can't use the handy-dandy **httpd** Apache startup script in the **/etc/rc.d/init.d/** directory to use it. Instead, you have to directly invoke the **httpd** binary located in **/usr/sbin**. Further, you have to qualify the location of the custom Apache configuration file:

```
/usr/sbin/httpd -f /home/userdir/www2/conf
```

Using this strategy, you can start multiple Apache instances, as long as each configuration file qualifies a different port number.

The **/etc/rc.d/init.d/httpd** script has a stop option to end the Apache server, but since you can't use the script with this strategy, you have to end the Apache job manually. To end a Linux process, use the **kill** command with the process ID of the controlling Apache process. To find that process ID, use the following **ps** command:

```
ps aux | grep /usr/sbin/httpd
```

The **ps** command lists all **httpd** processes, as shown in Figure 9.2. Note that Figure 9.2 lists, not one, but nine processes. Also note that the name of the user associated with the first process is the super user (root), while the other processes are the more ordinary nobody user. Finally, note that the process ID (the second column) is perfectly sequential.

This sequence is no coincidence. The first process, 2959 in this case, is the true server; the others are merely helper processes. The first process sits on the TCP/IP port waiting for Web-browsing requests. As soon as a request comes in, it hands the responsibility for handling it to its child processes. This does two things:

- It instantly frees the server process so that it can go back to waiting at the port for another request.

- It makes the Web server more secure because the request is handled by a process limited by the rights of the user qualified in the **httpd.conf** file with the User and Group directives.

```
root    2959  0.0  0.2  3748 1076  ?    S    09:37  0:00 /usr/sbin/httpd -
nobody  2960  0.0  0.2  3940 1268  ?    S    09:37  0:00 /usr/sbin/httpd -
nobody  2961  0.0  0.2  3928 1268  ?    S    09:37  0:00 /usr/sbin/httpd -
nobody  2962  0.0  0.2  3928 1268  ?    S    09:37  0:00 /usr/sbin/httpd -
nobody  2963  0.0  0.2  3892 1152  ?    S    09:37  0:00 /usr/sbin/httpd -
nobody  2964  0.0  0.2  3892 1152  ?    S    09:37  0:00 /usr/sbin/httpd -
nobody  2969  0.0  0.2  3900 1168  ?    S    09:37  0:00 /usr/sbin/httpd -
nobody  2970  0.0  0.2  3900 1168  ?    S    09:37  0:00 /usr/sbin/httpd -
nobody  2971  0.0  0.2  3900 1168  ?    S    09:37  0:00 /usr/sbin/httpd -
```

Figure 9.2: The ps aux | grep command string lists all httpd processes.

If you end the process that is running as the root user, all its child processes will automatically be terminated, also. So, based on the process IDs in Figure 9.2, you can end the Apache server with the following command:

```
kill 2959
```

The minimal configuration shown here is useful for gaining an understanding of how the Apache configuration process works. For production servers, it is probably a better idea to start with the default **httpd.conf** configuration file in the **/etc/httpd** directory and then to use the **/etc/rc.d/init.d/httpd** script to start and stop Apache. The **/etc/httpd/conf/httpd/conf** file is lengthy, but it contains plenty of comments that do a great job of explaining what each directive is for. Don't forget to also look at the documentation available at the *www.apache.org* site.

Support

If you are still a little wary of this unsupported Web server stuff (that's right, the authors of Apache didn't volunteer to answer tech-support phones), you might want to consider a commercial implementation of the Apache HTTP server. IBM provides such a product, IBM HTTP Server, shown in Figure 9.3. The IBM HTTP Server provides the quality and power of the Apache HTTP server, along with the support you'd expect from an IBM commercial product.

Think of IBM HTTP Server as a shrink-wrapped Apache HTTP server with simple installation and full support. Also, because IBM HTTP Server is a pay-for-view product, IBM is able to legally bundle support for SSL (although the U.S. government won't allow it to provide the source code for their SSL Apache module).

IBM keeps close ties with the Apache Group; the company pays the salaries for two full-time members of the Apache Group core team. IBM also has a complete team of programmers making enhancements to the IBM HTTP Server. To ensure compatibility with the Apache HTTP server, those enhancements are submitted to the Apache Group. Once those enhancements are accepted, they become a permanent part of both the Apache HTTP server and the IBM HTTP Server.

Figure 9.3: The IBM HTTP Server product logo clearly states that it is "powered by Apache" to show that it is based on the open-source Apache HTTP server.

Tomcat Apache Plug-in

Chapter 8 introduced Apache's open-source Web application server, Tomcat. In the exercises for that chapter, you installed and tested Tomcat. The Tomcat product contains a rudimentary HTTP server. For production use, Tomcat should be added as a plug-in to the Apache server. You can download that plug-in from Apache's Jakarta Project Web site (*http://jakarta.apache.org*). Take the download link for your version of Tomcat (note that 4.0 and higher uses a new plug-in strategy not covered in this session), and then follow the path **/bin/linux/i386/** to retrieve the file **mod_jk-noeapi.so**.

The module **mod_jk-noeapi.so** enables Apache to communicate with Tomcat. You'll need to move it to the directory **/etc/httpd/libexec/** with the following command:

```
mv <download-dir>/mod_jk-noeapi.so /etc/httpd/libexec/mod_jk.so
```

Note that you might have to create the **libexec** directory. Also note that the move renamed **mod_jk-noeapi.so** to simply **mod_jk.so**. (There is an eapi version and a non-eapi version of **mod_jk.so** available for download.)

Finally, include the entries required for Tomcat in the Apache configuration file by adding this line to the end of Apache's **/etc/httpd/conf/httpd.conf** file:

```
Include /opt/jakarta-tomcat/conf/mod_jk.conf-auto
```

Apache is now ready to work with Tomcat, and you're ready to test the installation. For these two packages to work together correctly, you'll need to start Tomcat first, then Apache. First, ensure that Apache is currently stopped. On a Red Hat system, you can accomplish this by issuing the following command:

```
/etc/rc.d/init.d/httpd stop
```

Next, start the Tomcat server by issuing this command:

```
/opt/jakarta-tomcat/bin/tomcat.sh start
```

Tomcat will send messages to the terminal session where it was started. Finally, start Apache with this command:

```
/etc/rc.d/init.d/httpd start
```

A test of the following URL should present an HTML page that simply states "HelloWorld":

```
http://localhost/test/jsp/HelloWorld.jsp
```

End of Chapter Review

Key Terms

AddModule	httpd	RedHat
Apache Server	httpd.conf	Tomcat
Deamon	Kill	
FRCA	Nobody	
HTTP Server	Port 8888	

Review Questions

1. What does the .org suffix stand for?

2. The term "Apache" is derived from what term?

3. List three reasons that the authors cite why someone or a company would devote their time and talents on improving a Web server without the promise of a return on their investment.

4. The AddModule directive performs what function?

5. The **httpd** Apache HTTP server is delivered with which program and modules?

Programming Assignment

Exercise 1: Start Apache

1. Using the **http** startup utility in the **/etc/rc.d/init.d** directory, start Apache.

2. Access Apache from Netscape:

```
http://127.0.0.1
```

Exercise 2: Customize Apache

1. Create the following directory structure under your home directory:

   ```
   www2
           conf
           htdocs
           logs
   ```

2. Place the minimal Apache directives shown in Figure 9.1 in a file called **httpd.conf** under the **conf** directory.

3. Create a home page (HTML page) under the **htdocs** directory.

4. Replace the DirectoryIndex directive in your **httpd.conf** file to qualify your home page.

5. Start Apache, qualifying the location of your custom configuration file.

6. Test Apache from Netscape. Note that the Port directive in Figure 9.1 qualified port 8888, so your URL needs to identify that port:

   ```
   http://127.0.0.1:8888
   ```

Exercise 3: Install the Apache Tomcat Plugin

1. Follow the directions in the chapter to download and install Tomcat's Apache plug-in.

2. Start Tomcat, then start Apache.

3. Test the plug-in from Netscape:

   ```
   http://localhost/test/jsp/HelloWorld.jsp
   ```

Exercise 4 (Optional): Download and Install IBM's HTTP Server

1. Download **HTTPServer.linux.1.3.19.0.EN.tar.gz** (where EN is the language identifier) from *www-4.ibm.com/software/webservers/httpservers/download.html.*

2. Use **gunzip** to uncompress the **.tar** file:

   ```
   $ gunzip HTTPServer.linux.1.3.19.0.EN.tar.gz
   ```

   The **gunzip** utility will replace **HTTPServer.linux.1.3.19.0.EN.tar.gz** with **HTTPServer.linux.1.3.19.0.EN.tar**.

3. Sign on as root.

4. Change your directory to **/opt**, then extract the **.tar** file using the **tar** utility:

```
# cd /opt
# tar -xf  where/ever/you/put/HTTPServer.linux.1.3.19.0.EN.tar
```

The **tar** utility will create a directory called **IHS-1.3.19.0** and fill it with about half a dozen RPMs.

5. Change your working directory to **IHS-1.3.19.0**:

```
# cd IHS-1.3.19.0
```

6. For each of the RPMs, run the **rpm** utility in the following format:

```
# rpm -U –nodeps <rpm file name>
```

7. Start IBM's HTTP Server:

```
# /opt/IBMHTTPServer/bin/apachectl start
```

or

```
# /etc/rc.d/init.d/ibmhttpd start
```

8. Test IBM's HTTP Server:

```
http://127.0.0.1
```

9. Stop IBM's HTTP Server:

```
# /opt/IBMHTTPServer/bin/apachectl stop
```

or

```
# /etc/rc.d/init.d/ibmhttpd stop
```

Take note that under the **/opt/IBMHTTPServer** directory, you'll find the same **conf, htdocs,** and **logs** subdirectories as the standard Apache Web server.

10

Linux Operation, Configuration, and Administration

The Linux system that results from your carefully planned installation will have everything you need to keep you off the streets for a long time to come. Eventually, though, you'll want to make some changes. You might want to alter the way your desktop looks and behaves, perhaps add some additional software, or make configuration changes to the base Linux system. If nothing else, entropy will eventually attack your system, forcing you to delve into the system configuration. This chapter introduces you to the tools for making these changes.

The User Interface

It might seem incongruous to have a section on user interfaces in a book that deals with Linux-based Web hosting. After all, most Linux servers run without benefit of a keyboard and screen (a.k.a. *headless*), so the only user interface available is via a browser or remote command-line shell. We realize that the first server you build will probably be hosted on your own workstation. With that in mind, let's take a quick look at the Linux GUI and find out why it is so powerful.

X in a Nutshell

Anyone who has used the Windows operating system is already familiar with a graphical user interface (GUI). Unlike Microsoft's offerings, where the GUI is an integral part of the operating system, the Linux GUI is an add-on called the X Window system (or just *X*).

The X Window system is based on a client/server architecture, with the various parts available as individual software components. At the heart is the X server, which runs on the computer to which is attached the hardware providing the basic requirements of X: a graphics card and monitor, a keyboard, and a mouse. Working in conjunction with the X server are two additional components: the desktop environment and the window manager. These two provide the basic functionality (like drag-and-drop) and window treatment (sorry—we just couldn't resist) that permit you to give your desktop a personalized look. The server, desktop environment, and window manager communicate with one another to provide you with the X Window experience.

The server is the one item within X that is not negotiable. You need to run one that is compiled for your particular CPU and operating system. There is an X server available for virtually every computer equipped with the basics, and your Linux distribution undoubtedly includes it. If your usual operating system is Linux, BeOS, MacOS, OS/2, or even Windows, chances are you can get an X server—if not an open-source (free) one, then a commercial one.

For the window manager and desktop environment, you have many choices. Included with your Linux distribution are various window managers, such as **sawfish**, **windowmaker**, and **enlightenment**, as well as desktop environments, such as KDE and Gnome. If you choose to install X and either or both KDE and Gnome, you already have some or all of these options at your disposal. Depending on which desktop you choose for your default, you'll find yourself in KDE or Gnome. If you are one of those itinerant GUI-twiddlers, you'll have lots of new toys to play with.

Before going any further, it would be helpful if you were currently at a computer that is in X. If you configured your computer to start in runlevel 5 (the graphical runlevel), you will have a graphical sign-on screen. If you are looking at the console **login:** prompt, you need to log on and, at the command prompt, enter the command **startx**, which brings up a graphical desktop. This, of course, assumes that you installed the X server and a desktop. If not, you can either go back and install them now, or simply skip this section if you don't plan to use X.

To start, click the KDE Control Center (on the toolbar at the bottom of the screen) or the Gnome Control Center (Foot->Settings->Gnome Control Center), and take a look at the vast array of options you can change. It's enough to make a geek drool. You can see what these control centers look like in Figures 10.1 and 10.2.

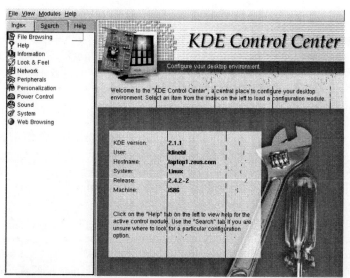

Figure 10.1: The KDE Control Center allows easy configuration of your desktop.

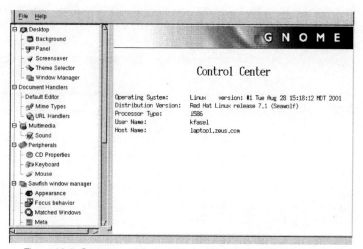

Figure 10.2: Gnome provides a control center similar to that of KDE..

You might want to try both desktop environments to see which on you like better. Red Hat seems to push Gnome, but KDE is reputed to be the easiest to convert to from Windows. We use both, although we're starting to lean toward KDE. Keep in mind that running a desktop environment is entirely optional; if you have a memory-constrained system, you can run without one.

At this point, you're probably wondering what advantages X provides over its embedded-GUI equivalent. After all, the job of any GUI is to make it easy for you to do your work, and if you are used to the Windows environment, you probably find it easiest to work there. Let's look, however, at some of the advantages of X.

First on the list, of course, is the freedom of choosing which window manager/desktop environment combination you want to use—including the choice to run none at all. If the selections provided with your distribution don't inspire you, there are more at *www.plig.org/xwinman/*. You are bound to find one that fits both your tastes and your hardware. The closest equivalent to this in the Windows world comes from Stardock, Inc. in a package titled "Object Desktop," which started as an OS/2 Workplace Shell extension. This product enables you to make your desktop "skinnable," allowing you to customize it to your content. The bloat inherent in the Windows GUI is still there, however; Object Desktop just adds to it. So, while X allows you to make choices to balance functionality with form, the Windows GUI only allows you to add a pretty facade at the cost of more bloat.

Another advantage of X is its *virtual desktop*. Both Gnome and KDE can have not only virtual desktops, but also separate desktops (pages) within the virtual desktops. For instance, let's say that, while you are sitting at work or in class, you want to play games. On one desktop, you can have Freecell running, while on another, you can have your work, switching between them with keystrokes or mouse clicks. On a more practical note, you can place your Web browser in one window to view your latest creation, while having the source open in an editor in another. The best Windows can do is stack one window on top of another. Any competent computer geek will want to have many windows open at once, and X provides an easy way to organize them. Granted, the Object Desktop product allows you to have multiple desktops, but it is a Windows add-on instead of an inherent trait. And, you have to pay for Object Desktop; X is available for free.

One of the big features touted in Windows XP is the "fast-switch" option. This feature permits a user to interrupt his or her work so that another may log on and do something else. When the new user logs off, the state of the original user's desktop is restored where he or she left off. In essence, Microsoft is finally attempting to create the multiuser operating system that it has been claiming as a function of Windows for a long time. Since X is built on an operating system that truly is multiuser, it has been able to do this since its inception. To demonstrate, press Ctrl-Alt-F2, and you'll find yourself at another console. Log on as someone else, and then enter the following to start another X server on console 1:

```
startx -:1
```

You can alternate between your two different users' sessions simply by pressing Ctrl-Alt-F7 for the original session, and Ctrl-Alt-F8 for the second session. And there you have it—the X Window fast-switch feature! You can't do that with any Windows version except XP.

Of course, you could argue that this isn't a big deal, so let's go one step further. Although it is not apparent to a user on a single computer, the X client/server architecture applies to two separate computers. The programs communicate with each other over TCP/IP sockets, whether they are within the same machine or on different machines. This makes it possible to run a program on one computer while controlling it from another, which is something you just can't do from a Windows desktop. Well, that's not completely true, since you can run a program like Virtual Network Computing (*www.uk.research.att.com/vnc/*). But VNC only gets you remote access to a Windows computer, and not remote *concurrent* access to the remote computer. This difference becomes apparent if you happen to seize control of a remote Windows machine without its current user being aware of the capability. In other words, you can remotely control the computer, but only to the extent that you would if you were sitting directly in front of it. A single Linux computer could easily be running programs on behalf of any number of users who are located anywhere on any network capable of reaching it. In fact, it is possible that the machine you use could be doing that right now! The good news: you will have an opportunity to experiment with all of this during the exercises at the end of this chapter.

Facility Configuration and Administration

There are so many different aspects to configuring and administering a Linux box that quite a number of books have be written on the subject. This section boils Linux configuration down to one simple fact: almost without fail, you can find the configuration files for the operating system and programs in the main **/etc** directory, or one of the other "etc" directories, such as **/opt/etc** or **/usr/local/etc**.

Our initial plan for this section was to show some examples from within the **/etc** directory, point out how to use vi to edit them, and then go on to talk about some of the various KDE, Gnome, or Linux utilities that you could use to accomplish the same task. The problem is, like so many things Linux, there are many ways to accomplish this, and there are some risks to advocating a particular method. For example, the **linuxconf** utility is mentioned in many books on Linux as the premier way of configuring your system. However, it is now officially *deprecated* by Red Hat, which is a polite way of saying that it's broken, it's not supported, and it's unlikely it will ever be fixed. As a matter of fact, it is so broken that, if you see any references to it anywhere on your system, you should go out of your way to avoid it. As we can both attest, its use is likely to destroy your current working configuration.

There have been other attempts to make configuring your system less of an arcane art and more of a science, but they all have been made obsolete by what has to be the finest configuration tool ever made: Webmin. Not only does it allow you to easily configure your system, it slices and dices and allows you to maintain it as well! Webmin is probably all you need to configure and maintain your Linux Web server. (If you aspire to be a Linux system administrator, however, you will still eventually want to purchase some Linux administration books to explore the guts of the system.)

Webmin is a browser-based application that allows you to configure and maintain your computer locally (from the same machine), or from another computer across a network. So complete is the implementation that you can virtually replace all other configuration tools with this one item. As a bonus, it is extensible, so that any software author can write a Webmin module to support his or her application. Webmin will, upon installation, determine the distribution of Linux (and some other operating systems) on which it is running and automatically configure itself to provide only the relevant options. But we digress. You first need to get and install Webmin.

Point your browser to *www.webmin.com/webmin/* to get the Webmin RPM. To ensure you don't have conflicts with the browser distinguishing between a RealPlayer file and an RPM file, hold down the Shift key while clicking the RPM link. You will be prompted to give the downloaded file a place to reside, which is probably your home directory, and a name, which is probably **webmin-0.90-1.noarch.rpm** (although the "0.90-1" portion could be different as the program is updated).

Once the file is downloaded, open a terminal window to get a command line, and then issue the **su** command to switch to the root user. (You aren't logged on as the root user already, are you? You shouldn't be!) At the prompt, enter the following command to install the package:

```
rpm -Uvh webmin-0.90-1.noarch.rpm
```

Tip: Enter everything through **webmin** in the line above, and press Tab. The file name will be completed for you through the magic of the **bash** shell.

After much wailing and gnashing of disk, you'll be rewarded with a prompt that says you can now log on to *http://localhost:10000*. That means the Webmin server is ready to accept connections, but is awaiting the connection on port 10000 instead of the standard HTTP port 80. You may now exit the terminal session (close the window or type **exit** at the command line) and fire up your browser (which we assume is Netscape). Enter that address into the Location field and press Enter. You will be prompted to log into Webmin.

It is important to note that the user name and password you use to log into Webmin will determine the level of access you are granted. Webmin honors Linux privileges, so log on as the root user. You should find yourself at the screen shown in Figure 10.3.

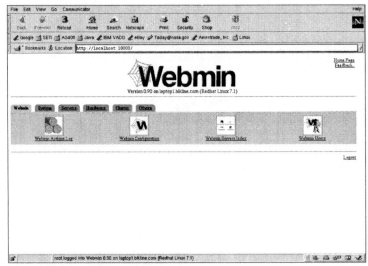

Figure 10.3: This is the first Webmin screen.

The very first task to perform is to verify that you have Webmin secured from the world. Upon initial installation, it should be configured to accept connections only from the *loopback interface*, meaning that you can connect to it from your local machine (localhost) on IP address 127.0.0.1. You want to ensure that this is the case. If you were to log into Webmin from another machine on an unencrypted connection, the user name and password would travel the network in plain text, so anyone with a packet sniffer would be able to configure your system for you very quickly. That would be a bad thing.

To verify that Webmin is listening on the loopback interface only, click the Webmin Configuration link, and then click Ports and Addresses. If the resulting display resembles Figure 10.4, you are ready to go. If it doesn't, make it do so, and then click Save.

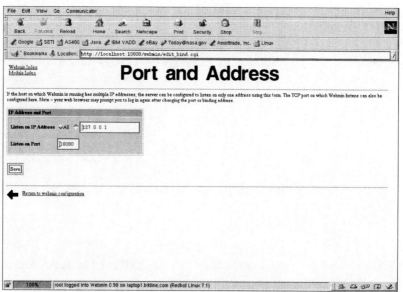

Figure 10.4: This screen shows Webmin listening on the loopback interface only.

To further increase your protection, click IP Access Control and make the adjustments in your browser window until you have things configured as shown in Figure 10.5. This tells Webmin to accept connections only if they come from 127.0.0.1, which is the local loopback address. In other words, you can only access Webmin from the same machine on which it is running, so you are doubly protected if you accidentally expose Webmin to connections from the network.

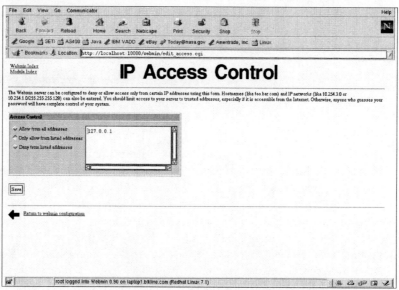

Figure 10.5: For added security, configure IP Access control as shown here.

If you ever want or need to configure your system from another machine, configure Webmin to use an encrypted link. That is beyond the scope of this book, but if the topic interests you, follow the SSL Encryption link on the Webmin configuration page..

File System Administration

Under normal circumstances, you will have little to do with file system administration. Linux systems, and servers in particular, run for months or even years without a reboot. Given that reliability, there are only three situations where you will need to worry about your file system:

1. You turn your computer off without issuing the **shutdown** command or the power goes off and you don't have a suitable uninterruptible power supply (UPS).

2. One or more of your partitions runs out of space.

3. Your hard drive fails.

The lack of a proper system shutdown is a very bad idea. The lack of a UPS is a stupid idea for a Web server. Linux, like most current operating systems, uses memory as a cache (temporary storage location) for data that is coming from or going to the disk drive. The premise is simple: as fast as disk drives have become, accessing data from them is still tremendously slower than a comparable data exchange from memory. So, the operating system will store changes in memory until a convenient time becomes available to flush the cache to disk. The result is a system that is more responsive to the user, or in the case of a Web server, has quicker response times. The trade-off is a certain exposure to the possibility that the system could die before the changes get written to disk. Rudely shutting the computer down is a glaring example of that exposure. The best-case scenario is an extended system boot time while a file system check is done (which will be explained shortly). The worst-case scenario is a loss of data, potentially with an unbootable or unusable system.

> **Note:** Never power off your system with the power switch; use **shutdown -h now** instead. Systems without power management can be turned off using the switch once the "power off" message appears on the screen.
>
> And, for crying out loud, buy a UPS! (Preferably one with a communications port for the computer—Linux can monitor for a lack of commercial power and shut itself down gently and cleanly.)

If you do manage to shut down your Linux system abruptly, you'll be introduced to the file system check (**fsck**) utility. Linux will automatically run **fsck** if it finds that the partition was not cleanly unmounted during the prior shutdown (because you turned off the power). This is where you will be punished for your mistake, because an **fsck** on a large partition can last quite some time. And since each one of your partitions is in the same state, you'll get to watch each partition being cleansed. (Either that, or you can start writing that ten-page paper you've been putting off.) Most of the time, you'll see a bunch of hateful messages listing the things that are being fixed and, if the stars are aligned properly, you'll get a "successful" message at the end of each partition. If not, you'll have to run **fsck** by hand. If that is the case, Linux will let you know and will guide you through the process.

Various journaling file systems are under development to help alleviate the trauma to file systems if you lose power, but you should try to avoid this situation altogether. One other thing about **fsck**: it gets run automatically every *n* times you reboot your computer (where *n* is some number that you can change with the **tune2fs** command) or when it has been a long time between restarts. Don't assume, therefore, that you had a power drop just because **fsck** runs during a bootup.

The second "oops" in the list is running out of space in a partition. This can have some interesting side effects. Assuming that it's not your root partition that has become full, the usual symptom is that your servers shut down or adamantly refuse to accept connections. If this ever happens, one of the first things you should check is that you still have some disk space available. One way to check is to use Webmin. Connect to *http://localhost:10000* and sign on. Click the Hardware tab, and then click Partitions on Local Disk. On the right side of the screen, you'll see a listing of each of your partitions and a percentage of the space still available. If any partition says zero percent, you've found the problem.

You might be wondering, "If my system is not accepting connections, how can I connect to Webmin?" Good question! The answer is that you might not be able to connect. In that case, you'll have to fall back to Plan B, which is to open a terminal session (or use Ctrl-Alt-F2 and sign on) and issue the **df** command, which is the tried-and-true Linux way to get at the same data. There is one caveat, though: **df** returns the percentage of the disk space *used*, which is just the opposite of Webmin. In this case, you're looking for a partition that's 100 percent used.

In either case, you have some housekeeping to do. The first thing you need to do is find where your disk space is going, by using the **du** command. Change to the mount point on the offending partition and issue the following to get a list of the directories and their sizes, in descending order of size:

```
du -x | sort -g -r | more
```

You can use the **man** command to figure out what each of those switches does. Once you've determined which directories are the drive-space hogs, examine each one and delete unnecessary files, such as those MP3s of copyrighted material that you downloaded from Napster or JPG files of...well, you get the idea.

If, after all of your housekeeping efforts, you still can't find enough room to run, your next solution is simple: reevaluate your partitioning scheme. Perhaps you can rob Peter to pay Paul by taking space from one partition and assigning it to another. Use one of the various tools available for this task, like the commercial product Partition Magic or the open-source program **partd**. If that isn't possible, you'll need to purchase and install another disk drive. (The steps involved with either partition resizing or disk installation are outside the scope of this book.)

The third pitfall, hard drive failure, is the least likely because of the reliability of the current generation of hard drives. When it does occur, however, the solution is straightforward: buy a new drive and restore the system from your last backup. Sometimes you can get lucky with a failed drive and be able to extract information from it, but don't try press luck. A disk drive is unable to heal itself, so when it starts to go, put it out to pasture. (Backups are discussed later in this chapter.)

Facility Monitoring

One of the most important functions of a system administrator is to maintain a vigil on the system to ensure that everything is going fine. Webmin provides the access to the information you need. Point your browser to your system, and click the System tab, then choose System Logs. To view a log, click the associated View link at the right side of the screen. Although you probably won't need to do it, you can configure the logging function using the link at the left of the screen.

Two of the logs are of particular interest. The first, **/var/log/messages,** is where almost all system daemon-logging takes place. When that disk drive starts to act flaky or a daemon is configured incorrectly, you'll probably find suspicious messages here. The second log, **/var/log/secure,** is where all security-related messages are stored. Of particular importance are those indicating that the system rejected the user ID or password multiple times, since this could indicate someone was trying to break into your system, albeit via a rather crude, brute-force method.

For the most part, facility monitoring is comprised mainly of knowing such things as the amount of disk space used in your system, how many users are on the system at one time, and what normal log messages look like. The next step is watching the logs for changes to the norm. For this task, Webmin is probably the easiest solution.

Routine Maintenance

One of the great things about the current crop of Linux distributions is that much of the tedium that was part of a system administrator's job has been automated. For example, we indicated earlier that quite a bit of information is logged to disk. That is simply space that continues to get eaten up as the system runs. Left to their own devices, the logging daemons would eventually eat up every available byte. The obvious solution to the problem is to occasionally archive the current log files and re-create them, thereby freeing up the space used.

This job used to be done manually whenever it appeared that drive space was becoming in precariously short supply. Now, the **logrotate** command takes care of it for you. If you are interested, display the contents of **the /etc/logrotate.d/** directory to see a list of logging daemons that are cleaned up by **logrotate**. You'd need to remember to run this command, if it weren't for the **cron** daemon.

In your Webmin window, click the System tab, then click Scheduled Cron Jobs for a list of what gets run automatically. Continuing with the **logrotate** task, click the **/etc/cron.daily/logrotate** link, and you'll find out that every day at a specific minute and hour (which, on our system, is 4:02 A.M.), the logs are rotated. If you examine the **/var/log/** directory, you'll note that the archived logs are numbered, the newest starting wth a **.1** extension and going up from there. Depending on the setting in the **/etc/logrotate.d** directory, the number of archived logs can vary. Most are kept for four generations, but some are kept even longer.

Backing Up

Even though most housekeeping is configured and maintained for you, the one thing that can't be automated is backup. That responsibility falls squarely on your shoulders. There are a number of different viewpoints on backup. To fully understand them requires a book on system administration, but to cut to the chase, there are certain basic things you need to consider when planning your backup strategy.

We use the following guidelines:

- Only back up those directories that you can't restore from the installation CDs. You already have a backup of your operating system on your distribution CD-ROMs, so don't feel you need to do a complete backup of your system.

- Since most configuration information is kept in **/etc**, it would make sense to include this directory in a backup.

- Obviously, you'll want a backup of your Web server's document root directory, which for a standard Apache installation on Red Hat Linux is **/var/www**. If you choose to back up this entire directory, you'll not only get the Web pages, but also any CGI programs in **/var/www/cgi-bin**.

- User home directories are likely candidates for frequent backup, if you have created any users (including yourself). If you simply request the entire **/home** directory, you'll be in good shape.

- Other directories that are possible candidates for backup include **/usr/local** and **/opt**. The frequency with which you back up these directories depends on the frequency with which you load software. If your system is stable, you can simply back them up whenever you add or remove software.

- Be sure to back up your databases! You'll need to check the database vendor's documentation to determine how to extract the information to a file and ensure it gets into your backup. For example, PostgreSQL has the **pg_dump** command to extract the schema and contents of an entire database. The output from this command can be redirected to an output file in one of the aforementioned directories, so that databases can be included in a normal backup schedule.

- Learn to use **tar**. This venerable program is the basis for almost all exchanges of software and data between Linux and UNIX systems, and it is extremely powerful. Although it is short for "tape archiver," **tar** can write its output to a file. Unfortunately, Webmin doesn't seem to have a "System Backup" tab (although one could be created), so you'll need to get cozy with the command-line version. Here is a sample command line that would save the directories listed in the previous items:

```
tar -cjf mybackup.tbz /etc /var/www /home /opt /usr/local
```

Keeping Current

Last on your list of maintenance items is keeping current on your distribution software. One of the really great things about open-source software is that bugs or security flaws are frequently fixed very soon after they are discovered. Red Hat and the other distribution authors quickly ensure that the patches are propagated throughout their software.

Red Hat posts all of its updates at *www.redhat.com/errata/*; check there for the latest packages. Also included with each fix package are the instructions for installation, so you won't be guessing how to do it. If you purchase a boxed set of a Red Hat distribution, you can take advantage of the **up2date** program, which automates the entire process. It connects to Red Hat's site and compares the list of available fixed packages there with the list installed on your system, keeping your system synchronized with Red Hat.

Chapter Summary

This chapter examined some of the tasks faced by a system administrator, such as monitoring logs, performing system backup and executing system recovery. Although Linux administration used to be something of an arcane art, programs such as Webmin have made it painless and straightforward.

End of Chapter Review

Key Terms

Backup	tar	webmin
File system check (fsck)	UPS	X server
linuxconf utility	Virtual desktop	X Window System
Loopback address	Virtual Network Computing	

Review Questions

1. List the three components of the X Window System.

2. Describe the benefit of having a virtual desktop.

3. List three situations that could corrupt or even destroy your Linux files. Of these, which do the authors deem most detrimental?

4. If your server shuts down unexpectedly, or stops accepting connections from browsers, what should you check? How can you check this (list two methods)?

5. What does the following command accomplish:

```
tar -cjf mybackup.tbz /etc /var/www /home /opt /usr/local
```

Programming Assignment

Exercise 1: Work with Webmin

1. Download and install Webmin's RPM from *www.webmin.com/webmin*.

2. Invoke Webmin's administrator panel from Netscape:

```
http://127.0.0.1:10000/
```

3. When the login panel is displayed, log on as root.

4. Review the Apache Web server configuration:

    a) Click Webmin's Servers tab

    b) Click the Apache Web server link.

    c) Under the Global Configuration section, review the settings for each of the configuration links.

5. Check disk usage from the Hardware tab. List the amount of available free space.

Exercise 2: Research UPS Products

1. Find three vendors of UPS products.

2. List the Web site address, price, and several features of each vendor's UPS.

Exercise 3: Monitor Facilities

1. Using Webmin, click the System tab.

2. Review the following system logs:

    *   /var/log/messages

- /var/log/secure

Exercise 4: Perform Routine Maintenance

1. Using Webmin, click the System tab, then click Scheduled Cron Jobs.

2. Click the Logrotate link to determine when the **logrotate** command is executed.

3. Back up, using the **tar** utility:

```
# tar -cjf mybackup.tbz /etc /var/www /home /opt /usr/local
```

   a) Explain why the **.tbz** extension is used.

   b) What does each of the **cjf** options do?

11

Linux and the Internet

Undeniably, the Worldwide Web has become an integral part of many peoples' lives. Most people who use it do not know or care how it works. To them, the inner workings of the Internet are as fascinating as the inner workings of their local phone service. They don't want the details, as long as it works.

While it's true that, with today's Web hosting services and HTML editors, you can become an active participant in the Web without much computer knowledge, we assume that because you are reading this book, you have more than a passing interest in the "plumbing" that makes your information flow across the world. This chapter gives you an extremely basic introduction to the Internet's infrastructure—how your data gets from "here to there." Don't expect to get enough information here to achieve guru status; that would take volumes of text and years of experience. You will, however, get enough information so that, when you finally decide to unleash your server onto the world at large, you won't sound like a complete idiot to the guru who will be "hooking you up."

The 60-second Internet History

The Internet as we now know it owes its existence to the paranoia of the 1950s. The ability of a single bomb to wipe out a large physical area greatly concerned the research and development community of the military. In a nutshell, the problem came down to creating a communications infrastructure for the Advanced Research Projects Agency (ARPA) and the various university and private labs working under its umbrella, which would continue to be effective even if parts were destroyed in a nuclear blast. The result was *ARPANET*, a communication system that would automatically route information around damaged parts of the network using a technique called *packet switching*.

As the years passed, ARPANET morphed and begat a slew of "somethingNETs": MILNET (Military Network), BITNET (Because It's Time Network), CSNET (Computer Science Network), and a host of others were built by specific groups for specific purposes. The standard communication protocols we use today (such as email and FTP) were developed so that users in one network could communicate with users in another (internetworking, as it were), creating the noun that describes the glue that put the networks together: the Internet.

The modern Internet is actually quite young; it didn't extend much past universities until the mid-1990s. In fact, the system known as "the Worldwide Web" didn't get released until 1991. Prior to that, computer hobbyists exchanged information via a piece of software known as a *bulletin board system* (*BBS*), which serviced calls coming into the modems connected to the computer on which the BBS software ran. A user connected to the BBS with terminal-emulation software and navigated it via textual menus, not the familiar browser screens we take for granted today. Typically, the BBS would offer a file-exchange area (we'll leave to your imagination what kinds of files were exchanged) and a message board (similar to the Internet's USENET newsgroups). Sometimes, chat sessions were provided.

Most BBSs were small-time operations that typically could handle no more than 16 callers simultaneously, since each user would tie up one phone line and modem. Since computer hardware wasn't as powerful or inexpensive as it is today, the small-time operator could ill-afford a massive BBS system. Typically, BBS operators funded their operation through the subscription fees paid by their members, which usually were limited to people within the local calling areas of their system. Soon, companies like CompuServe, SpryNet, and America Online (AOL) began to offer functions equivalent to those of the local BBSs, but on a much grander scale, covering a large geographical system. As these big boys started to provide local access numbers in more and more communities, the smaller operators became extinct. In its turn, though, the Internet made the services provided by companies like CompuServe look stale and archaic. AOL is still going strong, but one of its main services is a portal to the Internet, without which it would have surely died.

Even the great visionary Bill Gates and his company of innovators had to contend with the Internet. Their failed Microsoft Network was built as an alternative to the Internet and companies like AOL. Even when the access software for Microsoft Network was bundled with the Windows operating system, users weren't interested. Bill & Company finally saw the writing on the wall ("build it and they *won't* come") and decided instead to embrace the Internet—Internet Explorer being the primary result.

The history of the Internet makes fascinating reading. If you have an inclination toward the history of technology, plug the phrase "history of the Internet" into your favorite search engine.

TCP/IP Primer

By now, you've already been introduced to the concept of TCP/IP addresses. They are those 32-bit numbers that you type into the networking-parameters boxes during installation. You might be saying, "Huh? I never typed in any 32-bit numbers." Actually, though, you did. To make it easier to work with these addresses, they are typically broken down into four, eight-bit octets, separated by decimal points, providing numbers in the range 0.0.0.0 through 255.255.255.255.

An IP address is further broken down into two parts: the *network address* and the *node address*. Networks are grouped by class based on how much of the address is given to the network address and how much to the node portion. The zero in the following examples represents the node address.

Class-A networks are defined using the first octet, $X.0.0.0$, where X can have a value of one through 127, inclusive. There aren't many class-A addresses available, so only the biggest users can score one. Class-B networks use the first two octets for their definition, $X.Y.0.0$, where X has a value between 128 and 191. Class-C networks, which are what most end-users deal with, use the first three octets, $X.Y.Z.0$, and start with an X value between 192 and 223. The two node addresses of zero and 255 are reserved; the former represents an entire network, and the latter represents a broadcast address for an entire network. Compared to class-A networks, many more class-C network addresses are available, but each can have only 254 nodes. (Remember: zero and 255 are reserved.) In addition, some of the address ranges are reserved. For example, the $127.X.X.X$ series is reserved for a loopback device, used for testing computers without Internet connections.

Assume for the moment that you have two computers connected by a simple Ethernet hub. The first computer is an FTP and HTTP (Web) server. The second is a simple workstation that is a client to the first. For these computers to talk to each other via TCP/IP, they must have the same network address, and each must have a unique node address. In the case of a class-C network, this means that the first three octets must match, but the fourth octet must be unique.

Assuming everything is connected and configured properly, the question then becomes, "How does the server know which service the client is requesting when a connection request is made?" The answer is simple: logical ports. Within each TCP/IP packet is embedded not only the source and target (the sender and receiver) IP addresses, but also a from-port and to-port number. TCP/IP has provisions for 65,536 logical ports. Logical ports under 1,024 are the well-known ports, because the function of each has been defined in the IP specifications. In the case of the first computer in our example, the FTP server normally would be listening on port 21 (the FTP port), and the HTTP server normally would be listening on port 80.

These ports are not carved in stone. In fact, you can make adjustments to your server configurations to effectively change the port on which the server listens for a connection. However, once you deviate from the well-known ports to your own definitions, you'll need to specify the port number whenever making a connection request. For example, if you've configured your HTTP server to listen on port 2000, you'll need to append ":2000" to any URL that points to your custom server. Otherwise, your browser won't be able to connect. For example, "http://www.yourdomain.com" would become "http://www.yourdomain.com:2000" when attempting to connect to your server. A list of services and the ports on which they listen is on your computer (at **/etc/services**); you can browse this file if you are curious.

At this point, you are probably wondering asking yourself, "How is this relevant to my Web server? I always type in a URL, so why should I know this material?" Our answer is simple: You should know the basics so that you can more readily configure your server. But don't fret; the worst is over. There are just a few more terms with which you should become familiar.

You have already heard the term *IP address*, which is the unique address (on your network) assigned to your computer. The network administrator assigned the address and probably gave you a number in conjunction with another number, known as the *network mask*, or just *netmask*. Basically, the netmask indicates which of the bits comprise the network address. Each bit that is set to a logical one in the netmask is part of the network address. Those that are set to a logical zero are considered part of the node address. This topic can become quite esoteric, so we'll just leave you with the admonition to always double-check IP addresses and netmasks. An error in the IP address could cause your computer to conflict with another that has the same IP address, which can lead to some curious problems that are hard to troubleshoot. An error in the network mask can lead to the inability of your computer to communicate with any others. This error isn't nearly as difficult to find, however.

Another term of interest is *gateway*. As mentioned earlier, two computers can communicate with one another only if they are on the same network. If they are on different networks (say, your local network and the Internet), your communications will be brokered by a device called a gateway that has at least two interfaces: one on the network to which you are connected and another on another network. The gateway address given to you by your network administrator is the address to which it will send any packets destined for a computer that is not on your local network.

The next term to know is *Domain Name System*, or *DNS*. The simplest way to explain DNS is to use the analogy of IP addresses and phone numbers. If you know someone's phone number, you can easily call that person. If you don't know the phone number, but you know the person's name, you can call directory assistance to get the number.

DNS is the directory assistance of the Internet. When you enter a URL like "http://www.yourdomain.com" into your Web browser (the name you wish to call), your system will first look in its own address book (the file **/etc/hosts**) to see if it knows that name. If not, it will connect to a DNS server to retrieve the number. If the DNS system knows the name, it will transmit the number back to your computer, which will use it to make the connection. If the name is unknown, the DNS server will return an error message to that effect, which you see as a "Host Unknown" message from your browser.

The list of DNS servers to which you'll request information is in the file **/etc/resolv.conf**. If you look in that file, you'll see up to three "nameserver *xxx.xxx.xxx.xxx*" entries. They will be searched in the order in which they appear. Typically, you'll be given two DNS server IP addresses—a primary and a secondary address. If the primary one dies, the second will provide DNS services until the primary comes back online.

The final term is *Dynamic Host Configuration Protocol*, or *DHCP*. In a nutshell, it refers to a protocol whereby a computer that has just been turned on can automatically be configured with the correct IP/netmask, DNS, and gateway addresses. It does this by broadcasting a DHCP request to the network (using a different type of addressing because it doesn't know anything about the network at this point) and waiting for a response from a DHCP server in which all of the network parameters are provided. The DHCP server has a pool of available addresses from which it will choose one to send to the client. Once it does this, the address is said to be *leased*, which means that the server will not assign it to another client. The lease has a fixed lifespan, just as real-world leases do, and the client will occasionally be polled to see if the lease should be renewed. If the client responds, the lease is renewed. If not, the lease is cancelled and the address is placed back in the pool.

Most networks use DHCP for all machines but their servers (and some even use it for them, too!), simply because it requires much less effort on the part of the network administrator. If your net admin tells you to use DHCP when you initially connect your computer to the network, be sure to let him or her know that you are going to be running a Web server. You cannot be assured of receiving the same IP address every time your computer comes online unless the net admin either makes special adjustments to the DHCP server configuration or gives you a static IP address.

Figure 11.1 shows how all of these pieces fit together. Note that your communication will frequently go through a number of gateways until it gets to its destination. In fact, a file that is too large to make it in one TCP/IP packet will be split into many smaller ones. What's fascinating is that they may travel using different routes, arriving at the destination at different times and out of order. TCP/IP was designed to put them back together correctly. The beauty of TCP/IP is that the whole process ultimately appears like magic. You have to do nothing more than correctly configure your computer's IP address, netmask, gateway, and DNS entries, and the rest happens automatically.

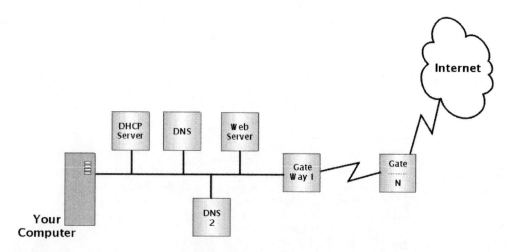

Figure 11.1: The various components of a TCP/IP network.

Protocols

An understanding of the term *protocol* is important because of the misconceptions most people have about the meaning of the URLs they type into their browsers. Take, for example, the URL "http://www.mydomain.com." Most people erroneously believe that the "www" in the URL indicates "Worldwide Web." Well, it does, but in name only. Actually, "www" is simply a host within the "mydomain.com" domain. The URL could just as easily have been "http://myserver.mydomain.com" and everything would have worked just the same. The use of "www" became a standard host name so that people could make assumptions as to the location of a company's Web site. Following this standard, a person wanting to find out more information about IBM's product would point a browser to *http://www.ibm.com*. It is actually the "http://" part of the URL that indicates you want to communicate using the Hypertext Transmission Protocol.

Simply put, a protocol is an agreed-upon language used to accomplish a given task. In the case of a Web server, your browser makes a connection to the port on which it is listening (port 80), and once connected, issues the specific commands to retrieve a single file. The Web server will return either the requested file or an error message indicating that it wasn't found. At that point, the connection is broken and the exchange is completed.

The browser will format the page sent to it and display it to you. Images embedded in the Web page will result in subsequent connections to the Web server, as will clicking on any links. Each connection is a separate transaction that ends with a response from the server. You can verify this simply by connecting to your computer's Web server. Ensure that you have the Web server running (using **/sbin/service httpd status**). Then, from a command line, type the following:

```
telnet localhost 80
```

This uses the telnet client to connect to the HTTP port of your computer. Once you receive the message **Escape character is '^]'**, the Web server is ready for your request. Type **GET / HTTP/1.0** and press Enter twice. You'll get a notification that the Web server received your request, along with a message indicating success or failure. In this case, you should receive the message **HTTP/1.1 200 Okay,** followed by some header information and the Web page. Contrast that with an error by typing **GET /failform HTTP/1.0** and pressing Enter twice. An edited version of this transaction appears in Figure 11.2.

```
Trying 127.0.0.1...
Connected to localhost (127.0.0.1).
Escape character is '^]'.
GET / HTTP/1.0

HTTP/1.1 200 OK
Date: Tue, 04 Dec 2001 02:08:16 GMT
Server: Apache/1.3.19 (UNIX)  (Red-Hat/Linux) mod_jk
Last-Modified: Thu, 29 Mar 2001 17:53:01 GMT
ETag: "1447d-b4a-3ac3767d"
Accept-Ranges: bytes
Content-Length: 2890
Connection: close
Content-Type: text/html

<!DOCTYPE HTML PUBLIC "-//W3C//DTD HTML 3.2 Final//EN">
<HTML>
 <HEAD>
  <TITLE>Test Page for the Apache Web Server on Red Hat Linux</TITLE>
 </HEAD>
<!- Background white, links blue (unvisited), navy (visited), red (active) ->
 <BODY BGCOLOR="#FFFFFF">

...

 <P>
  You are free to use the image below on an Apache-powered Web
  server.  Thanks for using Apache!
 </P>

 <P ALIGN="CENTER">
 <A HREF="http://www.apache.org/"><IMG SRC="/icons/apache_pb.gif" ALT="[ Powered
by Apache ]"></A>
 </P>

 <P>
  You are free to use the image below on a Red Hat Linux-powered Web
  server. Thanks for using Red Hat Linux!
 </P>

 <P ALIGN="center">
 <A HREF="http://www.redhat.com/"><IMG SRC="poweredby.png" ALT="[ Powered
by Red Hat Linux ]"></A>
 </P>
 </BODY>
</HTML>
Connection closed by foreign host.
```

Figure 11.2: Response from Apache on an invalid request.

Besides HTTP, you'll also occasionally see a URL in the form "ftp://ftp.domain.com," which indicates that communication should use the File Transfer Protocol connection to the FTP port (21) of the host "ftp" in the domain "domain.com." You'll typically see this in conjunction with a request to download a file, although HTTP is becoming more popular for downloading files.

Although most modern browsers can communicate using FTP, earlier computer users became familiar with the FTP client called, amazingly enough, *ftp*. You can get a taste of the FTP protocol by issuing the command **ftp** from a command line. At the **ftp>** prompt, type a question mark and press Enter. You'll be presented with a list of the commands included in the File Transfer Protocol. If you don't want to do that yourself, you can always look at Figure 11.3, where we've done the heavy lifting for you.

```
ftp> ?
Commands may be abbreviated.   Commands are:

!              cr            mdir          proxy         send
$              delete        mget          sendport      site
account        debug         mkdir         put           size
append         dir           mls           pwd           status
ascii          disconnect    mode          quit          struct
bell           form          modtime       quote         system
binary         get           mput          recv          sunique
bye            glob          newer         reget         tenex
case           hash          nmap          rstatus       trace
ccc            help          nlist         rhelp         type
cd             idle          ntrans        rename        user
cdup           image         open          reset         umask
chmod          lcd           passive       restart       verbose
clear          ls            private       rmdir         ?
close          macdef        prompt        runique
cprotect       mdelete       protect       safe
ftp>
```

Figure 11.3: Most FTP servers provide help with a simple request: **?**

Odds, Ends, and Email

One of the most widely used Internet facilities is email, and it may have been that function that first drew you to the Internet. When you first became "connected," your ISP or network administrator should have provided the names of your SMTP and POP servers, which you dutifully filled into the appropriate spaces in your email client's configuration screen.

Once your email started being delivered, you probably didn't give any more thought to the curious terms *SMTP* and *POP*. Not surprisingly, the last *P* in each of these terms stands for "protocols." The protocols primarily responsible for delivering your missives and Microsoft viruses are the Simple Mail Transfer Protocol (SMTP), the Post Office Protocol (POP), and, to a growing extent, the Internet Message Access Protocol (IMAP).

Let's begin this discussion with SMTP, which transmits your message to its destination. SMTP is the *protocol* used between programs to exchange email, not the program itself, so if you plan on running an SMTP daemon, you'll need to obtain an SMTP server program. The standard on Red Hat Linux is the venerable and very powerful sendmail program, notorious for its incredibly tricky configuration and infamous for security holes in older versions. Simpler and more secure programs include QMail and PostFix, either of which is readily available in RPM form for a Red Hat system. Regardless of which SMTP server you choose, they all operate in the same basic fashion. Upon startup, they check their configuration, decide where they are running and from whom they will accept mail, then patiently await a connection on TCP/IP port 25.

Suppose you've just heard a really bad joke and wish to inflict it on a friend via email. Opening up your email client, you enter "myfriend@hisdomain.com" into the "To:" field and, after filling in a subject like "I thought you might like this" (which might make your friend suspect that you just sent a Microsoft email virus), you start typing the lengthy text of the joke. When you click the Send button, your email client will connect with the SMTP server and, using the SMTP protocol, send the message through the ether to its intended recipient.

A standard Red Hat installation already will have sendmail running, with which you can communicate using telnet. Try typing the following:

```
telnet localhost 25
```

You should see a heading that begins with the digits 220 and then has your host name, the version of sendmail that is running, and the local date and time. You can then type **HELO localhost**. Sendmail will greet you, notifying you that you have successfully gotten its attention. Figure 11.4 shows the complete conversation.

```
Telnet localhost 25
Trying 127.0.0.1...
Connected to zeus2.
Escape character is '^]'.
220 localhost ESMTP Sendmail 8.11.2/8.11.2; Wed, 5 Dec 2001 21:46:52 -0500
HELO localhost
250 localhost Hello IDENT:userid@localhost [127.0.0.1], pleased to meet you
MAIL FROM: userid@localhost
250 2.1.5 userid... Recipient ok
Data
354 Enter mail, end with "." on a line by itself
This is a message to myself.
.
250 2.0.0 fB62mak11188 Message accepted for delivery
QUIT
```

Figure 11.4: Code showing complete conversation.

It's now ready to communicate with you. Feel free to experiment! When you are through, disconnect from sendmail by issuing **QUIT**. You should now be notified that you have new mail. You can work through this same procedure with your ISP's SMTP queue, and send mail to anyone.

It is no real mystery that the mail ended up in the right place, since you connected to the SMTP server on your own machine. You might be wondering, though, how mail ends up on the right machine in the real cyberworld, if you'll pardon the oxymoron. Actually, it's quite simple. If you send an email message addressed in the form "userid@hostname.domainname.com," you are asking for the mail to be delivered to a specific host with the given domain. You've done that before with your Web browser ("www.yourdomain.com"), so there's no magic there. But what happens to an email addressed simply to "userid@domainname.com"? On what host does that message finally arrive?

Although you haven't had occasion to see it, an entry in the DNS database specifies the host that handles mail for a given domain. In fact, there can be multiple hosts specified, so that delivery attempts can be made with each one, until the message is successfully received. That redundancy is to ensure that the mail doesn't "bounce" if the primary mail server fails.

Once the mail arrives at its final destination, you use your email client to retrieve it. If you haven't already viewed the message you sent to yourself earlier, find it in the **/var/spool/mail** directory of your system, in a file that has your user name. One method to view the message is to simply issue the command **cat /var/spool/mail/***username* (substitute the appropriate username).

"But wait!" you exclaim. "What is all that other stuff at the top of the message?"

That "stuff" is heading information added by sendmail, per RFC 1869, which describes SMTP. Each SMTP server, from the SMTP server you connected to through the last SMTP server to handle the message, adds its own heading information, so you can always see the route your message took. Most email clients hide that information from you, but you can configure them to show entire headers, if you wish.

Using the **cat** command to view your message isn't very practical, since each new incoming message is appended to this file, so you'd be seeing the same messages over and over. Instead, you can access your messages using your email client. On your local machine, you can configure your client to manipulate the mail spool file directly. If your mail were located on another machine, though, you would not have access to the mail spool file. Instead, your email client would connect to a POP server.

Like SMTP servers, POP servers are pieces of software that listen on a TCP/IP port (in this case, 110) and await connections from client software. However, unlike SMTP, which requires no user or password information, POP will connect to your client immediately and wait for it identify you (with **USER** and **PASS** commands) before proceeding. Once your identity has been authenticated, the POP server will respond to commands from your client. These include instructions to the POP server to send a count of your waiting messages, send one of the waiting messages, or delete a message, unless you've configured your email client to keep the messages on the server.

You can experiment with POP servers by issuing the following command:

```
telnet yourPopServer 110
```

Once connected, issue **USER** *username*, then issue **PASS** *password* for your account. The **HELP** command will give you a list of commands to which the POP server responds.

Once you've received your messages, they exist nowhere else but in your local mailbox. This isn't much of a problem, unless you use multiple computers. Then, it seems that the email message you want to review is always "where you ain't." Sure, with a little creativity, you can configure all of your computers but one to leave messages on the server. The better solution, though, is to use IMAP. This is typically no more complicated than telling your email client to use an IMAP server (assuming your ISP provides one) instead of a POP server. The difference, though, is that the mail is left at the server. This is more convenient for the user who has many computers, since the mail is in one spot. Most ISPs do not offer IMAP simply because of the space requirements on their end. They're more than happy when you connect and delete your messages from their disk drives. Fail to do that for too long, and people who sent you messages will start getting them bounced back.

No discussion of Internet email would be complete without a mention of *MIME*, the *Multipurpose Internet Mail Extension*. You have probably attached some kind of file to an email message before. Unless the attachment was pure text, it was sent using MIME.

When email was first created, the messages were pure ASCII text. Although a byte is one eight-bit character (for a total of 256 characters), ASCII only defined the first 128. The upper characters were "extended" for printing cute symbols on printers, or for printer-control characters, or for some of the characters used in non-English languages. Actually, only the lower seven bits would be passed through email systems.

Today, it's not at all unusual to send pictures and other files that have ASCII values that are in the upper 128 characters. These *binary files* wouldn't be able to pass normally through the email system without MIME. Simply put, MIME maps the single nonroutable characters present in binary files into roughly two-byte strings that are routable. These pass flawlessly through email systems.

Most email clients take care of the conversion for you automatically. If you attach a picture to one of your emails, the client will convert it, and the recipient's email client will convert it back. If you look at the raw data in your mail file, you'll see how this is done, assuming that you've ever received a MIME-encoded attachment (which you probably have).

Chapter Summary

This chapter looked at some of the protocols that make the Internet function. You learned that TCP/IP is used for transmitting and routing the information, and protocols are used to facilitate the communication between the types of information servers and their clients.

End of Chapter Review

Key Terms

ARPANET	FTP server	Network mask
ASCII	Gateway	POP
BBS	HTTP server	Protocol
Binary files	IMAP	SMTP
Class A network	Internet	TCP/IP address
Class B network	ISP	TCP/IP packet
Class C network	Logical ports	telnet
DHCP	Loopback device	USENET
DNS	MIME	World Wide Web

Review Questions

1. Prior to the launch of the World Wide Web as we know it today, how did users exchange information?

2. What is the purpose of a network gateway?

3. On a Linux system, how can you ensure that 1) your web server is running, apart from testing it from a browser, and 2) the web server is receiving requests?

4. At times, you may be directed to web sites that *ftp://* versus *http://* in the URL. Explain the difference between FTP and HTTP. In your answer, make sure you mention the TCP/IP port that each protocol connects to by default.

5. List the names of the three protocols that enable email to be delivered.

Programming Assignment

Exercise 1: Perform Domain-Name Resolution

Using the **nslookup** command, list the IP addresses of six Web sites.

Exercise 2: Send Manual Email

In this exercise, you'll use the telnet utility to connect to an email server and send someone an email. To complete this exercise you'll need the following:

- The domain name of an email server

- A sender email address

- A receiver email address (which can be the same as the sender, if need be)

1. Telnet to an email server, replacing *servername* in the following with your actual email server:

```
$ telnet smtp.servername.net 25
```

You should get a 220 response message if all went well

2. Identify yourself, replacing *username* with your actual user name:

```
HELO username
```

3. Say who the mail is from, replacing *me@myisp.net* in the following with your email address:

```
mail from: me@myisp.net
```

You should get a 250 message saying "Sender ok."

4. Say who the email is being sent to, replacing *you@yourisp.net* with the receiver's email address:

```
rcpt to: you@yourisp.net
```

You should get a 250 message saying "Recipient ok."

5. Enter the **data** command. You should get the following 354 message:

```
Enter mail, end with "." on a line by itself.
```

6. Enter the following email message, terminating the message with a dot on a line by itself.

```
From: me@myisp.net
To: you@yourisp.net
Subject: Chapter 11 email test
This is a test message from me
.
```

You should receive a 250 message saying "Message accepted for delivery."

7. Enter the **quit** command. You should receive the following 221 message:

```
... closing connection, Connection closed by foreign host.
```

8. Verify that the email was successfully sent.

    a) If you were the recipient, use your email client.

    b) If someone else was the recipient, ask that individual to check his or her email.

9. Repeat steps 1 through 8, but this time send a message to *elvis@graceland.com* and take note of how the server handles the email address.

Exercise 3: Diagram Your Network Topology

Using information provided by your instructor or network administrator, diagram your network topology and explain how the topology works. You may use the phone-system analogy in your description.

12

Using the Bash Shell

In the Microsoft Windows world, after you've booted the system, you are presented with a sophisticated graphical user interface. Everything in Windows is done through that GUI. In fact, the GUI components of Windows are hard-wired into its operating system. Even if your Windows system has no monitor attached at boot time (because, for example, it's a server), the operating system still loads all the GUI components. UNIX systems, on the other hand, load GUI components as an option.

For optimal performance of Linux server systems, you really don't want the unnecessary baggage of a graphical desktop environment slowing down your server. How then, do you control the system? How do you start, stop, and reconfigure the Apache Web server? How do you add users? On Microsoft Windows, this would all be done from a sophisticated GUI. On UNIX, your "window" to the operating system is the bash shell.

What's a Shell?

Actually, saying that the bash shell is Linux's window to the operating system is not completely true. Like many things in UNIX, you have many options for the type of shell you use; the bash shell is simply the default. Once Linux is booted, the terminal screen displayed is under control of the bash shell, unless you selected a desktop environment to automatically start. Even if a desktop environment is loaded on your system, however, a bash terminal session is available as an application window. Either click the terminal-emulator icon, or, from a non-GUI terminal screen, press Ctrl-Alt-F1 (or F2, F3, F4, F5, or F6).

The first UNIX shell was called simply *shell*. It was a text-based screen that allowed the user to enter system commands. That first shell was only about as powerful as the limited DOS shell of Microsoft operating systems. In 1978, Stephen Bourne replaced the original UNIX shell with a new one that added advanced scripting capabilities and command-line editing. The Bourne shell, as it is called, is still available; you can try it from your Linux machine by entering **/bin/sh** from a terminal screen.

Bill Joy (more recently known as one of the Sun scientists who created Java), while he was at the University of Berkeley at Southern California, created the C shell. The C shell has more job-control features than the Bourne shell and sports a C-like syntax. And, yes, the C shell is available on Linux. You can try it by typing **/bin/csh**. This "shell game" goes on: there is a shell called Korn; OS/400 has one called Q; and there are many others. Eventually, a group of UNIX programmers combined the features of several popular shells into one called *bash* (a play on words that stands for the "Bourne Again Shell"). The bash shell, because of its powerful features, was selected as the default Linux shell.

If you become attached to a shell other than bash, you can change to it by modifying your user profile in the **/etc/passwd** file. Each entry in the **passwd** file contains a semicolon-separated list of options:

username:password:userid:groupid:user_description:home_dir:shell

The following line qualifies the shell as **/bin/bash** in one of the authors' **passwd** file entries:

```
donat:x:500:500::/home/donat:/bin/bash
```

To give you an idea of the powerful yet quirky features of bash, rather than using an editor or the **less** command to view the **/etc/passwd** file, you can use the following command to list your default shell (replacing *username* with your user name):

```
$ cat /etc/passwd | grep ^username: | cut -d : -f 7
```

It responds by listing **/bin/bash** to your terminal screen.

> **Note:** The dollar symbol is the bash shell prompt when you are logged on as a normal user. When you are logged on as root, the shell prompt will have a pound symbol (#). Commands that require root privileges are identified in this chapter with the # symbol; otherwise, the $ symbol is displayed.

Another way to list your default shell is by echoing the **SHELL** environment variable:

```
$ echo $SHELL
```

Once again, it simply lists **/bin/bash** to your terminal screen.

These **echo** and **cat** commands use some of the powerful features of the bash shell: piping and environment variables. In this chapter, you'll learn not only about environment variables and piping, but also about features like file redirection, filename globbing, and substitution mechanisms—in other words, how to become a power shell user.

Command Execution

Linux commands follow a common structure:

command option(s) argument(s)

Command arguments qualify information that is necessary for the command to execute. For instance, the **cd** command requires the name of the directory you wish to make current:

```
$ cd books/linux/
```

Command options modify how the execution of a command is to proceed. For example, the **-l** option of the **ls** command tells the list command to show verbose information about files:

```
$ ls -l
```

Command options are identified with a hyphen, followed by a single character. Some commands, however, also have options that require a double hyphen followed by a word. For instance, the **ls** command has an option that will recursively descend into lower-level directories:

```
$ ls —recursive
```

The number of files listed with this version of the **ls** command will probably fill more than one screen. Most power bash users use a pipe to the **less** command to show just one screen worth of data at a time:

```
$ ls | less
```

You probably won't remember all the options of the myriad of Linux commands, so don't forget to use the **man** command to get help. If you enter the following, for example, you'll get a nice Linux manual for the **ls** command:

```
$ man ls
```

Foreground/Background

When you execute a command, bash creates a new Linux process and executes it in the foreground. A *process* is simply a program running on the system. While a command is executing in the foreground of your terminal session, you will be unable to enter other commands. If you want to execute a command that might take a long time, you can force it to run as a background process by adding an ampersand (&) to the end of the command. For example, suppose you want to edit a file using Gnome's gedit. If you just enter **gedit** followed by the name of the file you want to edit, the terminal session will not accept any other commands. For that reason, you will usually want to launch gedit as a background process. For instance, to edit **/etc/lilo.conf** you would enter the following:

```
gedit /etc/lilo.conf &
```

This is shown at the top of Figure 12.1. Notice in Figure 12.1 that Linux assigned and then listed a process ID for the background gedit task. You can end the process by issuing the **kill** command and qualifying the process ID (in this case, 5920). Arguably, it would be better to end gedit by simply closing the application window because that ensures file modifications are saved. Sometimes, though, you need to manually terminate processes, and the **kill** command is the only way to do it.

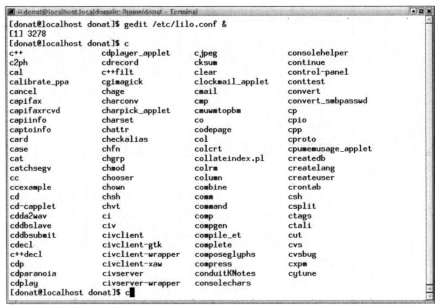

Figure 12.1: The ampersand at the end of a command tells Linux to run that command as a background process (or subprocess).

Word Completion

Sometimes, as consultants, we have the unfortunate requirement of working in a Microsoft Windows environment. Microsoft's DOS is itself a shell, although one with a limited set of commands and features. When in DOS, we miss the powerful features of bash. The feature we miss most is *word completion*. In bash, if you forget the name of a command, directory, or file (remember that commands and directories are implemented as files on UNIX), you can simply type the first few characters and press Tab. Bash will flesh out the rest of the name if there is only one match, or list all the files that start with those letters if you press Tab again. For instance, if you type the letter *c* and press Tab, bash will beep to tell you an exact match wasn't found. If you press Tab a second time, bash responds with the list of commands that start with *c*, as shown in Figure 12.1. In fact, if you press Tab twice without typing any character at the bash prompt, it will list the several thousand commands that are available.

Using word completion for directory and file names comes in quite handy. For instance, we had a consulting gig where the production files existed in **/opt/tomcat/webapps/manta/WEB-INF/classes/com/manta**. To change to that long-winded directory, we would enter **/opt/tom** and press Tab to flesh out **tomcat**, then **we** and Tab to flesh out **webapps**, and so on.

History Repeats Itself

Another useful feature of bash is its ability to retrieve, edit, and re-execute previously entered commands. By simply pressing the Up arrow key, you retrieve the last command executed. If you keep pressing the Up arrow, bash will continue to retrieve the commands executed. If the command you're looking for flashes past the terminal screen, use the Down arrow to go in reverse direction. Once you've retrieved the command you want, you can edit it with the help of the Home, End, Delete, Backspace, and arrow keys, and press enter to execute the modified command.

If you type two exclamation points, bash will retrieve and immediately execute the previously entered command. If you type one exclamation point followed by a number *n*, bash will retrieve and execute the command entered *n* times ago. Perhaps the coolest feature of bash history, though, is the search-and-execution feature. If you type an exclamation point and a question mark followed by a string, bash will scan history for the command that contained that string, and then execute it. For instance, suppose you like to use the **rdate** command to set your system date to equal that of an Internet time server. Instead of trying to remember the URL for the time server, you simply type the following:

```
# !?rdate
```

Bash pulls from history and executes something like this:

```
rdate -s tock.usno.navy.mil
```

To delve a little deeper into the mechanics of bash history, consider the results of the following command:

```
$ set | grep HIST
HISTFILE=/home/donat/.bash_history
HISTFILESIZE=1000
HISTSIZE=1000
```

The **set** command is discussed a little later in this chapter, but, from the list, you can surmise that the user's personal history file is **/home/donat/.bash_history**. The history file is simply a text file, so you can open it with your favorite text editor or use **less** to display its contents:

```
$ less /home/donat/.bash_history
```

The history file will become especially handy when you start to create bash scripts to automate the execution of a series of bash commands under a single, home-grown, custom Linux command, as covered in the next chapter.

I/O Redirection and Piping

Enough of the history lesson. It's time to move on to another bash power feature: input/output redirection and piping. In a few commands already shown in this chapter, you've see the pipe operator (|) used. Let's review those commands:

```
$ cat /etc/passwd | grep ^username: | cut -d : -f 7
$ ls | less
$ set | grep HIST
```

The simplest of these three commands is **ls**. When you execute this command, the | operator tells bash to *pipe* the output from **ls** into the **less** command. You already know that **less** shows the contents of a file one page at a time. The file, in this case, is a virtual one created from the output of the **ls** command.

The stdin, stdout, and stderr Files

In UNIX, all programs have three standard files: **stdin**, **stdout**, and **stderr**. Unless otherwise qualified, the standard output file (**stdout**) is your terminal session. When you run the **ls** command by itself, all the files that exist in the current directory are listed on the terminal screen. The | operator tells bash to pipe standard output of **ls** to the standard input of **less**. The **less** command, when it doesn't have a file name as an argument, displays the data from **stdin**.

The other two commands that used the pipe operator, **cat** and **set**, work similarly. The **set** command lists all the environment variables currently set on your system. (You'll find out about environment variables later in this chapter.) The standard output of **set**, in this case, is piped to the **grep** command. The **grep** command is a simple utility that scans for strings. The argument to **grep** in this example is **HIST**, so the **set** command pipes the entire list of environment variables (about two dozen) to **grep**, which then lists to its standard output all the environment variables with the string **HIST** in them. Note that the standard output for **grep**, in this case, was not piped, so it simply went to the terminal session. Alternatively, **grep**'s standard output could have been piped to the **less** command:

```
$ set | grep HIST | less
```

The **cat** command in the example also piped to **grep**, the standard output of which was piped to a powerful command called **cut**. We'll leave it up to you to research **cut** but, to summarize, it removes extemporaneous sections of a text line, resulting in standard output that contains only meaningful pieces of data. In this case, the line was an entry from the **passwd** file and the only piece of information we are interested in (with pieces determined by the colon separator) is the seventh—the user's default shell.

Redirection

Whereas the pipe operator allows you to force the standard output from one command to be the standard input of another command, the redirection operators in Table 12.1 allow you to force standard output and errors to a particular file.

Table 12.1: Input/Output Redirectors	
Redirector	**Function**
>file	Redirects standard output to the specified file.
2>file	Redirects standard error to the specified file.
>>file	Redirects standard output to the specified file, appending existing data.
2>>	Redirects standard error to the specified file, appending existing data.
&>file	Redirects both standard output and standard error to the specified file.
<file	Redirects standard input to the specified file.
<<text	Redirects standard input until a line matching *text* is found.
cmd1 | cmd2	Uses the standard output of *cmd1* as the standard input to *cmd2*.

The following **ls** command will place a verbose list of the files in our home directory into a file called **listhome.txt**:

```
$ ls -l /home/donat > listhome.txt
```

If the file did not exist before the execution of the command, it would have been created; if it already existed, its contents would have been overwritten. To append to a file, you can use the double less-than redirection operator: >>.

Suppose you want to add to **listhome.txt** the files that exist in a subdirectory called **java**. You would use the following command:

```
$ ls -l /home/donat/java >> listhome.txt
```

However, the list doesn't differentiate between the files in your home directory and the subdirectory of Java. To handle that, use the **cat** command to add a subdirectory header line to **listhome.txt**. The **cat** command normally takes input from a file name argument, but if no file name is qualified, **cat** will use the standard input of the screen. The **cat** command's standard output, unless redirected, also lists to the screen.

To add that subdirectory header line with **cat**, use the following command, and after the text entry, press Ctrl-D:

```
$ cat >> listhome.txt
The java subdirectory contents:^D
```

Note that the **^D** is not added to the file; it represents the Ctrl-D keystroke combination that forces standard input to the **cat** command to close. Obviously, you have to re-execute all three commands in the proper sequence so that the subdirectory header precedes the output in the **listhome.txt** file.

UNIX Filters

The most frequent use of redirection is for standard output. However, there will be occasions when you will want to redirect standard input, especially when using UNIX *filters*. Filters are utility programs that are used as command building blocks; each one performs a specific type of filtering on standard input. Table 12.2 shows a few of the more common UNIX filters.

Table 12.2: UNIX Filters	
Utility	Purpose
cat	Copy stdin to stdout.
grep	Search for strings in stdin.
sort	Sort lines in input.
cut	Extract columns from input.
sed	Perform editing operations on input.

Each of the filters in Table 12.2 defaults to using the terminal screen as **stdin**, **stdout**, and **stderr**. For instance, if you enter the **sort** command with no arguments, it will accept input from the terminal. The sort utility will then, after you close terminal input with Ctrl-D, sort the entries and list them to **stdout** (the screen). The following example shows what happens if you enter **sort**, then four lines that contain the numerals 4, 3, 2, and 1, and finish by pressing Ctrl-D:

```
$ sort
4
3
2
1
^D
1
2
3
4
```

The sort utility, by itself, is not all that useful. When you redirect or pipe standard input or output to it, however, it becomes very useful. For instance, you could quickly sort the entries in a password file as follows:

```
$ sort < /etc/passwd
```

If your reason for sorting the password file was to find a specific user, **grep** would be even better:

```
$ grep username < /etc/passwd
```

The output from this command contains the complete line from the password file. If you want one section of a line, such as the section of that contains the user's default shell, you'd use the **cut** utility. For instance, at the beginning of this chapter, you saw the following command:

```
$ cat /etc/passwd | grep ^username: | cut -d : -f 7
```

This uses **cat** to pipe the contents of **/etc/passwd** to **grep**. The **grep** utility then finds the line containing the specified user name, and pipes it to **cut**. The **cut** utility then extracts the seventh field, as determined by colon separators, and lists it to standard output, the screen. Although this process sounds complicated, it illustrates how filters can be combined to create useful and powerful utilities—in a single bash statement.

To better understand how the combination of these three UNIX filters work, let's break the previous command into two statements:

```
$ grep ^username: < /etc/passwd > temp.txt
$ cut -d : -f 7 < temp.txt
```

The **grep** utility's **stdin** is redirected to the password file, and its **stdout** is redirected to a file called **temp.txt**. Then, **cut** reads from the temporary file, which contains a single line, extracts the seventh field of that line, and lists it to standard output. Whereas this version uses temporary files to store the results of a UNIX filter, the one-line command bypassed the need for creating a physical file on disk by piping **stdout** from one utility right into **stdin** of another.

When you can use redirection and pipes with ease from the bash shell, you will be a power Linux user.

Variables

At the beginning of this chapter, you saw a much easier way of listing the default shell for a user than with a combination of **cat**, **grep**, and **cut**:

```
$ echo $SHELL
```

The word **SHELL** is a variable. Variables are simply symbols that represent pieces of information, just like in algebra, where changing the value of *X* changes the results of an equation. The value of a shell variable can be set and then later retrieved. The variable called **SHELL** is a symbol that contains the default shell for a user. You retrieve and use the values of variables in bash commands. The **echo** command simply writes to standard output the value of the string argument passed to it. In the above example, the value of the string is stored in the contents of a variable. The dollar sign tells bash that the string, **SHELL**, is not a literal string, but is instead a symbol to a string, so bash knows to get the value of that variable.

Note: You can list all currently existing variables with the **set** command.

You can set variables by using the simple syntax *name=value*. For instance, if you wanted to create a variable called **LASTNAME**, set its value to *Denoncourt*, and later list that variable's value, you'd use the following commands:

```
$ LASTNAME=Denoncourt
$ echo $LASTNAME
```

Note: It is a standard to name variables using all uppercase characters.

You can create as many variables as you like, but Linux ships with many variables already created. There is one standard variable that you should know about: **PATH**. We've already mentioned that Linux has thousands of commands (programs) in various directories on your system. How does bash find those programs so it can execute them? Through the **PATH** variable, which contains a semicolon-separated list of directories that bash uses to search for programs. If you issue a command from bash that doesn't exist in any of the directories in the **PATH** variable, you get a "command not found" error.

Consider a new Linux user called **donat**. If you listed the user's **PATH**, you would get something like the following:

```
$ echo $PATH
/bin:/usr/bin:/usr/X11R6/bin:/usr/local/bin:/home/donat/bin
```

When that user first begins to compile and test Java applications with the **javac** and **java** commands, he or she would have to fully qualify those commands with their directory locations:

```
$ /opt/java/jdk1.2.2/bin/javac SomeJavaApp.java
$ /opt/java/jdk1.2.2/bin/java SomeJavaApp
```

To avoid wasting time entering directory paths, the user would modify the **PATH** to contain the locations of **javac** and **java**:

```
$ PATH=$PATH:/opt/java/jdk1.2.2/bin/
```

Note: Variables are appended by setting them equal to their existing value (with the dollar operator and variable name), followed by the value to be appended.

The topic of Java programming brings up another important variable that is not created by default: the Java **CLASSPATH** variable. **CLASSPATH** is to Java what **PATH** is to bash. The Java Virtual Machine (JVM) looks for Java classes (which you can think of as Java programs) by searching through the semicolon-separated list of directories and Java archives (compressed Java classes) in the **CLASSPATH** variable.

At the time of this writing, we were working on a project that required the classes contained in the files **jdom.jar** and **xerces.jar**. Our **CLASSPATH**, at that point, was as follows:

```
$ echo $CLASSPATH
.:/opt/java/jdom-b6/build/jdom.jar:/opt/java/jdom-b6/lib/xerces.jar
```

Note: The dot operator by itself in **PATH** or **CLASSPATH** refers to the current directory.

Dot Profile

By qualifying the location of **java** and **javac** in **PATH** and various **.jar** files in **CLASSPATH**, we had set up a Java development environment in bash. But whenever we signed off, our **PATH** and **CLASSPATH** modifications were lost. That meant each time one of us logged in, we would have to reset the Java environment. There is a better way.

Whenever you log on, Linux runs a couple of special scripts. It first executes the commands in a script called **profile** located in the **/etc** directory. It then executes a script called **.bash_profile** in your home directory. To have our Java environment set every time we logged onto our Linux system, we modified the **.bash_profile**, as shown in Figure 12.2.

```
# .bash_profile

# Get the aliases and functions
if [ -f ~/.bashrc ]; then
    . ~/.bashrc
fi

# User specific environment and startup programs

PATH=$PATH:$HOME/bin
BASH_ENV=$HOME/.bashrc

export BASH_ENV PATH
unset USERNAME

# denoncourt added:
JAVA_HOME=/opt/java/jdk1.2.2
TOMCAT_HOME=/opt/tomcat
PATH=$PATH:$JAVA_HOME/bin

CLASSPATH=$CLASSPATH:.
CLASSPATH=$CLASSPATH:/opt/java/jdom-b6/build/jdom.jar
CLASSPATH=$CLASSPATH:/opt/java/jdom-b6/lib/xerces.jar

export JAVA_HOME TOMCAT_HOME PATH CLASSPATH
```

Figure 12.2: The .bash_profile file is where you place user-specific environment settings.

The next chapter covers script programming in detail. For now, simply look at the last part of the code in Figure 12.2, below the "denoncourt added:" comment. This code sets the variable values for **JAVA_HOME**, **TOMCAT_HOME**, **PATH**, and **CLASSPATH**. **JAVA_HOME** is used by many Java utilities, and **TOMCAT_HOME** is used by Apache's open-source Tomcat Web application server.

You've probably spotted a command in Figure 12.2 that hasn't yet been mentioned: **export**. Whenever you create a variable, it is available to that process, but not to any subprocesses. Linux uses subprocesses heavily, as most commands execute as subprocesses. The **export** command tells bash that the space-separated list of variables is to be made available to subprocesses.

> **Note:** To test or otherwise use enhancements to your **.bash_profile**, you must log off and log back on.

Advanced Shell

Using the techniques shown thus far in this chapter, you'll be a shell power user. By understanding a few other features of bash, though, you become a *master* shell user. These features are filename globbing, quoted strings, and aliases. *Filename globbing* is a UNIX term that describes the use of wildcards and sets in commands. Table 12.3 shows a list of the metacharacters that can be used as wildcards in commands.

Table 12.3: Filename Globbing Operators	
Metacharacter	**Matches**
?	Any single character
*	Any string of characters
[*set*]	Any character in *set*
[!*set*]	Any character not in *set*
~	The home directory of the current user
~*userid*	The home directory of the specified user
~+	The current working directory
~-	The previous working directory

We use filename globbing regularly when searching for files with the **find** command. For instance, if you want a list of all the Java source in a specific directory under your home directory, you can use the following command:

```
$ find ~/manta/*.java
```

The asterisk wildcard tells **find** to list all files that have the string ".java" as the file name's extension. If you wanted to drill down further and find the Java source for a file that contained the string "DTD" in the file name, you could use the following command:

```
$ find ~/manta/*DTD*.java
```

If you wanted to look for any Java source that starts with an uppercase alphabetical letter and finishes with a numeric, you could use the following command:

```
$ find ~/manta/[A-Z]*[0-9].java
```

Quoted Strings

The bash shell interprets quote strings, depending on the type of quote character, in a variety of useful ways. When bash sees a chunk of text contained within a pair of single quotes, it interprets those characters literally—whether or not shell variables or metacharacters are in that quoted string. If a chunk of text is contained within double quotes, the shell replaces any shell variables with their values. If a chunk of text is within a pair of back quotes, that text is executed as a subcommand, the output of which is used in the enclosing command. Table 12.4 summarizes the way bash interprets quotes.

Table 12.4: Special Characters in Quoted Strings	
Character	Meaning
'	Text within a pair of single quotes is interpreted literally. Shell variables and metacharacters are not replaced with their interpreted values.
"	Similar to single quotes, except that shell variables are replaced with their values.
`	Text within a pair of back quotes is executed as a subcommand, the output of which is then used in the enclosing command.
\	Characters that follow a slash are interpreted literally; any metacharacter meaning is ignored. If the backslash is the last character in a line, it signals to the shell that a continuation line will follow.

The quote characters in the following three commands cause the results of the commands to vary greatly:

```
$ echo '$PATH'
$PATH
$ echo "$PATH"
/bin:/usr/bin:/usr/X11R6/bin:/usr/local/bin:/home/donat/bin
$ echo `$PATH`
/bin:/usr/bin:/usr/X11R6/bin:/usr/local/bin:/home/donat/bin: No such file or directory
```

In the first command, the fact that **$PATH** refers to a shell variable is completely ignored, and the string is simply listed to standard out. The second command encloses **$PATH** within double quotes, so bash retrieves the value for the **PATH** variable and lists it. In the last command, bash assumes the text within back quotes contains a valid command.

A better example of using back quotes in commands follows:

```
$ CLASSPATH=$CLASSPATH:`pwd`/xml4j.jar
```

In this command, the string within back quotes contains the name of a UNIX command, **pwd**. The **pwd** command lists the current working directory. During Java development, we are always modifying **CLASSPATH** to contain various Java archives. One simple way to modify **CLASSPATH** is to change the current directory to where desired **.jar** files are stored and then use the above command, as shown here:

```
$cd /opt/java/jdom-b6/lib
$ls *.jar
ant.jar collections.jar xerces.jar
$ CLASSPATH=$CLASSPATH:`pwd`/xerces.jar
```

Aliases

The last advanced shell feature covered here is aliases. The **alias** utility allows you to assign a name to a command string. A good way to learn about aliases is to look at the ones that Red Hat has set up for you. You can review all the aliases on your system by using the **alias** command with the **-p** option. The following shows the results when signed on as root to our Red Hat 7.1 system:

```
$alias -p
alias ls='ls —color=tty'
alias ll='ls -l —color=tty'
alias l.='ls -d .[a-zA-Z]* —color=tty'
alias rm='rm -i'
alias mv='mv -i'
alias cp='cp -i'
alias which='alias | /usr/bin/which —tty-only —read-alias —show-dot —show-tilde'
```

When you think you are using the **ls** command on a default installation of Red Hat, you are actually using an alias called **ls**. The alias invokes the actual **ls** command, but not before it sets the default options of **—color-tty**. Red Hat also creates an alias called **ll** that calls the **ls** command with the "long listing" option set.

Red Hat creates aliases for the dangerous shell commands **rm**, **mv**, and **cp**, to set their default option to **-i**, which makes those commands interactively prompt for verification that the user really, really, wanted to remove, move, or copy that file. If you never, ever make mistakes, you might want to remove those aliases from **/root/.bash_profile** (or simply use the **-f** option to force them to run without prompting—but only when you are sure the command will work as expected).

We use aliases to save from typing the fully qualified names when we're changing directories. Sure, word completion helps you type out a directory name quickly, but it's nowhere near as quick as a simple alias. Earlier in this chapter, we talked about word completion to avoid typing the long directory **/opt/tomcat/webapps/manta/WEB-INF/classes/com/manta**. Instead, you could create an alias called **cpmanta** that would make changing to that directory a breeze:

```
alias cpmanta='cd /opt/tomcat/webapps/manta/WEB-INF/classes/com/manta'
```

After testing this alias, you could put it in your **.bash_profile** so it would be available every time you logged on.

End of Chapter Review

Key Terms

aliases	CLASSPATH	piping
bash shell	dot profile	Q shell
Bourne shell	grep	recursive
C shell	Korn shell	redirection
cat	PATH	variables

Review Questions

1. In a command, what does the ampersand do?

2. What does "GUI" stand for?

3. What is a shell, in the UNIX environment?

4. What is "bash" short for?

Programming Assignment

Exercise 1: Create Directory Reports

1. Create a report file that lists the contents of your home directory.

    a) Put a header in the report file that contains your full name and the name of your directory.

    b) Make sure the list contains the size of each file.

2. Using the Java **jar** utility, list the contents of the **servlet.jar** in **/opt/tomcat/lib**.

3. Using the **find** command:

    a) List all the HTML files under **/opt/tomcat/webapps/examples**.

    b) List all the JSP files under **/opt/tomcat/webapps/examples**.

4. Practice piping output:

    a) The file listing from step 2 is overly verbose. Often, you will have to look in **.jar** files to see if a particular Java class is in that file. Pipe the output from step 2 to **grep** to search for the HttpServlet class.

    b) Pipe step 3's output through the **xargs** utility. (The **xargs** output, without qualifying a command, doesn't do much. It just takes input and, delimited by spaces or lines, iteratively invokes the command that follows.)

    c) To make use of **xargs**, run the **find** commands from step 3 again, piping the output through **xargs**, but this time, qualify the **grep** command as an option to **xargs**. Ask **grep** to list the JSP files that contain a reference to the special **request** variable.

        Hint: Here's how you would list all the HTML files that have a **<FORM>** tag:

        ```
        $ find /opt/tomcat/webapps/examples -name '*.html' | xargs grep FORM
        ```

Exercise 2: Use Environment Variables

1. List all environment variables.

2. Create a new environment variable using your last name. (Remember, use all uppercase for environment variables.) Set that environment's value to be your first name.

3. Append to the special Java **CLASSPATH** environment variable a qualifier to Tomcat's **servlet.jar** file, using the following strategy:

    a) Change your current directory to **/opt/tomcat/lib**.

    b) Modify **CLASSPATH** using the "print working directory" command in back quotes:

        ```
        $ CLASSPATH=$CLASSPATH:`pwd`/servlet.jar
        ```

        The `pwd` command should be interpreted as **/opt/tomcat/lib** and the **CLASSPATH** should be modified accordingly.

4. List all environment variables again. Pipe the output to the printer.

Exercise 3: Practice File Globbing

1. Find all HTML files under **/opt/tomcat/webapps/examples** that have "lo" in their names. Pipe the output to the printer.

2. Find all files that have a number in their names. Pipe the output to the printer.

3. Find all files that have an uppercase alphabetical character in their names. Pipe the output to the printer.

Exercise 4: Create an Alias

1. List all the current aliases.

2. Create an alias that starts Tomcat. Note that Tomcat starts with the following command:

```
# sh /opt/tomcat/bin/startup.sh
```

3. List all the current aliases. Pipe the output to the printer

13

Shell Programming

The last chapter introduced you to the power of UNIX shells. This chapter goes a step farther, by showing you the power of shell scripts. There are two reasons why you need to understand how to program a shell script:

- You might need to revise or enhance an existing shell script.

- You might want to create your own script to relieve the tedium of keying the same set of commands over and over again.

A good example of an existing shell script to enhance is Apache's Tomcat startup script, **tomcat.sh**. Later in this chapter, you will review the startup script in detail. Right now, you will learn how to create your own shell scripts.

One simple way of reducing the keystrokes necessary to execute a complex shell command is to create an alias, as discussed in chapter 12. However, aliases are limited because they cannot operate on parameters and they do not support conditional statements. A shell condition might be based on an input parameter or on some state of that machine (such as the existence of a file or directory).

There are four special variables available to scripts:

- $0 refers to the name of the shell script.

- $1 through $9 refers to the value of parameters 1 to 9.

- $@ returns the values of all arguments in a single string.

- $# gives the parameter count.

For example, here is a script called **say.sh** (**.sh** being the default extension for shell scripts):

```
#!/bin/sh
echo "This shell script is called $0"
echo "Parameter 1 is equal to $1"
```

When executed from the command line and passed a single parameter, it produces the following output:

```
$ sh say.sh hey
This shell script is called ./say.sh
Parameter 1 is equal to hey
```

Comments in shell scripts start with the pound symbol (#). The first line of the **say.sh** script is a special comment line. The exclamation point followed by **/bin/sh** in this line identifies the shell that is to run the script. You could change it to **/bin/bash** (for the bash shell), but you'll find that **/bin/sh** (for the original, Bourne, shell) is more standard because any UNIX system that might execute your script will be guaranteed to have the Bourne shell. If you don't expect your script to run on other systems, you can omit the special comment.

Command Execution

To run the **say.sh** script, you pass it as a parameter to the **sh** command. (You could also use the **bash** command.) To be able to run **say.sh** from some other script, or to otherwise work like other UNIX commands, you would have to put its path qualifier in your **PATH** environment variable (or copy it to one of the directories already in your path) and change its permissions to allow it to be executed:

```
$ PATH=$PATH:`pwd`
$ chmod u+x say.sh
```

Then, you could execute the **say.sh** command without the **sh** command processor:

```
$ say.sh hey
This shell script is called ./say.sh
Parameter 1 is equal to hey
```

Optionally, instead of modifying the path, you could use the dot operator to qualify that the script exists in the current directory:

```
$ ./say.sh hey
This shell script is called ./say.sh
Parameter 1 is equal to hey
```

One final way of executing a script is by *sourcing* the script. You source a script by using the **source** command followed by the name of the script. When you source a script, the current shell executes it line by line as if you were entering each line manually into a terminal session. When you execute a script with the **sh** command, that script runs as a subprocess, in its own shell:

```
$ source say.sh hey
This shell script is called ./say.sh
Parameter 1 is equal to hey
```

Another way to source a script is to use a dot, a space, and the name of the script:

```
$ . say.sh hey
This shell script is called ./say.sh
Parameter 1 is equal to hey
```

> **Note:** Environment variables set in a subprocess are not automatically available to the process that spawned them. Linux programmers often source a script when they want the environment variables set by that script to be retained in the existing shell.

You will see all of these methods used in various scripts.

Predicates

Predicate is a fancy term for a condition. One condition typically used in shell scripts is to check for required parameters. Let's enhance the **say.sh** script to tell users that a parameter is required. To do that, use a conditional **if** block:

```
#!/bin/bash
if [ -z $1 ]; then
        echo 'Usage: say.sh <word>'
fi
echo "This shell script is called $0"
echo "Parameter 1 is equal to $1"
```

Then, if you omitted passing a parameter to the **say.sh** script, you'd get the following message:

```
$ ./say.sh hey
Usage: say.sh <word>
```

The predicate used in this new version of **say.sh** uses the following scripting:

```
if [ conditional ]; then
fi
```

The conditional, in this circumstance, uses the **-z** operator to see if string $1 is zero. Table 13.1 shows a several other string-comparison operators that can be used in conditional expressions.

Table 13.1: String Comparison Operators	
Operator	True if...
str1 = *str2*	*str1* matches *str2*
str1 != *str2*	*str1* does not match *str2*
str1 < *str2*	*str1* is less than *str2*
str1 > *str2*	*str1* is greater than *str2*
-n *str1*	*str1* has a length greater than zero
-z *str1*	*str1* has a length of zero

Conditional expressions can also contain some sophisticated file operators, such as those in Table 13.2. For instance, in a Red Hat installation, each user's **.bash_profile** startup script checks to see if the user has a **.bashrc** file in the home directory. If **.bashrc** exists and is a regular file, the script executes it, as shown in the following code snippet:

```
if [ -f ~/.bashrc ]; then
        . ~/.bashrc
fi
```

Note that the tilde (~) refers to the user's home directory.

Table 13.2: Partial List of File Attribute Operators	
Operator	True if...
-a *file*	*file* exists
-d *file*	*file* is a directory
-e *file*	*file* exists
-f *file*	*file* is a regular (text) file
-h *file*	*file* is a symbolic link
-r *file*	current user has read permissions on *file*
-s *file*	*file* has a size greater than zero
-w *file*	current user has write permissions on *file*
-x *file*	current user has execute permissions on *file*
-O *file*	current user owns *file*
-G *file*	current user is a member of *file*'s group

Exit Codes

One of the strengths of shell scripts is that they can use other commands. Most commands return an integer value, called an *exit code*, that tells its invoker if it ran properly. An exit code with a value of zero normally means that the command ran as expected. A non-zero exit code typically means the command did not work as expected. That non-zero value, depending on the command, might further describe to its invoker what went wrong.

Using the special environment variable **$?**, you can look at the exit code of the previous command. For instance, if you attempt to change your current directory to one that doesn't exist, the exit code value will be one:

```
$ cd bogus
$ echo $?
1
```

When the current directory is valid, the exit code value is zero:

```
$ cd /opt
$ echo $?
0
```

Your shell script can predicate blocks of code based on the value of an exit code. For instance, the following script snippet lets the user know if a directory-change worked:

```
if cd $1
then
        echo "Now in directory $1."
else
        echo "Sorry, $1 does not exist."
fi
```

Looping

In addition to supporting conditional logic, all programming languages have a facility that allows a program to perform a block of code, to *loop,* until some condition is met. Shell scripts have **do/until**, **do/while**, and **for** loops. The format of each of these loops is shown in Figure 13.1.

```
while condition; do
    statements
done

until condition; do
    statements
done

for variable in list; do
    statements that use variable
done
```

Figure 13.1: Shell scripts can iterate through blocks of code using while, until, or for loops.

The difference between a **while** and an **until** loop is that the **while** loop executes as long as the condition is true, and the **until** loops as long as the condition is false. Here is a simple example of a **while** loop:

```
while true; do
        echo 'looping...'
done
```

The condition of the loop is simply **true**, which effectively makes the loop execute forever. (If you enter this example and test it, you'll have to press Ctrl-C to abort the loop.) If you replace **while** with **until** in the example, the conditional code never executes.

For loops are handy for processing the elements of a directory list. The following example simply echoes the contents of the current directory:

```
for elem in ./*; do
     echo $elem
done
```

Note that **elem** in this example is a variable that takes the value of the current list element being processed.

There might be times when you want to prematurely exit out of a loop before the loop's condition has been met. The reserved word **break** may be used for this. Some programmers use a **while true** loop with an **if** condition inside the body of the loop that terminates the loop with **break**. There might also be times when you do not want to finish executing the body of the loop for the current iteration, but instead want to move on to, or continue with, the next iteration. The reserved word **continue** can be used for this purpose.

Case Statements

The last script-control construct to cover here is the **case** statement. There are times where you want to predicate a variety of code paths based on the value of the same variable. For example, consider a script that uses a parameter to predicate whether to start up a process, list the current status of that process, end that process, or list the proper usage of the script. A nested **if**, such as the one in Figure 13.2, could handle that, but **case** could also be used.

```
#!/bin/sh
if [ "$1" = 'start' ]; then
    echo 'start it'
elif [ "$1" = 'status' ]; then
    echo 'list status'
elif [ "$1" = 'stop' ]; then
    echo 'stop it'
else
    echo "Usage: $0 start|status|stop"
    exit 1
fi
```

Figure 13.2: A nested *if* could be used in a script that started, stopped, listed status, and provided help for a process.

Case statements have the following format:

```
case expression in
    pattern1 )
            statements  ;;
    pattern2 )
            statements  ;;
    * )
            statements that handle drop-through cases ;;
esac
```

The asterisk handles those circumstances where the value of *expression* has no associated *pattern*. Programmers typically call this portion of the case statement the *drop-through* code.

A working example of a script that uses the **case** statement is Apache's **httpd** script (which, on a Red Hat system, can be found in the **/etd/rc.d/init.d** directory). The portion of the script that predicates processing based on parameter 1 is shown in Figure 13.3.

```
case "$1" in
  start)
    start
    ;;
  stop)
    stop
    ;;
  status)
    status $httpd
    ;;
  restart)
    stop
    start
    ;;
  reload)
    echo -n $"Reloading $prog: "
    killproc $httpd -HUP
    RETVAL=$?
    echo
    ;;
  condrestart)
    if [ -f /var/run/httpd.pid ] ; then
            stop
            start
    fi
    ;;
  *)
    echo $"Usage: $prog {start|stop|restart|reload|condrestart|status}"
    exit 1
esac
```

Figure 13.3: Apache's httpd script uses a case statement to handle its various parameter options.

Tomcat Code Review

A good way to show the power of shell programming is to review Apache's Tomcat script. The script is called **tomcat.sh** and is located under the **bin** directory where Tomcat is installed (**/opt/jakarta-tomcat** on our system). The **tomcat.sh** script shown in Figure 13.4 is devoid of comment (except for the first line), so it might be worthwhile to add comments to the script as you step through the code.

```
#!/bin/sh
#
# $Id: tomcat.sh,v 1.17.2.2 2001/01/10 22:55:48 glenn Exp $

# Shell script to start and stop the server

# There are other, simpler commands to startup the runner. The two
# commented commands good replacements. The first works well with
# Java Platform 1.1 based runtimes. The second works well with
# Java2 Platform based runtimes.

#jre -cp runner.jar:servlet.jar:classes org.apache.tomcat.shell.Startup $*
#java -cp runner.jar:servlet.jar:classes org.apache.tomcat.shell.Startup $*

if [ -f $HOME/.tomcatrc ] ; then
  . $HOME/.tomcatrc
fi

if [ "$TOMCAT_HOME" = "" ] ; then
  ## resolve links - $0 may be a link to  home
  PRG=$0
  progname=`basename $0`

  while [ -h "$PRG" ] ; do
    ls=`ls -ld "$PRG"`
    link=`expr "$ls" : '.*-> \(.*\)$'`
    if expr "$link" : '.*/.*' > /dev/null; then
     PRG="$link"
    else
     PRG="`dirname $PRG`/$link"
    fi
  done

  TOMCAT_HOME_1=`dirname "$PRG"`/..
  echo "Guessing TOMCAT_HOME from tomcat.sh to ${TOMCAT_HOME_1}"
    if [ -d ${TOMCAT_HOME_1}/conf ] ; then
     TOMCAT_HOME=${TOMCAT_HOME_1}
     echo "Setting TOMCAT_HOME to $TOMCAT_HOME"
    fi
fi


if [ "$TOMCAT_HOME" = "" ] ; then
  # try to find tomcat
  if [ -d ${HOME}/opt/tomcat/conf ] ; then
    TOMCAT_HOME=${HOME}/opt/tomcat
    echo "Defaulting TOMCAT_HOME to $TOMCAT_HOME"
  fi

  if [ -d /opt/tomcat/conf ] ; then
    TOMCAT_HOME=/opt/tomcat
    echo "Defaulting TOMCAT_HOME to $TOMCAT_HOME"
  fi

  # Add other "standard" locations for tomcat
fi

if [ "$TOMCAT_HOME" = "" ] ; then
    echo TOMCAT_HOME not set, you need to set it or install in a standard location
```

Figure 13.4: Apache's Tomcat script uses many of the features of shell script programming (part 1 of 4).

```
        exit 1
    fi

    if [ "$TOMCAT_OPTS" = "" ] ; then
      TOMCAT_OPTS=""
    fi

    if [ "$ANT_OPTS" = "" ] ; then
      ANT_OPTS=""
    fi

    if [ "$JSPC_OPTS" = "" ] ; then
      JSPC_OPTS=""
    fi

    if [ -z "$JAVA_HOME" ] ;  then
      JAVA=`which java`
      if [ -z "$JAVA" ] ; then
        echo "Cannot find JAVA. Please set your PATH."
        exit 1
      fi
      JAVA_BINDIR=`dirname $JAVA`
      JAVA_HOME=$JAVA_BINDIR/..
    fi

    if [ "$JAVACMD" = "" ] ; then
        # it may be defined in env - including flags!!
        JAVACMD=$JAVA_HOME/bin/java
    fi

oldCP=$CLASSPATH

unset CLASSPATH
for i in ${TOMCAT_HOME}/lib/* ; do
  if [ "$CLASSPATH" != "" ]; then
    CLASSPATH=${CLASSPATH}:$i
  else
    CLASSPATH=$i
  fi
done

if [ -f ${JAVA_HOME}/lib/tools.jar ] ; then
    # We are probably in a JDK1.2 environment
    CLASSPATH=${CLASSPATH}:${JAVA_HOME}/lib/tools.jar
fi

# Backdoor classpath setting for development purposes when all classes
# are compiled into a /classes dir and are not yet jarred.
if [ -d ${TOMCAT_HOME}/classes ]; then
    CLASSPATH=${TOMCAT_HOME}/classes:${CLASSPATH}
fi

if [ "$oldCP" != "" ]; then
    CLASSPATH=${CLASSPATH}:${oldCP}
fi

export CLASSPATH

# We start the server up in the background for a couple of reasons:
```

Figure 13.4: Apache's Tomcat script uses many of the features of shell script programming (part 2 of 4).

```
#   1) It frees up your command window
#   2) You should use `stop` option instead of ^C to bring down the server
if [ "$1" = "start" ] ; then
  shift
  echo Using classpath: ${CLASSPATH}
  if [ "$1" = "-security" ] ; then
    shift
    echo Starting with a SecurityManager
    $JAVACMD $TOMCAT_OPTS -Djava.security.manager
-Djava.security.policy==${TOMCAT_HOME}/conf/tomcat.policy
-Dtomcat.home=${TOMCAT_HOME}  org.apache.tomcat.startup.Tomcat "$@" &
  else
    $JAVACMD $TOMCAT_OPTS -Dtomcat.home=${TOMCAT_HOME}
org.apache.tomcat.startup.Tomcat "$@" &
  fi
#   $JAVACMD org.apache.tomcat.shell.Startup "$@" &

elif [ "$1" = "stop" ] ; then
  shift
  echo Using classpath: ${CLASSPATH}
  $JAVACMD $TOMCAT_OPTS -Dtomcat.home=${TOMCAT_HOME}
org.apache.tomcat.startup.Tomcat -stop "$@"
#   $JAVACMD org.apache.tomcat.shell.Shutdown "$@"

elif [ "$1" = "run" ] ; then
  shift
  echo Using classpath: ${CLASSPATH}
  if [ "$1" = "-security" ] ; then
    shift
    echo Starting with a SecurityManager
    $JAVACMD $TOMCAT_OPTS -Djava.security.manager
-Djava.security.policy==${TOMCAT_HOME}/conf/tomcat.policy
-Dtomcat.home=${TOMCAT_HOME} org.apache.tomcat.startup.Tomcat "$@"
  else
    $JAVACMD $TOMCAT_OPTS -Dtomcat.home=${TOMCAT_HOME}
org.apache.tomcat.startup.Tomcat "$@"
  fi
#   $JAVACMD org.apache.tomcat.shell.Startup "$@"
  # no &

elif [ "$1" = "ant" ] ; then
  shift

  $JAVACMD $ANT_OPTS -Dant.home=${TOMCAT_HOME} -Dtomcat.home=${TOMCAT_HOME}
org.apache.tools.ant.Main $@

elif [ "$1" = "jspc" ] ; then
  shift

  $JAVACMD $JSPC_OPTS -Dtomcat.home=${TOMCAT_HOME} org.apache.jasper.JspC "$@"

elif [ "$1" = "env" ] ; then
  ## Call it with source tomcat.sh to set the env for tomcat
  shift
  echo Setting classpath to: ${CLASSPATH}
  oldCP=$CLASSPATH

else
  echo "Usage:"
```

Figure 13.4: Apache's Tomcat script uses many of the features of shell script programming (part 3 of 4).

```
        echo "tomcat (start|env|run|stop|ant)"
        echo "        start - start tomcat in the background"
        echo "        run   - start tomcat in the foreground"
        echo "             -security - use a SecurityManager when starting"
        echo "        stop  - stop tomcat"
        echo "        env  -  set CLASSPATH and TOMCAT_HOME env. variables"
        echo "        ant  - run ant script in tomcat context ( classes, directories, etc)"
        echo "        jspc - run jsp pre compiler"

        exit 0
    fi


    if [ "$oldCP" != "" ]; then
        CLASSPATH=${oldCP}
        export CLASSPATH
    else
        unset CLASSPATH
    fi
```

Figure 13.4: Apache's Tomcat script uses many of the features of shell script programming (part 4 of 4).

The script begins by checking to see if a special file called **.tomcatrc** (Tomcat resource) exists under the user's home directory. (Refer to Table 13.2 to find the meaning of the file operators used in the **tomcat.sh** conditionals.) If **.tomcatrc** file exists, **tomcat.sh** executes it with the dot sourcing operator.

The next three blocks of code are all predicated with the same condition:

```
 if [ "$TOMCAT_HOME" = "" ] ; then
```

The first two code blocks attempt to set the value of **TOMCAT_HOME**, while the third echoes a message to the user and gives up (exits with an error code of one). That first block uses the qualified name of the script (with the $0 variable) to guess where **TOMCAT_HOME** should be. The **while** loop that begins with the following condition is decidedly complex:

```
 while [ -h "$PRG" ] ; do
```

It handles circumstances where the qualified **tomcat.sh** file name is a link, by back-peddling links until the real file is found. The **while** loop uses the **expr** command and an odd search string passed to retrieve the name linked file from a directory listing:

```
 link=`expr "$ls" : '.*-> \(.*\)$'`
```

Note that a long directory listing will show that a file is a link by listing the name of the linked file after the -> operator.

The **while** loop also uses **basename** to strip the directory and extension from $0 and **dirname** to strip the nondirectory extension from a qualified file name. After the **while** loop terminates (because there are no more links), Tomcat checks to see if the directory, so laboriously found by back-peddling links, contains a directory called **conf**. If it does, Tomcat assumes that's the proper directory and sets **TOMCAT_HOME** to it.

If the Tomcat home environment variable was not set, the next block tries to see if it is under the conventional **opt** directory, either under the user's home directory or the root directory, with the following two conditionals:

```
if [ -d ${HOME}/opt/tomcat/conf ] ; then
if [ -d /opt/tomcat/conf ] ; then
```

In the third and final "Tomcat home is blank" block, the **tomcat.sh** script echoes a message and gives up, with an exit code of one. Tomcat then checks for the existence of three optional environment variables: **$TOMCAT_OPTS**, **$ANT_OPTS**, and **$JSPC_OPTS**. If any of those environment variables does not exist, Tomcat creates it by setting it with empty string values.

Which Java

The next problem that the Tomcat shell script has to handle is finding Java's home directory. If the system already has the **JAVA_HOME** environment variable set, this isn't a problem at all. When the following predicate is true, however, **tomcat.sh** attempts to find Java's home directory by asking the **which** command to find the **java** command:

```
if [ -z "$JAVA_HOME" ] ;  then
```

So long as the Java home block of code doesn't exit, the next block checks for the existence of an environment variable called **JAVACMD**. Tomcat allows users to qualify the Java command string with site-specific Java command flags. If the **JAVACMD** variable doesn't exist, **tomcat.sh** sets it to equal the qualified location of the **java** command.

Classpath

The next four blocks of code set the special Java environment variable, **CLASSPATH**. Tomcat begins this chunk of code by politely saving the existing value of **CLASSPATH** in **oldCP**. When **tomcat.sh** completes processing, **CLASSPATH** is set back to its original value.

After the value for **CLASSPATH** is saved, the environment variable is destroyed with the **unset** command. The **for** loop that follows then rebuilds **CLASSPATH**:

```
for i in ${TOMCAT_HOME}/lib/* ; do
```

The body of the **for** loop appends the name of every file in Tomcat's **lib** directory to **CLASSPATH**. Those files are the Java archives that contain the Java code required to run Tomcat.

The next code block handles a discrepancy between the way Java works between JDKs 1.1 and 1.2. JDK 1.2 requires the **tools.jar** file to be in **CLASSPATH**. Tomcat determines a JDK1.2 environment with the following predicate:

```
if [ -f ${JAVA_HOME}/lib/tools.jar ] ; then
```

The block of code conditioned by the following clause could safely be deleted, as it is only required by developers who are modifying Tomcat's code:

```
if [ -d ${TOMCAT_HOME}/classes ]; then
```

The last conditional in the **CLASSPATH** code blocks appends the original **CLASSPATH**, if it exists, to the new one. Finally, **CLASSPATH** is exported so that the subshell that will be running Tomcat can access it.

Command Parameters

The next block of code is a nested **if** that handles the command-line parameters to **tomcat.sh**. If you look at the **else** clause to the nested **if**, you'll see that **tomcat.sh** accepts **start**, **env**, **run**, **stop**, **ant**, and **jspc**. We'll only cover **start** and **stop** in detail. However, just so you know, **ant** is a facility for compiling the entire Tomcat product, and **jspc** is a utility that precompiles JavaServer Pages.

The top of the **if** block checks to see if the first parameter is **start**. If it is, Tomcat does a shift. The **shift** utility takes the parameter list and bumps the first one out. So, if your parameter list were *1, 2, 3, 4, 5*, **shift** would reset your parameter list to *2, 3, 4, 5*. After shifting, Tomcat checks to see if the second parameter (which is now actually the first) is **security**. If so, Tomcat shifts parameters again and starts the Tomcat Java application, with the **JAVACMD** environment variable with security options set. If the security parameter is not set, the Tomcat Java application is started without the security options.

The next clause in the nested **if**, the **else-if**, checks to see if **tomcat.sh** was invoked with a parameter value of **stop**. If so, **tomcat.sh** starts the Tomcat Java application with options to end Tomcat. If the Tomcat Web application server is not running in some other process, the Tomcat Java application ends with an error; otherwise, the Tomcat Web application server is shut down.

The very last clause of **tomcat.sh** resets **CLASSPATH** to its original value, which **tomcat.sh** had earlier saved in an environment variable called **oldCP**.

End of Chapter Review

Key Terms

case statements	exit codes	script
commands	for loop	sourcing
conditional expressions	parameters	tilde (~)
execution	predicates	while loop

Review Questions

1. Why might you need to understand how to program a shell script?

2. List two of the four special shell variables.

3. What symbol starts a comment in a script?

4. Explain what "sourcing the script" means.

5. Define the term *predicate*.

Programming Assignment

Exercise 1: Add Descriptive Comments to the tomcat.sh Startup Script

Using the discussion in the chapter, provide extensive comments in the **tomcat.sh script**. (You will probably want to copy them to a working directory first.)

Exercise 2: Fix say.sh to Echo Parameters without Script Errors

1. Test the **say.sh** script using several methods to invoke a script:

    a) With a dot.

    b) With the **source** command.

    c) With the **sh** command.

Exercise 3: Look for Loops in Scripts

Provide comments to several scripts. Suggested scripts are a few from **/etc/rc.d/init.d**, such as **httpd** and **postgresql**. (You might want to copy them to a working directory first.)

Index

Note: Boldface numbers indicate illustrations.

Note: Boldface numbers indicate illustrations.

Note: Boldface numbers indicate illustrations.